D0114602

PRIDE AND PINSTRIPES

PRIDE AND PINSTRIPES

The Yankees,
Mets, and
Surviving Life's
Challenges

MEL STOTTLEMYRE

WITH JOHN HARPER

HarperEntertainment
An Imprint of HarperCollinsPublishers

PRIDE AND PINSTRIPES. Copyright © 2007 by Mel Stottlemyre. All rights reserved. Printed in the United States of America. No part of this book may be used or reproduced in any manner whatsoever without written permission except in the case of brief quotations embodied in critical articles and reviews. For information address HarperCollins Publishers, 10 East 53rd Street, New York, NY 10022.

HarperCollins books may be purchased for educational, business, or sales promotional use. For information please write: Special Markets Department, HarperCollins Publishers, 10 East 53rd Street, New York, NY 10022.

FIRST EDITION

Designed by Laura Kaeppel

Library of Congress Cataloging-in-Publication Data has been applied for.

ISBN: 978-0-06-117408-7
ISBN-10: 0-06-117408-4

07 08 09 10 11 WBC/RRD 10 9 8 7 6 5 4 3 2 1

To my lost son, Jason, who taught us how to live . . . one day at a time

Contents

Cheeseburgers with George

It was the World Series of a lifetime for millions of New Yorkers, but even more so for me. The Yankees and Mets: For all but a few of my forty years in professional baseball, theirs were the only two uniforms I wore. So many memories. So much emotion. If only I could have soaked it all in from my usual front-row seat next to Joe Torre in the dugout. But as the Series began on a chilly Saturday night in the Bronx, I had to rely on recall to experience the feel of Yankee Stadium in October, the buzz inside the big ballpark that is unlike anything else I've seen or felt in baseball.

Oh, I was there that night in the fall of 2000. I wouldn't have missed it for the world. But because it had been barely more than a month since my stem-cell transplant that enabled me to survive multiple myeloma, a rare bone marrow cancer, my doctor would only allow me to attend the game if I stayed in the relatively closed environment of the manager's office. As it was, I had to beg the doctor for that much, since it would be months before my immune system was again strong enough to be exposed to the everyday germs that I would encounter being around people.

So although this was my first time at the ballpark since entering the hospital in early September, I hadn't exactly made a grand entrance. I was driven right up to the press gate, helped down the stairs, and from there I made the walk around the winding corridor, finally entering Joe's office through the side entrance. I was wearing latex gloves to further protect me from exposure to germs, and feeling a bit out of place because of my condition. I wanted so badly to offer some pregame encouragement to our Game 1 starter, Andy Pettitte, one of my all-time favorite pitchers whom I've coached. But the doc wouldn't budge: no contact whatsoever with the players in the clubhouse. Actually, Andy and I were so close that it probably wouldn't have been a good idea to throw such an emotional curve into his preparation anyway. I was just hoping that knowing I was there would offer him a bit of inspiration.

In Joe's office, I settled in on the couch to watch the game on TV. From there I could feel the rumble from the roars in the stadium above, but as close as I was to the field, just a short walk up the tunnel from the dugout, I still felt strangely detached as the game began. At least I'd been allowed to see and talk with Joe before the game. He had been a lifesaver during my absence, speaking to me almost daily by phone to keep me up to date and ask for my opinion on pitching matters, and I'll always be grateful for that. But then, I wasn't surprised. Over our years together with the Yankees, Joe had become like a brother to me, one of the most loyal, trusting people I've ever known in or out of baseball. Just seeing him briefly had lifted my spirits, and now as the first pitch was thrown I sat alone, trying to concentrate on the TV, just in case I saw something that I might want to relay to either Andy or Joe. Other than an equipment man or clubhouse kid occasionally popping in to see if I needed anything, I assumed I'd be watching the game by myself.

Then, suddenly, none other than George Steinbrenner came striding into Joe's office, asking me how I felt, which was nice of him, and deciding that he wanted to watch the game with me, which wasn't really what I wanted to hear. George had been great to me during my illness, offering to help me in any way that he could. It is times like this, when any member of the Yankee family is ailing, that George can be the most kindhearted man in the world. He'll use his clout as the owner of the most famous franchise in sports to make sure the person gets whatever he or she needs. When I was in Memorial Sloan-Kettering Hospital for three weeks in September, my only complaint was that I couldn't see the Yankee games on TV because the Madison Square Garden network wasn't available in the hospital. I mentioned that to Joe Torre over the phone, and one day later, I had MSG on my TV in my room. I was told that Joe had called George, who promptly called Mayor Rudy Giuliani, and, like magic, my TV was the only one in the hospital that picked up the Yankee games. I'm sure it didn't hurt that the mayor was a huge Yankee fan, but I have a feeling that George would have convinced him to make it happen for me even if he were a Mets fan.

Of course, as everyone knows, George has a bully side to his personality as well, famous as he is for his impulsive fits of temper during his thirty-plus years as owner of the Yankees. Little did I know at the time that I would begin to see more of that side of him in the coming years, when we stopped winning championships and he began looking to place blame on one of his favorite targets over the years: the pitching coach. As it was, our relationship was cordial but George and I already had quite a history. I held a grudge against him for about twenty years after I was released from the Yankees as a player in late March of 1975, two years after George had bought the team. At the time I was stunned at first, then furious, because I'd been promised by then-GM Gabe Paul that I would have until at least May to take my time rehabbing a shoulder injury incurred the previous year.

As it turned out, I never made it back from my rotator cuff injury, after hurting the shoulder again while trying to strengthen it with weight training a couple of months later. But that wasn't the point. The Yankees had flat-out lied to me, telling me not to even try to be ready for opening day, and then they cut me just a couple of days before spring training ended. George was suspended from baseball at the time, after being found guilty of making illegal contributions to Richard Nixon's presidential campaign, and wasn't around the team that spring, but I still blamed him for my release. Eventually I came to believe that Gabe Paul was behind the decision as a cost-saving measure for the club, but that was only after I'd avoided virtually all contact with the club for two decades, annually tearing up the invitation I received to Yankees Old-Timers Day.

Finally, it was George himself who convinced me he wasn't the bad guy all those years ago, during a phone call he made after the 1995 season to inquire about my returning to the Yankees as pitching coach. George sort of apologized for the way my Yankee career had ended, about as much as George can apologize for anything, I guess. He explained that because of his suspension, he truly was not involved in the day-to-day decision making at the time. He did a pretty good selling job, and as I told my wife, Jean, when I got off the phone, if George was big enough to finally call me, maybe I could be big enough to forgive and forget.

In addition, what I could never forget was how much my youngest son, Jason, loved the Yankees. Life had changed forever for me and my family in 1981 when he died at the age of eleven from leukemia. Besides the devastating effect Jason's death had on our daily lives, it eventually helped me reconcile my feelings toward the Yankees. I found that you look at life a little differently after experiencing that kind of tragedy. My other sons, Mel Jr. and Todd, were old enough at the time I was released to pick up on my bitterness, but Jason was only five years old, and to him the Yankees were Dad's team, even if I wasn't playing anymore, so he continued to root for them enthusiastically. Even when I went to work as a roving pitching instructor for the Seattle Mariners, which was close to my home in Yakima, Washington, Jason wouldn't budge. I took the boys to see a Mariners-Yankees game in Seattle one time, and Jason said to me, "Sorry, Dad, I know you work for the Mariners, but I'm rooting for the Yankees."

Those memories softened my feelings enough so that I might have been willing to make peace with the Yankees had George approached me in the years after Jason's passing. Finally, twenty years later, when the opportunity presented itself, I felt like I owed it at least partly to his memory to return to the Yankees, and it turned out to be maybe the best decision I ever made. By October of 2000, three championships in my first four years already had more than made up for my unfortunate timing as a player, coming up as a rookie in 1964, just as the Yankees of the Mickey Mantle and Whitey Ford era were getting old, while the club's farm system was finally running dry. When I lost Game 7 of the World Series to the St. Louis Cardinals in a duel with Bob Gibson that year, my only consolation was being reassured by all the veterans that I'd have plenty of other chances to win a championship. Turned out the Yankees didn't get back to the World Series until 1976, the year after they released me.

Call it bad luck, I guess, to be the ace of the pitching staff during what was then the longest postseason drought for the franchise in some fifty years, or since the pre–Babe Ruth era. But I never dwelled on it when my career was over. I enjoyed every minute of my time in the big leagues and felt blessed to have such talent, but I have to admit, finally winning a championship with the Yankees in 1996 gave me the biggest thrill of my baseball life. I had won a ring as pitching coach with the Mets in 1986, and that was gratifying, but winning one with the only team I ever played for was truly special, at least partly because it finally closed that wound Gabe Paul had opened the day he ended my Yankee career.

Of course, as pitching coach I had to establish some ground rules,

I guess you might say, in my second go-round with George. When I agreed to take the job at the same time Joe Torre was hired as manager, I was fully aware the pitching coach position had long been a favorite target for George anytime the club wasn't playing well. So, much as Joe did, I took the job with no illusions of long-term employment, and as such I fully intended to do it my way. My first moment of truth with George came in late August of that first season, 1996, when the team was experiencing its first prolonged slump, and our twelve-game lead in the AL East over the Orioles had shrunk to just a few games. As is his habit during such times, George summoned the manager, coaches, and top executives upstairs to his office for a meeting after a game one day. Our pitchers had been struggling, especially in the early innings, so I knew I'd hear about it. Sure enough, George vented on everybody, starting with me. When he's agitated, his voice tends to rise a bit, and he speaks in rapid-fire fashion. It's kind of funny, at least when he's not rapid-firing at you. In these types of meetings he always addressed me by my last name.

"Stottlemyre," he snapped, "are you aware of how many first-inning runs your pitchers have given up lately?"

"Yeah, I'm aware, George," I said. "It hasn't been very good."

"Well, dammit," he said, "you've gotta try something different—warm 'em up longer or warm 'em up twice. Something different."

"I've tried all those things," I said. "We're just going through one of those spells right now, but we'll be fine, it'll work itself out."

"No, no, that's not good enough," he said. "We've gotta do something different. I'll tell you what you do: Get on their ass. Get on 'em."

"George, I've tried that, too," I said. "I've made them aware we need them to be better. They're aware of it."

"No, no, no," he said again, becoming more animated. "You've gotta do better than that. Goddammit, go to the press. Blast their ass in the papers. That'll get their attention."

At that point I knew I had to make a stand, literally.

"Wait a minute, George," I said, getting up out of my seat to make my point. "If that's what you want, you've got the wrong guy. Before I do that, I'll go home and sit in my boat in the middle of the river and be happy fishing. That's not how I coach. It's not me, I won't do it."

I think George was a bit stunned.

"What do you mean, you won't do it?" he said.

"I won't do it," I repeated. "I'll lose those guys. They won't ever trust anything I tell them again. I've never done it before, and I'm not going to start now. So if that's what you want, you've got the wrong guy."

Now George didn't seem to know what to say. He was quiet for a few seconds, and I guess he sensed how serious I was.

"Well, by God, I can get on 'em. I can blast them," he said.

"You can do anything you want, George," I said, "but I can't and I won't do it."

I wasn't loud, but I was forceful enough that I guess George decided not to push it any further.

"All right, all right, sit down," he said, "and let's talk about this some more."

And just like that, he got off the pitching, went on to start talking about the hitting problems. That was my first real head butt with George, and I think it made an impression. He never said any more about it, and I never mentioned it again, but from that point on, he kind of left me alone. Our pitchers turned it around fairly soon after that, and we went on to win the championship.

Now, four years later, in 2000, it was hard to believe we were in the World Series for the fourth time in five years. It was a remarkable run, more than I'd ever dreamed of when I'd taken the job. But, sitting in Joe's office as Game 1 with the Mets began, I was thinking this was it for me. For weeks I'd been contemplating retirement after the season, because of the way I was feeling. Months of chemotherapy, followed by the stem-cell transplant, had drained me physically and emotionally, and I just didn't think I'd have the strength or even the desire to return the next year.

With these kinds of thoughts in my mind, I wasn't really in the mood for company as I watched the game. George's intentions were good, but it just wasn't very comfortable sitting there with him because he was terribly uneasy watching the game. He didn't say much during the early innings of Game 1, just commenting occasionally, but you could see how he lives and dies with every pitch. And then, suddenly, he got an urge to eat. He called one of the clubhouse kids into the office, whipped out a $100 bill, and sent the kid on a mission to get some cheeseburgers. He went back to watching the game, but after about fifteen minutes or so he jumped up from his seat and started yelling at no one in particular, demanding to know, "Where's that kid with my $100?" When the cheeseburgers arrived, George insisted that I eat with him, and I did, even though it probably wasn't the best food for me at the time. Then he grabbed a couple of red Gatorades out of the cooler, and he seemed fascinated when I told him I'd never tried that flavor, but now that I had, I liked it. He couldn't believe I'd never had one, and he told Rob Cucuzza, our equipment manager, to go get a couple of cases of the red Gatorade from the storage area for me. He then had a couple of the kids working in the clubhouse carry them out to my car in the parking lot. Finally, about the seventh inning I had to leave to beat the crowd at game's end, and George walked me out to my car, made sure I got out okay. That's George. He can be the greatest guy in the world, as long as things are going his way.

I was glad I wasn't there with him for the nerve-racking finish, as we won in twelve innings, but the win gave George a little more swagger the next night for Game 2. I was back in Joe's office again, because being at the stadium made me feel more like a part of the Series, but this time George was acting a little more like the Boss. He was reacting to plays, making comments. I don't know if he tempered them somewhat with me there, but I can only imagine what he's like when he's alone in his office watching these games. At one point he did take issue with our lineup, griping about Joe's decision to use Chuck Knoblauch as our designated hitter.

"What the hell is Joe doing?" he said. "We can't have Knoblauch at DH. We're the Yankees. You don't have a little guy at DH. You need somebody who can hit the ball out of the ballpark. Can't you talk to Joe and tell him?"

"But, George," I said, "he just hit a sacrifice fly his last time up."

"Ah, you're just like Joe," he said, and he dismissed me with a wave of his hand.

I laughed because it was just George being George. He'll have that football mentality forever, thinking the Yankees should be able to overpower everybody like the Green Bay Packers under Vince Lombardi. It goes back to George's younger days, when he worked for a couple of years as an assistant football coach at Purdue and Northwestern in the 1950s, and in some ways it's at the root of his impatience as a baseball owner. Deep down he thinks we should win all 162 games in a season, or at least come close, the way a powerhouse football team might go 11-1 in college or, say, 14-2 in the NFL.

Anyway, it was quite an experience sitting with George for those two nights, and fitting, I thought at the time, considering that I was contemplating retirement. After all, he has influenced my life in important ways, good and bad, going back thirty years. Watching a game with him just isn't something I'd want to make a habit of doing. When the Series moved to Shea Stadium for the next three games, I didn't have to worry about that because I stayed at home in my New Jersey apartment and watched on TV. I watched the final one by myself because I insisted that my wife, Jean, go to Shea with some relatives and enjoy the game. It was hard not being there, especially when we finished off the Mets in Game 5, but the guys were great, calling me on the phone from the clubhouse as they were celebrating. As I talked to Joe, and then Andy Pettitte and a couple of the other guys, I was kind of emotional, thinking I wouldn't be back with them the next year.

It wasn't the way I wanted to leave the game, but on the other hand, I thought, maybe it was the perfect way to go out. We'd defeated the Mets in the first Subway Series since 1955, and with four championships in five years, we'd not only returned the Yankees to glory, but established a dynasty to match almost any in the franchise's storied history. For me, personally, the championships had provided a new place in Yankee history, as well. For a long time it seemed I was destined to be remembered as Poor Mel. As in Poor Mel, if he'd only come along with the Yankees five years sooner, or five years later, he would have won his share of championships as a player. Now I was assured of a happier legacy, I guess you might say, and while it's never been something I lay awake at night worrying about, it made me feel good to know I now had contributed to the franchise's total of twenty-six world championships, the most in sports.

Still, I hadn't stayed in baseball this long because I wanted to leave a legacy. I loved being around the game, working with my pitchers, feeling the rush of adrenaline for big games even after all these years. By the end of that 2000 World Series, however, I wasn't feeling any of that because I was so weak. That's mainly why I was thinking I would have to walk away from the job. But as weeks and months went by, I gradually regained my strength and my feelings began to change. The Yankees were good enough not to push me for a decision, and by January or so I began to feel that old urge to be at the ballpark again. I was also motivated by the hundreds and hundreds of letters I had received from people suffering from the same cancer as me, people saying they were pulling for me and telling me I was an inspiration because I had continued to work at my job through most of my treatment. As I recovered during the winter and continued reading the letters that had piled up at Yankee Stadium, I began to feel that, as someone in the public eye, I owed it to people to show them you could overcome the disease and continue to live a normal life.

So I did come back, and I stayed five more seasons before deciding to retire after the 2005 season. Though we played in two more World Series during that time, we didn't win another championship, and by my final season, George and I weren't sharing cheeseburgers. Though he never challenged my coaching in person after that meeting in 1996 in which I'd refused his suggestion to publicly criticize my pitchers, I'd heard the rumblings about my job status coming out of Yankee headquarters in Tampa during my last couple of years and figured the time was right to say good-bye. After all the great times and grand success as pitching coach, I didn't want this second run with the Yankees to end in the same manner as my playing career. I'd enjoyed wearing the pinstripes too much to leave with any bitterness this time. On that count I'd learned a lasting lesson from my son, Jason, a Yankee fan forever.

2

From Mabton to the World Series

The last World Series in which Mickey Mantle, Whitey Ford, and, as it turned out, a twenty-two-year-old rookie pitcher from the Great Northwest would ever play had been over for about seven hours. Midnight was approaching on the East Coast, and as I loaded my Chevy Chevelle for a cross-country drive home, I could only guess where Mickey and Whitey might be, probably lamenting our loss to the St. Louis Cardinals together over a cold one somewhere in Manhattan, after our long, quiet flight back from the heartland. For that matter, I was struck by the thought that I was surely the only member of the New York Yankees preparing to drive off into the night, from my rented house in New Jersey west through Pennsylvania, Ohio, Indiana, and eventually all the way to my hometown of Mabton, Washington.

Before you ask what a major leaguer, even a rookie, was doing making such a drive, with my wife, Jean, and one-year-old son, Mel

Jr., in tow, remember, this was 1964. Plane fares were costly but gas was only 29 cents a gallon, and my salary for the year was $7,500. After New York state taxes were deducted from my paycheck, in fact, I was actually making less as a Yankee than I had been making in Richmond, Virginia, for the Yankees' Triple-A affiliate. Free agency was still eleven years from becoming a reality in baseball, which meant that ball clubs had complete control over player salaries. Suffice it to say a guy like Scott Boras, superagent in the twenty-first century, might have wound up selling insurance for a living in those days.

So I was driving, not flying, home to an off-season where I would work a nine-to-five job in a Safeway Grocery plant because I needed the money to support my family. You should have seen the looks on the faces of guys like Andy Pettitte and Mariano Rivera when I would tell them how it was in those days. It was a different world for professional athletes, and to me there was no choice when it came to driving. Of course, I should have been too tired, exhausted really, to even think about beginning the drive that night, since earlier that day I had been the starting and losing pitcher in Game 7, making my third start of that World Series. But I was still wired, angry at myself for not pitching better that day, yet exhilarated from the most re-markable two months of my life.

My wife, Jean, had packed up our belongings in the house in New Jersey, and when I arrived home I realized I wasn't going to be able to sleep, so I said what the heck, let's go. We piled everything into the car and I started driving. And driving. And driving. I prob-ably drove for eighteen hours, through the night and the next day, before finally stopping at a motel, probably somewhere in Iowa, though I don't even remember for sure. All I know is that the miles flew by as I spent those hours reflecting on my two months in the big leagues, how I'd gone from a minor-league nobody to the toast of New York in the blink of an eye.

It still seemed hard to believe. The Yankees had called me up from Triple-A in mid-August when they were in third place behind the Baltimore Orioles and Chicago White Sox, unable to sustain any kind of hot streak. I had been in a zone for months, with a record of 13-3 for Triple-A Syracuse and a streak of ten straight wins at the time of my call-up, and, fortunately I didn't know enough to be nervous. I just kept throwing my trademark sinking fastball, and to my surprise, it was just about as effective in the big leagues as it had been in the minors. In my first start I induced nineteen ground-ball outs in beating the White Sox 7–3, and before I knew it, we had played our way to October.

Though I was just a wide-eyed kid, truly in awe of guys like Mickey and Whitey, Elston Howard and Bobby Richardson, I turned out to be the spark the Yankees needed. I posted a 9–3 record as the team finally did get hot, running off a 17-3 streak in September to win a fifth straight AL pennant. Then, because Whitey hurt his shoulder in Game 1 against the Cardinals, I wound up starting Games 2, 5, and 7 in the World Series, all of them against Hall of Famer Bob Gibson. I won Game 2, then pitched a solid seven innings in a ten-inning loss in Game 5, and, finally, lasted only four innings in Game 7. What nobody ever really knew about that last game, however, was that while I came out for a pinch-hitter after giving up three runs in the fourth, it was largely because my shoulder stiffened up after I fell on it reaching for an errant throw as I covered first base. Al Downing relieved me and gave up three more runs the next inning in what turned out to be a 7–5 loss, so I always wondered if that World Series might have turned out differently had I been able to stay in the game that day.

Now I finally had the time to reflect on my whirlwind tour of duty with the Yankees, and I was still so wound up that I made what was usually a five-day drive to Washington in just over three. In fact, I drove so relentlessly that I nearly spoiled a surprise welcome-home party the good folks of Mabton had decided to throw for me. Fortunately, our next-door neighbors were the only ones to notice when we pulled into our driveway. They came running to tell us about the party, how everyone was planning to meet us outside the city limits and escort us to our house. So we left the car packed and hid it in our neighbors' garage overnight. The next day we got back in the car and drove it outside of town while our neighbors alerted everybody we were on our way. Then we pretended to be surprised as we made our reentry into town.

It was really a nice gesture. They held a big ceremony for me at the city park. They knew I liked to hunt, and they presented me with a new rifle. Having a local boy make it to the big leagues was a great moment for a little town. Having one make it to the Yankees, who seemed to play in the World Series every year, was practically unthinkable. I know I hadn't even dreamed of it myself. Growing up in a rural area out west in the 1950s, when the closest big-league team was located in another time zone, and the Saturday Game of the Week was the only baseball you could see on TV until the World Series, made the idea of someday playing major-league baseball seem as far-fetched as traveling to the moon.

That was my world as a kid. Mabton is a tiny town in southern central Washington, just north of the Oregon border. I grew up there from about the eighth grade on, after our family had moved around a bit. My dad worked as a pipefitter on construction jobs, and he went wherever he could find the best work. We lived in Oregon and South Carolina before my dad took a job at the Hanford Atomic Energy plant in Washington and found a house to rent in Mabton. It's a farming town now, as it was then, with a transient population that fluctuates around 1,000, because immigrant workers arrive in the spring but then leave in the fall after the crops have been harvested. There wasn't much for a kid to do in Mabton, especially in the 1950s, but fortunately, all I needed to be happy was a baseball, a couple of gloves, and my younger brother.

Keith, who passed away in 2000 after a battle with brain cancer, was seventeen months younger than me, and we both loved baseball above all else. We spent countless hours in the backyard, playing our own little game of pitch and catch. I was always the Yankees, he was the Brooklyn Dodgers. Even three thousand miles away, it made perfect sense. We had no local major-league team to root for, and the Yankees and Dodgers were the two most high-profile teams during that era, playing each other in the World Series a number of times. Keith would make up his Dodger lineup, and I'd pitch to each imaginary hitter. As the catcher, Keith would call balls and strikes, and after three outs, Keith would pitch to my Yankee lineup as I called balls and strikes. The Yankees won most of the time, and not just because I was the big brother. I always had a pretty accurate arm, and even then I could always throw strikes. I guess all of that catching paid off, too, because Keith became a very good catcher who played a few years in the minors for the San Francisco Giants, but he never quite made it to the big leagues.

Ours was very much a blue-collar family. My dad, Vernon, worked hard to support us, and though we didn't have a lot of money, he made sure we always had what we needed. Baseball equipment definitely fell into that category because my mom, Lorene, as well as my dad, was a big sports fan. My dad loved baseball and introduced me to the game. He had played sandlot ball in Missouri, where he was raised, and he spent a lot of time with my brother and me in the backyard, throwing or hitting baseballs to us. He'd take us to see local games between semipro teams. I guess the Cardinals were his favorite major-league team, though he just followed them from a distance, and mostly through the newspapers. Without a team in the area, I became a Yankee fan, I'm sure because they were on TV so often. My favorite player was Mickey Mantle, and I always loved watching Whitey Ford pitch. I never dreamed that someday I'd get to play with them.

I have an older sister, Joyce, who lives in New Mexico, and another brother, Jeff, who came along seventeen years after I was born.

Jeff was a good pitcher, too, who signed with the Seattle Mariners when I was working for them as a roving pitching instructor after my playing career ended. He got as high as Double-A, but then was farmed out to the Mexican League when the Mariners had too many players on their Double-A team. He did well there, pitching for a team in a border town, but when he was sold to a team in an interior town in Mexico, he said no thanks and went home. I thought he still had potential, but about that time he wrecked his knee stepping in a coyote hole while fishing with my dad, and he never played again.

My mom and dad encouraged us to play any sport but football. Dad loved watching football on TV, but he said he'd seen too many kids get hurt and told us, point-blank, don't even think about it. He was a disciplinarian, and I didn't fight him on it. Mom was the softie of the two, but both of them made sure we knew right from wrong and learned not to cross that line. None of us were any trouble, but kids were different then, too. The world was different. We'd spend hours and hours outside playing ball without an adult anywhere in sight, and if there was an argument we worked it out ourselves. Nobody was looking for trouble because it meant catching hell at home from your parents, no matter what your excuse might be.

For much the same reason, I was a pretty good student. I was always in the top 10 percent of my class, but that wasn't necessarily such an accomplishment, considering my graduating class at Mabton High numbered 24. There were probably 175 students total in the four grades, but the graduating class was extra small because a number of seniors dropped out to work in the fields. We only had ten players on the baseball team in my senior year, but that was partly because we had a coach, Jim Rodgers, who believed in conditioning. We started in preseason with more kids, but a bunch of them quit because of all the running we did.

The small numbers helped give me a chance to start on the varsity all four years in high school. I played shortstop and pitched, and as a pitcher I only lost once during my four years, as a junior to Sunnyside High, by a score of 2–1 in nine innings—two extra innings. As a senior I went 13-0, and we only played about twenty games, so I won some games in relief as well as starting, when the coach would bring me in from shortstop sometimes in the later innings. I threw the same sinking fastball then that I did later with the Yankees, as well as a roundhouse curveball, one of those big sweepers that is effective in high school. Nobody used radar guns in those days, but I'd guess I was throwing 84, 85 miles per hour with my fastball, because I know I threw considerably harder later as I grew and gained weight. I didn't know it at the time, but a couple of scouts found their way to our games to take a look at me, but nothing came of it. This was 1959 and there was no amateur draft, so any major-league club was free to try and sign any high school or college player it deemed worthy, but no one showed that kind of interest in me as I finished my senior year.

By then I was dreaming of a major-league career, although it still seemed like something unattainable to me. Jim Rodgers encouraged me to continue playing, but he only talked about going on to the college level. He'd always tell me, "You can play a lot of baseball if you want to," but he never talked about pro ball. Maybe it would have been different if I had played in a more populated area, or if I wasn't such a skinny kid in high school, but as it turned out, I was just happy after graduating high school to get a baseball scholarship to Yakima Junior College. The school had a highly regarded baseball program, coached at the time by a guy named Bobo Brayton, who eventually was inducted into the NCAA Hall of Fame.

I didn't get off to a great start with him, however. I pitched well enough during the informal fall season that he was counting on me in the spring, but winter grades came out just before the season began and I wasn't eligible because I'd failed an engineering class. Actually, I didn't so much fail as I just didn't show up because of some poor planning and the distraction, ahem, of having a girlfriend at home. That would be Jean, my lovely wife, whom I've known since I was a teenager. Jean's older brother, Pete Mitchell, was my best friend in those days, and he loved baseball as much as I did. During the summer we'd play pickup games at the city park, and Jean was always there, too. She was athletic and just kind of became one of the players, and I don't even remember how we started going out. I think I gave her a ride home from the park one time, and then I asked her if she wanted to go to a movie. Jean was three years younger than I, and it was kind of funny because my brother Keith had dated her briefly before I did. We hit it off and went out all through my senior year, and that was a factor when I decided I would commute to Yakima Junior College.

Yakima was about an hour's drive, and I made the mistake of scheduling an engineering class at eight in the morning. In addition, I was working at a gas station at home some nights so that I'd have spending money, and eventually the hours caught up with me. I couldn't seem to make it to that eight o'clock class very often, and that wound up costing me my eligibility. My father was real upset with me, and I was disappointed myself. I wound up pitching for an all-Mexican team in a summer league, just to have somewhere to play, and transferred to Central Washington, a four-year school a little farther away, forcing me to live there in a dorm. But that didn't work out, either, because the baseball coach there reneged on a promise to pay my tuition, and I wound up back at Yakima JC in the spring of my sophomore year.

This time I was eligible to pitch at least, and I had a good season. I finished with a record of 7-2, but the best thing that happened to me was pitching the second game of a bunch of doubleheaders after a left-hander named Andy Erickson pitched the first game. Andy was a very good pitcher with an excellent breaking ball, and he had attracted the attention of a Yankees scout named Eddie Taylor. Eddie would show up every time Erickson pitched, and he wound up seeing me as well because he'd stay for the second game of our doubleheaders. By then I was throwing harder, getting more sinking movement on my fastball, and pitching some strong games against pretty good competition. I was starting to think seriously that I could play pro ball, and toward the end of the season my coach told me that Hub Kittle wanted to take a look at me. Kittle, who coached in the St. Louis Cardinals' system for years, was managing the Milwaukee Braves' minor-league team in Yakima at the time, and I went over to their ballpark to throw for him. I thought I threw pretty well, but after about twenty minutes he called me over and said, "Sorry, kid, I'd like to sign you but you don't throw hard enough."

So I went back home to a summer job, working on a farm that primarily grew and harvested mint. One morning I was out in the field, spreading mint slugs, when a big white Cadillac pulled up out of nowhere, sending dust flying everywhere. Eddie Taylor stepped out of the car and yelled to get my attention. He'd talked to me once late in the season at Yakima, told me he liked the way I threw, and now he asked if I'd be interested in signing with the Yankees. It was kind of funny, with all of these workers standing around, wondering what in the heck was going on. He told me to talk to my parents and get back to him. My mom and dad weren't all that excited about the idea of giving up on school. It wasn't like we were talking about signing for much money. But my dad knew that I was more interested in baseball than school, and after we talked he made the decision easy for me.

"If you don't try it," he said, "you'll wonder for the rest of your life how far you could have gone with this."

There was no negotiating for my services. No bonus, either, just a standard minor-league contract for $400 a month and a bus ticket to Modesto, California. After a couple of minor-league coaches watched me throw batting practice there for a few days, the Yankees put me on a plane to Harlan, Kentucky, where they had a team in the Appalachian League. That was culture shock for me, suddenly living in a coal-mining town in the Southeast. I was kind of homesick, and Jean couldn't visit me, as she was still just going into her senior year in high school. I spent a lot of time on the phone with her and wrote letters often. But I was so excited about playing professionally that I handled being on my own pretty well. I got along with the guys on the team, but I didn't hang much with them off the field. I wasn't a party guy. I was serious about baseball, and there wasn't much to do anyway in that little town. Everybody stayed in a run-down hotel with showers at the end of the hall. Some guys would go down to the radio station in town just to be able to listen to some music. It was definitely a place that tested your desire to play baseball, but that was fine with me. I pitched well enough to earn a promotion in a couple of months to Auburn, New York, where I finished out my first season. Between the two stops I compiled a 9-4 record, which was good enough for the Yankees to skip me from Class D to Class B in the minors for the 1962 season.

Class B for the Yankees was Greensboro, North Carolina, where I had a breakthrough season, going 17-9 with eight shutouts, throwing 250 innings. Over the course of my first year in the minors, I had learned that I would have more success by keeping the ball down in the strike zone rather than trying to throw it by everybody. I gained more command with my sinker and by now I was throwing a hard slider rather than my old high school curveball. That season earned me an invitation to the big-league camp in the spring of '63, and that was the first time I really thought that maybe I could pitch for the Yankees.

By then I was taking my career more seriously than ever because Jean and I had gotten married after the 1962 season. We had been talking about it since I'd returned from Greensboro in September. Jean had graduated from high school and didn't have any real desire to go to college, so we decided to do it during the Thanksgiving break. We were both young, but we'd been going together for four years, and it just felt like the right time. By then I had the confidence that I was going to continue progressing with the Yankees and make a career out of baseball that could support a family. Jean's family was happy and supportive about it, as was my mother. I can't say the same about my father, however. He thought I was too young to be getting married, and though he didn't say much about it, I'm sure he thought taking on such a responsibility would interfere with my baseball career. He was so upset that he refused to attend the wedding. He just stayed at home, probably had a drink or two that day. I'm sure he regretted it, as he and Jean developed a good relationship over the years. Eventually we could all laugh about it, and Jean teases him about it to this day.

We had the ceremony on November 23, the day after Thanksgiving. We did it then to take advantage of the four-day weekend, since I was working in the Safeway plant and couldn't just take time off. It was a small wedding, with a handful of family and friends, a nice affair. We didn't have much of a honeymoon, just a quick drive across the mountains to Seattle for the weekend, because I had to be back to work on Monday. I needed that job at Safeway because I still only made $500 a month at Greensboro that year, and that was only for the months of the baseball season. It was grunt work, operating a forklift to move inventory, running apple pulp through a press to make apple juice, things like that. I worked a minimum of forty hours a week, usually more, and it was no fun, but I needed the money. I wasn't making enough money for Jean to come to spring training in '63, but I did get a raise to $800 a month when I made the Triple-A team, and Jean joined me in Richmond, Virginia, when the season began.

That year I went to big-league spring training for the first time, and it was a huge thrill for me. I was very much in awe of being around guys like Mickey and Whitey, my boyhood idols. I was scared to death to even talk to them, and though I watched every move they made, I don't think I got close enough to say a word to them for at least a couple of weeks. Actually, it was fairly late in spring training before I remember any interaction with either of them. By then I'd already lasted longer than I expected, as they'd made a couple of cuts, sending players back to the minor-league camp. I'd made a start in one of the early exhibition games, against the Minnesota Twins, and pitched three shutout innings. That earned me a couple of other chances to pitch, and I still hadn't given up any runs. So while most of the nonroster players had been sent down, I was still hanging around, and I remember Whitey joking with me, saying, "Would you hurry up and give up a run so they can send you down." Finally I did give one up, in relief against the Kansas City A's, and, sure enough, I was sent down the next day.

That spring was a great experience for me. I had enough success to realize that if I continued to improve, there was no reason why I couldn't become a Yankee within a couple of years. And eventually I grew comfortable being around the veteran players, mainly because they made a point of helping young players. They were a very proud, unselfish group that only wanted to win championships, and veterans were willing to work with young players for the good of the club. It was the Yankee way. I saw guys like Tony Kubek and Bobby Richardson instructing young infielders, and Whitey was great with me and other young pitchers. Those guys didn't talk about personal goals, or what kind of numbers they wanted to put up that year. All they talked about was winning another championship.

So I went to Triple-A instilled with confidence, but I only had a so-so year there. I was having some trouble with my control, learning how to harness the natural movement on my sinker, and I was sent to the bullpen for a while. Pitching in relief helped me get back on track, because I came into situations where I had to throw strikes, and I learned to be a little more aggressive with my fastball. It was a learning year, pitching at the highest minor-league level against a lot of older, experienced hitters. I had to learn how to set up hitters, use one pitch as a way of setting up the next to finish a guy off. In those days there were no pitching coaches on the minor-league clubs, just a roving instructor who moved around to the different minor-league levels and spent several days at a time with about seven or eight clubs. So you had to learn your craft more on your own, though I have to give credit to Billy Muffett, a veteran pitcher who was something of a player-coach in Triple-A during my two years there. He was a tremendous help to me, pushing me to be more aggressive in the strike zone, and talking to me about the mental part of pitching.

I finished that '63 season with a 7-7 record, but only threw about 150 innings, and I guess the Yankees weren't terribly impressed, because they didn't invite me to big-league camp in 1964. The good news was that at least I got a raise, to $1,200 a month, but I went back to Triple-A camp feeling as if I had something to prove. At that time, with only sixteen teams in the majors, it wasn't uncommon for a number of players to stall at the Triple-A level and be there for years. Throughout spring training that was my motivation, to make sure I wasn't going to be one of those guys. My season at Richmond didn't start out well, however, as I struggled with my control and once again found myself moved to the bullpen. I pitched in relief until getting a start during a Memorial Day doubleheader. I think the Yankees intended to send me back to the bullpen after that start, but I pitched a shutout and sort of forced them to keep me in the rotation. Four days later I pitched another shutout and went on to win ten straight decisions. I was getting more movement than ever on my sinker, and I'd learned to just throw it down the middle and watch as it danced toward the corner. I created some of the movement with my delivery and the way I held the ball, but mostly it was just natural. I couldn't throw the ball straight if I wanted to.

By late July the Yankees were looking for pitching help, especially when Whitey Ford had to miss a few starts with a hip injury. Ralph Houk, the GM at the time, had come to see me pitch at the end of July, and two starts later our manager, Preston Gomez, called me into the office when we were in Syracuse and told me I was going to New York in the morning, and pitching the following day. That was an emotional time for me. Wow, I was going to the big leagues. I had a million thoughts banging around in my head, not the least of which was figuring out what to do about my wife being in Richmond. I was reasonably sure I would be with the Yankees the remainder of the season, since in those days teams didn't shuttle players up and down from the minors the way they do now. So Jean decided she'd pack up our apartment in Richmond, rent a U-Haul, and drive the seven hours to New York. It wasn't easy, especially with Mel Jr. now eighteen months old, and the fact that she had no idea where she was going, but she made it, driving up the day after I pitched. I'd flown into the big city on August 11, and it was my first look at New York City. I remember just kind of staring in disbelief from the plane at the size of the buildings in Manhattan. I'd never seen anything quite like it. I went to Yankee Stadium that day, got a feel for my surroundings, and checked into the Concourse Plaza Hotel, which was only about six blocks up River Avenue from the stadium.

Taking the mound at the stadium the next afternoon was a memorable moment, but it wasn't as if Yankee fans came flocking to see me. Officially, 16,945 fans attended the game against the White Sox, and considering the old Yankee Stadium seated nearly 70,000 people, the place seemed practically empty. But that wasn't really unusual then. Baseball may have been the American pastime, but fans didn't fill the ballparks the way they do now, when the Yankees draw 50,000 or more for just about every home game. Still, it was by far the biggest crowd at a game where I'd pitched, and I remember being tremendously excited. Extra adrenaline is not usually such a good thing for a sinkerballer, because overthrowing tends to make the ball straighten out, but my sinker was working nicely and the White Sox hitters kept beating it into the ground that day. As a result, I got nineteen ground-ball outs and pitched a complete game, allowing seven hits and one walk, as we beat the White Sox 7–3. I even managed to get a hit, a single up the middle against Ray Herbert, so it was quite a day.

My debut was overshadowed, however, by the longest home run I'd ever seen, and one of the longest that Mickey Mantle ever hit. He hit one from each side of the plate that day, but the one he hit left-handed against Herbert was just stunning to see. The Yankees measured it at 500 feet, which is remarkable enough, but even that distance didn't seem to do it justice. The center field wall was 461 feet from the plate in the old stadium, and a 15-foot high screen that served as a batter's background sat atop the wall, in front of the bleachers that were kept empty for background purposes as well. There was some wind blowing out that day, but it was still hard to imagine Mantle hitting a shot that carried over the screen, finally landing fifteen rows up in the bleachers. At the time he was the only player ever to hit a home run over that screen, and the funny thing is, I remember him flipping the bat disgustedly as he left the plate, thinking it would be an out in dead center.

Mickey's home run was the talk of the locker room after the game, but everybody also made a point of congratulating me. Yogi Berra, in his first and only year as manager, was a man of few words, and indeed he came by my locker and said simply: "Nice game, kid." Photographers asked Mickey and me to pose for pictures after the game, and Mickey patted me on the shoulder, said I'd pitched a great game. That was quite a feeling, after all those years of idolizing him. Mickey made everybody feel good. As the season went on he'd joke around, calling me a rook, but basically he treated me like everybody else.

The win brought us within three and a half games of the first-place Orioles, and a half game of the White Sox. Four days later I beat the Orioles 3–1 in Baltimore, pitching eight and two-thirds innings, but from there we went to Chicago and got swept in a four-game series by the White Sox. The sweep, in which I didn't pitch, moved the Sox into first place, four and a half games ahead of us, and was probably the low point of the season for the Yankees.

That set the stage for the infamous harmonica episode. The team was on a bus from Comiskey Park to the airport when utility in-fielder Phil Linz, for some reason, decided to practice on his har-monica, which he was just learning to play. He started trying to play "Mary Had a Little Lamb," which he said later was the only song he knew. Considering the mood after the sweep, Yogi didn't appreciate hearing it. From the front of the bus he yelled for whoever had the harmonica to shut the damn thing up. Linz was in the back of the bus, and I guess because he was playing the harmonica at the time, he couldn't make out what Yogi said.

"What'd he say?" he said, as he stopped tooting.

At that point, Mickey decided to have some fun.

"He said 'play it louder,'" Mickey said.

I don't think Mickey meant any disrespect toward Yogi. He just liked to see if he could put one over on a teammate. In this case, I doubt if he expected Phil to actually start playing again. But he did, and this time Yogi came storming to the back of the bus, so mad that you could almost feel the heat from his body as he went down the aisle. I'd been in the big leagues for about a week, and I'm sitting there scared to death, as Yogi told Phil he was going to shove the harmonica up his ass if he kept playing, along with a few other choice words. It was all the more shocking because Yogi was always such an even-keeled guy—it's still the only time I've ever seen him snap. I guess he must have scared Phil a little because Linz tossed the harmonica to him, but rather than catch it, Yogi slapped it out of the air, sending it flying off Joe Pepitone's knee.

Yogi and Phil then went back and forth a bit, with Linz demand-ing to know why he couldn't play the harmonica.

"I give it everything I've got on the field," Phil said. "Why pick on me? I want to win. I'm always trying. I should be able to do what I want on my own time."

"Play it in your room," Yogi snapped.

At that point, veteran third-base coach Frank Crosetti jumped into the argument, scolding everyone on the club: "You act like you just won the pennant, with all this clowning around. You should be ashamed of yourselves after the exhibition you put on."

Phil yelled back at Crosetti, but then the bus quieted quickly, and there was silence the rest of the way to the airport. I'm not sure what got into Phil that day, because it was out of character for him, and I got the feeling later that he was embarrassed by it. It was the type of incident that the public might not hear about these days, because newspaper reporters have long since stopped traveling with the ball club, but at the time, with at least a few newspaper reporters on that bus, there was no hiding from it. In Boston the next day, then, after Phil met with Yogi and apologized, Yogi announced to the press that Linz had been fined $200, and he declared the matter over. As ugly as those few moments were on that bus, some of the players who had been on the team all season thought it may have been helpful in the long run because it gave Yogi, normally so mild-mannered, an opportunity to show he could be tough on the players. Whether it was coincidence or not, we started winning.

It didn't happen immediately, however. We lost that next night in Boston, and again in the first game of a doubleheader the following day. I was scheduled to pitch the series opener, but I was in terrible pain because my wisdom teeth were impacted and I had to have a dentist in Boston pull them for me. My start was pushed back a day, to the second game of the doubleheader, and by then we had a six-game losing streak, the longest of the season. Fortunately, I was probably too young to get caught up in any crisis mentality, and pitching too well to feel any pressure. In any case, I threw a six-hit shutout as we won 8–0 to break our streak, and that seemed to relieve a great deal of tension around the ball club. From there we got hot, made a strong September run, and clinched the pennant on the second-to-last day of the season, finishing one game in front of the White Sox and two ahead of the Orioles.

I received my share of media attention, though nothing like it would be today, when everything is so magnified. I probably would have gotten even more, but I wasn't real comfortable with it. I just wanted to pitch and be left alone. I wasn't exactly a colorful personality. I'm sure the writers in those days found me boring.

Off the field I was the same way. I was never a big drinker or carouser, and I gravitated toward the family-oriented guys. However, my first roommate on road trips was veteran pitcher Stan Williams, and, let's just say he kept later hours than I did. Long before Frank Thomas came along with the Chicago White Sox, Stan carried the nickname the Big Hurt, only his was based on the way he felt many a morning. I can vouch for how he got the nickname because he liked to come back to the room in the middle of the night and wake me up. It was a bit of an eye-opener, that's about all I can say, and I didn't room with him very long.

Fortunately, catcher Jake Gibbs was called up from the minors in September, when rosters expanded, and I roomed with him. Otherwise, I became very friendly with Tom Tresh. He was only a couple of years older than me, and he had young kids of his own. When Jean arrived we stayed with Tom's family for a week or so while we found a house to rent. On the road that first year, I'd go to dinner as part of a group with Mickey and Whitey occasionally, and it would always be fun. A few guys would let their hair down, you might say. I just enjoyed the show and went back to my room after dinner rather than go out with the guys. I was more interested in finding something to do to kill the time during long days on the road when we were playing night games. If I was pitching I'd almost always find a movie to go see, just so I wasn't sitting around all day thinking about the game.

By the end of the season, I'd compiled a 9-3 record but the games were all so important down the stretch that I never really stopped to think I had become something of a phenom, an untouted rookie suddenly dominating in a pennant race. I just kept throwing my sinker and relying on the great infield defense that Clete Boyer, Tony Kubek, Bobby Richardson, and Joe Pepitone provided. Man, could they turn a double play and get a pitcher out of trouble. So I rolled right into the World Series, on top of my game, and Yogi decided to start me in Game 2. It all seemed to be happening so quickly, but it was a huge moment for me, and it was even bigger back in Mabton.

Even at home it was as if I had come out of nowhere to be in the World Series. There hadn't been much written in the local newspaper about my progress in the minors, and then suddenly I was pitching for the Yankees against the Cardinals. My dad was working on a construction job in Oregon at the time and went into a local pub to watch me pitch in Game 2. He told the guy sitting next to him, "That's my son pitching for the Yankees." The guy said, "*Sure* it is, pal." So he didn't say another word to anybody, just watched the game quietly.

By the time I took the mound we were down a game, after the Cardinals beat Whitey 9–5 in Game 1. I was nervous and didn't sleep well the night before my start, but my sinker was moving well for me once more, and I held down a very tough lineup, mostly by getting eighteen ground-ball outs. It was a tight game, 1–1 after five innings, and then we scored one in the sixth to go ahead, two more in the seventh, and finally broke the game open with three in the ninth as we won 7–3. In addition to my sinker, I was able to use my backdoor slider effectively against their left-handed hitters. Elston Howard, our catcher, had convinced me it was a good pitch, and I dropped it on the outside corner to their lefties to get some key strikes. I'd have to say it was the best game I ever pitched, considering the circumstances. It made me feel proud that I'd gotten us even in the Series. Even though I'd won some big games down the stretch, this one truly made me feel like I was an important part of the ball club.

I hooked up with Gibson again in Game 5, and by then the Series was 2–2. Jim Bouton had thrown a gem in Game 3, winning 2–1 when Mickey ended the game with a home run off knuckleballer Barney Schultz, but then the Cards beat us 4–3 in Game 4, thanks to a grand slam by Ken Boyer off lefty Al Downing. This time I was pitching at home, and I recall thinking what a sight it was to see the Stadium completely full. I pitched pretty well again in Game 5, allowing two runs in seven innings before coming out for a pinch hitter in the bottom of the seventh trailing 2–0, as Gibson was just fantastic. Tom Tresh took me off the hook for the loss by hitting a game-tying home run in the bottom of the ninth, but Gibson stayed in and won 5–2 in ten innings when Tim McCarver hit a three-run home run off Pete Mikkelsen.

So we were down 3–2 in the Series, going back to St. Louis. I didn't know I was pitching Game 7 until after we won Game 6 by the score of 8–3, as Bouton pitched well again and Pepitone hit a grand slam. Yogi told me right after the game that I was pitching the next day, as he decided to skip Downing, who had struggled late in the season. I was pitching on two days' rest, but I felt strong and knew that being a little fatigued might even help my sinker. I tried not to think too much that night about it all coming down to this one game, and I remember Elston Howard, in particular, talking to me before the game, encouraging me to just pitch my game, nothing more, and everything would be fine.

I sailed through three innings, but in the fourth a single and a walk put Cardinals runners on first and second with no outs. I got McCarver to hit a ground ball to Pepitone, and we had a chance to turn a 3-6-1 double play. Pepitone threw to Linz, who filled in for an injured Kubek at shortstop the entire Series, for the force at second, but Phil's return throw to me at first was wide of the bag. I stretched out up the line, and finally had to dive for the ball, but couldn't get to it. The error allowed a run to score from second, but it also left me with a jammed right shoulder after I'd landed awkwardly trying to make the catch. I gave up two more singles in the inning, as the Cardinals took a 3–0 lead, and between innings the shoulder quickly began stiffening up. I remember my shoulder problem being communicated to Yogi somehow, and with a runner on first and one out, he decided to pinch-hit for me. I can't be certain if it was because of the shoulder, but I think it had to be a factor. In any case, it proved costly when Downing immediately gave up a home run to Lou Brock and wound up giving up three runs to give the Cardinals a 6–0 lead. We came back against Gibson but he hung in there to go the distance and beat us 7–5 to win the World Series.

It was quite a blow to be tagged with the loss in the deciding game, but what I remember most is so many guys coming over to tell me how important I'd been to the club, and not to worry because I'd have plenty of more chances to pitch in the World Series. I had no doubts myself about that, since the Yankees had just played in their fifth straight World Series, and fifteenth in the last eighteen years. When I received my full World Series share, as voted by my teammates, of $4,300, I thought how nice it would be to be able to count on such money every year. Little did I know the Great Depression, as it applied to the most famous sports franchise in the world, was just over the horizon.

3

The End of a Dynasty

The sting of losing Game 7 of the World Series lingered for weeks, but as spring training in 1965 rolled around, that feeling had given way to a sense of pride. Then, as now, the Yankees measured themselves by what they did in October, and those three starts against the Cardinals made me feel as if I truly belonged as a member of the most famous team in baseball. Little did I know, however, that in those days you didn't officially earn your pinstripes until you survived an important spring training initiation: a night out with Mickey Mantle and Whitey Ford.

I was just getting to the point where I wasn't in complete awe of the two Yankee legends when they cornered me in the locker room one late afternoon after we'd beaten the Mets in an exhibition game.

"Come on, Mel," Whitey said, "we're taking you out."

"Whether you like it or not," Mickey chimed in, with a laugh.

The Yankees held spring training in Fort Lauderdale at the time, but we were on our annual swing through Florida's west coast, staying in St. Petersburg, where the Mets were then based. So we went to dinner at Bern's Steakhouse, a famous restaurant in nearby Tampa. They ordered a drink for me, said I'd like it. They knew I wasn't a big drinker, so they got me something that tasted sweet—vodka and anisette. I didn't even know what anisette was, but it tasted like licorice, and I remember thinking it was something my wife would like. The first one went down easy, so I had another, and another, as Mickey and Whitey told baseball stories and made me laugh a lot. I was feeling good, a bit giddy even before the first drinks came, just to be having dinner with my two baseball idols. We were there for a couple of hours, and as we finished dinner, they made it clear the night was just beginning.

"It's early," Mickey said. "Let's go have a couple of drinks somewhere."

When I got up from the table I realized that my licorice-tasting drink had packed a punch. But I couldn't ask Whitey and Mickey to take me home just yet, or I knew I'd never hear the end of it. So I went with them to a place called The Congress Inn, and again they ordered vodka and anisette for me. After a few more drinks, I felt like my head was starting to spin. I weaved my way to the men's room and ran into Spud Murray, our batting-practice pitcher. I told him I was hurting and practically begged him to take me back to our hotel. He said he would, and I snuck out without telling Mickey and Whitey.

I got back to the hotel just in time. I've never been so sick in my life, and everything tasted like licorice. When I got up the next morning for our workout, my head was pounding. I went and had some eggs, hoping the food would settle me down, but the eggs tasted like licorice. Man, I was hurting. Mickey and Whitey were howling when they saw me come dragging into the clubhouse.

"Welcome to the big leagues, kid," Whitey said.

I don't know how I made it through the day. But I learned my lesson. I never let them gang up on me again. I also never drank anisette again. To this day, I can't even eat licorice candy. Just the smell of licorice still makes my stomach queasy. I never became much of a drinker, so I didn't go out on the town much with those guys, even after I was there for a while. Yet I became pretty close to each of them. They were both great teammates.

Whitey and I had almost nothing in common off the field. He was a guy from New York City—hence his nickname, Slick—who liked to shoot pool and play golf. I was an outdoors guy who enjoyed hunting and fishing. Yet he took a special interest in me at the ballpark because he loved to share his knowledge of pitching, and he saw me as someone who was able to pitch the way he did, getting hitters out by keeping the ball down in the strike zone, with movement. At that time he could make the ball move maybe more than any pitcher in the game. He was the first guy I ever saw who, as a left-hander, could start the ball at a right-handed hitter's hip and make it move back over the inside corner for a strike. It's a pitch that Greg Maddux became famous for mastering, as a right-hander to left-handed hitters, but Whitey was doing it three decades earlier. If Maddux were left-handed, in fact, he would be very similar to Whitey as a guy who dominated with precision pitching.

During my early years, especially, I watched other pitchers and tried to pick up things here or there. Bob Gibson had made a huge impression in the '64 World Series because he pitched so aggressively, intimidating hitters with his fastball and his willingness to come inside. He had an aura about him that made me realize how important it was to bring a little swagger to the mound, but he wasn't a guy I could imitate because I wasn't a power pitcher, and I knew better than to try to pitch that way. Jim Lonborg was a tall right-hander with the Boston Red Sox whom I watched carefully because he had a sinker similar to mine, and I paid attention to how he set up hitters to get easy outs with his sinker.

But the guy I watched and learned from the most was Whitey. I spent a lot of time picking his brain, and he enjoyed talking about the science of pitching. In that respect he personified his other nick-name, the Chairman of the Board, because he was a pro's pro who really studied hitters, knew their strengths and weaknesses, and was always looking for signs of whether he needed to change his pattern of pitching to individual hitters. He made me appreciate how such knowledge could be put to use. When we'd talk, he'd tell me about certain hitters whom he had pitched the exact same way for ten years because they didn't make adjustments. Meanwhile, he'd talk about other guys who made him change his pattern constantly because they adjusted, looked for a certain pitch after he'd gotten them out with it.

Both Whitey and Mickey were always looking for ways to have a little fun, keep the guys loose. They liked to pull little pranks, espe-cially on rookies. For years Whitey told new guys about a Mr. Lyons, whom he described as a huge Yankee fan who put together deals for players and rewarded them with $50 handouts for good games. He'd set them up and then have the clubhouse guy, Pete Sheehy, put a mes-sage in their locker, telling them that Mr. Lyons had called. When they called the number on the piece of paper, they got the main of-fice at the Bronx Zoo. Whitey never got me with his little joke, I guess because I came up late in the year when we were in a tight pen-nant race, but I saw him do it to a bunch of guys. He told me that after a while, the people at the zoo got in on the joke. When a player would ask if Mr. Lyons was there, they'd say yes, he's resting in his cage. Okay, so it wasn't the most sophisticated prank in the world, but it never failed to get laughs in the clubhouse.

My connection with Mickey was fishing. He enjoyed going out in a boat to some quiet spot. He was such a huge star, and fishing gave him a place where he could get away from everything. He liked to go with me because I knew my way around in the water. He was scared to death of alligators and didn't want to be out in the Everglades with somebody who didn't know where he was going. He used to get mad at me because I'd let the boat get a little too close to the alligators sometimes. Fishing was like everything else with Mickey—he was very competitive. If I caught more fish, which I usually did, it used to burn him up.

We'd go into the Everglades to a place called Loxahatachee. If we had a night game, we'd fish in the morning until about noon, then go to the ballpark. Even out in the Everglades, Mickey was instantly recognized. One time I remember another boat going by us and I could hear a guy say, "Look, it's Mickey Mantle." His friend said no, it wasn't, and the first guy said, "Yeah, it is. Look, he's got some dumb rookie to row for him."

As big a celebrity as he was, Mickey always made you feel comfortable, to the point where you could give and take with him. One morning Mickey was a couple of hours late, so to get even I told him that I wanted to go out earlier than usual the next morning, only I didn't show up at all. He came to the ballpark that afternoon and smiled that big smile of his and said, "All right, we're even."

When we were out in the boat we talked about fishing, maybe a little baseball. He'd always ask me about my family, my wife and kids, but he never said too much about his family. He wasn't one to talk much about his personal life. But he loved being around the guys, trading locker-room insults. Even though he was injured often, he always seemed to enjoy every minute at the ballpark, at least until his last couple of seasons. When he stopped being able to hit like Mickey Mantle, it was almost like he was embarrassed that he wasn't helping the team the way he had for all those years. That last year he played, 1968, he stopped going to dinner with us on the road. He had a lot of room service. It was sad because you could see how much it bothered him.

Occasionally over the years I saw that side of him when he drank too much. It seemed like we'd always go out as a group for dinner in Baltimore, and sometimes he'd drink so much that it was all he could do to get back to the hotel. But even then he was always giggly, laughing, having a good time. I never saw the nasty side that I've heard people talk about over the years—maybe that started after he retired and he couldn't be Mickey Mantle the ballplayer anymore. When I was around him, you always had a good time when you were out with Mickey. There were times when he'd come to the ballpark for a day game pretty hungover. It didn't happen as often as you might think, the way the stories have grown over the years. Then again, those stories about Mickey getting up off the training table after sleeping for most of the game, and coming out to pinch-hit a game-winning home run, that really happened from time to time.

It bothered me a lot to see that Mickey had problems with drinking after his career. I think it was because he truly didn't expect to live to be fifty. Both his father and grandfather had died young from Hodgkins disease, and as he got older Mickey was famous for saying, "If I'd known I was going to live this long, I'd have taken better care of myself." It was a one-liner he recited to get laughs, but I truly believe Mickey meant it. Whatever his problems, I'll always remember Mickey most for being such a great teammate. Everybody loved the guy. That was what rubbed a lot of us the wrong way about Jim Bouton's celebrated book, *Ball Four*. Bouton wrote that Mickey could have been a much better player if he hadn't kept such late hours. I don't think that's fair because you had to see the pain in his knees and legs that Mickey endured on a daily basis. It hurt just to watch him wrap his legs with tape and support bandages every day before games. Maybe he needed to drink to deal with that pain. Obviously the alcohol had to take a toll on him over the course of his career, but maybe he needed it just to play as long as he did. That's what I want to believe, anyway, because Mickey meant so much to me.

Mickey was so popular that it was hard to fathom anyone messing with him, yet that's what happened in 1965, my first full season with the Yankees. We went to spring training aware that there was a new sheriff in town, after Johnny Keane had been hired as manager during the winter to replace Yogi Berra. Yogi had been very much a players' manager, and I was shocked when he was fired after the '64 season, his first as skipper. During my two months as a Yankee in '64, Yogi seemed to have the players' respect, perhaps a little more so after he snapped at Phil Linz during the infamous harmonica incident, but in any case, I was shocked to hear that he was fired soon after we lost that '64 World Series.

We knew Keane had a reputation as a tough guy, and the atmosphere in that first spring training with him as manager was much different from life with Yogi. A few of the veterans told me it was unlike anything they'd ever experienced with the Yankees. On our trip to Florida's west coast, Keane announced that he would be having curfew checks at the hotel, and the veterans were nothing short of flabbergasted. This wasn't the regular season, after all, and some of the guys thought this was the time when they should be allowed to have their fun. Keane didn't want to hear it.

What really turned players against Keane was the way he treated stars, especially Mickey. I think he wanted to show everybody who was boss, that things would be done his way, but treating Mickey almost like a rookie was a huge mistake. Fairly early in spring training it almost seemed as if he wanted to embarrass Mickey. Late in games, he'd let Mickey jog out to his position in center field to start an inning, and then send a replacement out for him. That used to burn everybody pretty good. We never could figure out what he was thinking, why he didn't show a guy like Mickey more respect. I never had any problems with Keane, but he was not a real personable guy. He was all business, and he wasn't one to communicate his thinking with the players. His style created tension around the club. Even so, the veterans had a lot of pride as Yankees who were accustomed to winning, and I don't know that Keane's style could be blamed for the way we played that season, as we fell all the way to sixth place, a whopping twenty-five games behind the first-place Minnesota Twins.

I'd have to think it played a small role, but looking back, age and injuries just seemed to catch up with the Yankees almost overnight, and for the first time in decades, the organization didn't have the talent in its farm system to either survive injuries or replace some of the fading stars.

Still, everything revolved around Mickey in those days, and maybe it was coincidence, but his decline began when Keane took over as manager. As it turned out, 1964 was his last big season—he hit .303 with 35 home runs and 111 RBIs. The next year injuries limited him to 122 games, and he wasn't the same offensive force, hitting .255 with 19 home runs and 46 RBIs. Mickey's numbers stayed in that range for three more seasons before he finally retired at age thirty-seven.

Those were difficult years for all of us, as the franchise collapsed in shocking fashion. The Yankees didn't finish higher than fifth in the American League again until 1970, the year after MLB went to a two-division setup in each league, and we didn't return to the postseason until 1976. I don't think anybody saw it coming; certainly I didn't. I had no reason to doubt all those promises everyone had made after I lost Game 7 against the Cardinals about how I'd have plenty of more chances to pitch in the World Series. Mickey had been so impressive during my six weeks with the club, but it wasn't just him. Roger Maris had pounded the ball; Elston Howard was still very productive; Tom Tresh looked like a star in the making; Bobby Richardson was still smooth as silk at second base. And then there was Joe Pepitone.

Pepi was only twenty-four years old when he hit 28 home runs and drove in 100 runs during that 1964 season, and he looked like he might become a superstar. He went on to have some pretty good years, but nothing like what was projected for him. As it turned out, we needed somebody to carry the club at times the way Mickey did in his prime, and Pepi never reached that level. I know he wrote in his autobiography that he failed to make good on his potential at least partly because he spent too much time carousing at night and not enough working on his game. He was quite a character, a guy from the streets of Brooklyn who loved dressing and acting like he owned New York.

Joe and I didn't cross paths off the field very often, but I remember one time having a drink with him after a game in Detroit with Earl Wilson, and some fan was giving him a hard time, trying to get under Joe's skin. I tried to intervene, keep things from getting out of hand. But before we could just sort of sneak out of there, the guy said something else and the next thing you know we were holding Joe back. He wanted a piece of the guy but we basically pushed him out the door before he could start swinging. Joe had grown up on the streets and he could take care of himself. Put it this way: He didn't go looking for trouble, but he didn't run away from it either.

You always hear that Joe was the first player to bring a hair dryer into the clubhouse, and it was true. The first time I saw him using it I didn't even know what the hell it was, but Joe was proud of it. Mickey liked to mess with him, putting talcum powder in the hair dryer and watching with delight when the powder came flying at Joe's face when he turned it on. The thing was, most of the hair he was drying and styling wasn't his own. Even at that time Joe wore a hairpiece, although it took us awhile to figure that out. We didn't understand at first why Joe would wrap a sanitary sock around his head when he'd shower after the game. He was either trying to protect his hairpiece or he didn't want anybody to see him without it. At first he didn't wear his hairpiece during games because he thought it made his hat look too big, but he hated having to be on the field and take his hat off for the national anthem. Eventually he started wearing his hairpiece during games, and he was rather paranoid about it.

I remember he was in the middle of a fight with the Red Sox one night. He and Red Sox shortstop Rico Petrocelli went at it after a takeout slide at second base. It was a typical baseball fight, with players piling on one another. When the digging out began, Joe and Petrocelli were at the bottom of the pile. Most people in that position would have been protecting their face from getting cleated or whatever. But Pepi had both of his hands on the top of his head, trying to hold the piece on. I'll never forget that. We were all laughing at the sight of it.

The hairpiece was a touchy subject, so it was pretty much off-limits as far as clubhouse humor went. Pepi was very sensitive about his appearance. He took great pride in the way he looked in and out of uniform. He was a big, strong guy who always looked good in uniform, but he was constantly checking himself in the mirror before games, making sure that his pants were long enough, that the top of his stirrup socks—remember those?—lined up evenly. And off the field Joe spent a lot of money on suits. You'd never see him with a pair of jeans on, or anything like that. He was always dressed to kill.

Hairpiece aside, Joe took a lot of needling, mostly about his flashy clothes, but also about his habit of disappearing into the night. For all the carousing he did, Joe was pretty much a loner. You'd never see him out to dinner in a big group with Mickey or Whitey. I guess because he was from Brooklyn, he had plenty of friends to hang out with in New York. But as much as he liked carousing, Joe wasn't a big drinker. For the most part, when he came to the ballpark he was ready to play. Still, his late nights became so legendary around the club that guys were constantly kidding him, saying there was no telling what he could do if he got some sleep occasionally. And surely his late nights took a toll on his career. I think Joe would be the first one to tell you that he could have and should have been a truly great player if he had dedicated himself to the game a little more, because he had tremendous talent.

From 1965 on, the Yankees needed somebody like that to lift the team on his shoulders, but nobody ever did it. Mantle and Maris were both injured too much. Elston Howard hurt his arm and couldn't catch for a while. Tony Kubek retired, and it seemed we were always looking for a worthy replacement at shortstop. Whitey had surgery the next year and never dominated again before retiring in 1968. Bouton hurt his arm, had a terrible season. Everything just seemed to fall apart at once in 1965, and the season went downhill quickly.

Despite the losing, I had a great season. I won twenty games for one of three times in my career, finishing 20-9, with an ERA of 2.63. We seemed to play pretty well in the games that I pitched, so I felt I was more fortunate than some of our other starters. Then again, the Yankees were surely getting their money's worth out of me, considering I only made $12,500 that season. In those days the club always tried to lowball the players. Every winter I was fighting for a raise, at first just to support my family. Even after I won twenty games in 1965 I went back to work in that Safeway plant during the winter.

Finally, in 1966, the Yankees doubled my salary, from $12,500 to $25,000, and that was enough for me to justify giving up my off-season job. In one sense I enjoyed seeing how far I could push the Yankees in negotiations. At the same time, I always had a nagging fear that if I pushed too far, the Yankees would tell me they didn't need me. Even after winning twenty games, it was hard to escape that feeling in those days because basically the ball club owned you. But with each year I felt I could push a little harder.

One winter we'd closed a significant gap in negotiations down to a difference of $1,000, but I was holding firm. Finally, it was time to pack the car for my drive across the country to Florida for spring training, so the night before I left with Jean and the kids, I signed the contract, drove it over to my parents' house, and asked my mom to mail it the next day. The next morning, before we left, Lee MacPhail, the GM at the time, called me at home.

"Are you still holding tight?" he asked me.

"Yes, I am," I said, trying to sound convincing.

"Okay, come on down here," he said, "and we'll give you that last thousand you're after."

I couldn't hang up the phone fast enough so that I could call my mother and say, "Mom, please tell me you didn't mail that contract yet."

Fortunately, she hadn't, so I went over and tore up the contract, just to make sure, before I left. It sounds funny now, when you think about the kind of money players make in today's game, but believe me, $1,000 was meaningful when you're twenty-five years old, with a wife and two kids, and you're making $25,000.

One year I became so frustrated with negotiations that I even tried to use an agent—before anybody had heard of such a thing. I was coming off back-to-back twenty-win seasons in 1968 and 1969, and I was asking for a $10,000 raise, from $65,000 to $75,000. MacPhail said I didn't need a raise after the '69 season because I was already being paid as a twenty-game winner. So this time I really did hold out. I missed a week of spring training while I hired an agent, Ed Keating, to negotiate for me.

I had signed with Mark McCormick's agency earlier that year to have them handle my overall finances, and Keating worked for the agency. McCormick became famous as Arnold Palmer's agent, and his agency handled some big-name athletes at the time, but more for endorsement opportunities than contract negotiations. It wasn't until the Major League Players Association negotiated arbitration and free agency into baseball's collective bargaining agreement in the coming years that players had any real leverage, and at the time I signed with the agency I wasn't even thinking of using somebody to negotiate my contract.

Finally, I figured it was worth a try. MacPhail at least took Ed's phone call and listened to him negotiate on my behalf. But it was just out of courtesy. There was no real negotiating. In fact, MacPhail called me and told me I'd never get anything done as long as I was using an agent. After a week of spring training I was becoming impatient, and I finally told Keating thanks, but I would handle it my-self. Maybe as a reward for dumping the agent, MacPhail finally gave in and agreed to the $10,000 raise I wanted. My goal by then was to get to the magic $100,000 figure that several of the game's superstars were making. I got as high as $90,000 in 1974, and I would have cracked that six-figure barrier if I hadn't blown my shoulder out that season, essentially ending my career right then and there.

Anybody who played in my era can't help but be a little envious of the money that players make these days. It was frustrating fight-ing for even small raises, but at the time you just accepted it as part of the deal. After all, was there a better way to make a living? I got to live my dream, playing for the Yankees. I just never imagined that I wouldn't pitch in another World Series, until it became obvious in the mid-1960s that somehow the franchise had allowed the talent cupboard to go bare. The timing couldn't have been worse, either, because Major League Baseball created the amateur draft in 1965, meaning the Yankees could no longer go out and sign any high school or college kid in the land. For years the prestige of playing for the Yankees was such that they could sign just about anybody they wanted, but the draft changed all that.

The scouting department didn't do so well with the new way of doing business either. With their first-round pick, nineteenth overall, in the very first draft, the Yankees selected Bill Burbach, a pitcher who went on to win a total of six games in the majors. Somehow they overlooked future Hall of Famer Johnny Bench, picked thirty-sixth by the Cincinnati Reds. To make it worse, Bench was from Oklahoma, the state with famous ties to the Yankees as the home of Mickey Mantle and Bobby Murcer.

Because of the way we were floundering in the standings, the Yankees had several high picks in the first ten years of the draft, but the only gem the club selected in the first round during that time was Thurman Munson in 1968. More forgettable picks included Jim

Lyttle, Charlie Spikes, Dave Cheadle, Terry Whitfield, Doug Hein-hold, and Dennis Sherrill. In 1967 the organization had the number one pick in the entire draft, thanks to our last-place finish in 1966, and we took Ron Blomberg, known for being the first player to come to bat as a designated hitter, but a disappointment overall who played only a handful of years for the Yankees in a part-time role. To make it worse, consider the list of other players selected in the top thirty after Blomberg: Ted Simmons, John Mayberry, Jon Matlack, Bobby Grich, Vida Blue, Dave Kingman, and Jerry Reuss. I know the draft is far more of a crapshoot in baseball than football or basketball, but obviously we weren't drafting much better than we were playing in those years.

That helps explain why the Yankees didn't get back to the post-season again until 1976, but, in truth, the draft only magnified the dropoff in efficiency on the part of the organization's scouting de-partment. During the two years I was playing in Triple-A I had seen for myself that the Yankees had precious few top prospects at their highest minor-league level, and sooner than probably anyone expected, thanks to age and injuries, it became painfully obvious to Yankee fans everywhere. By 1967 our regular lineup included Jake Gibbs, Horace Clarke, Charley Smith, Ruben Amaro, and Steve Whitaker, in addition to Mantle, Tresh, and Pepitone, the holdovers from the championship era. Doing most of the starting pitching that year, besides myself, were Al Downing, Fred Talbot, and Fritz Peterson.

Suddenly we were losing every year, and searching for answers. The club admitted its mistake on Johnny Keane, firing him early in the 1966 season and replacing him with Ralph Houk, who had taken the Yan-kees to the World Series in his only three seasons as manager, from 1961 to 1963. Houk had moved upstairs to replace MacPhail as GM in 1964, but his return to the dugout proved to have no effect, other than making the veteran players very happy.

My first year with Ralph back in the dugout, in 1966, proved to be a disaster. For some reason, pitching coach Jim Turner wanted me to come up with an overhand curveball, to go with my sinker and slider. I couldn't make it work, but I spent so much time on it that I lost the touch and feel on my slider, and suddenly I was struggling a bit. I'm not sure why Turner messed with me after I'd won twenty games in 1965, but it was a lesson that came in handy as a pitching coach. I became a big believer in the old adage, don't fix it if it ain't broken. I certainly wasn't broken, but by trying to add that over-hand curveball I wound up developing bad habits, losing confidence, and instead of winning twenty games, I wound up losing twenty.

The funny thing was, I made the All-Star team that year. I was 8-12 at the break, but Baltimore Orioles manager Earl Weaver, who was managing the All-Star team, selected me to pitch. I'd made the All-Star team in '65, and now I was so embarrassed at the idea of going to the game with a losing record that I called Weaver and told him I didn't think I should go. He wouldn't hear of it, though. Bobby Richardson made the team as well, so it wasn't as if I was picked because someone had to represent the Yankees. Earl said I'd pitched much better than my record showed, and he insisted that I come to the game. It was true, I had lost a lot of low-scoring games, so I agreed to go, and I wound up pitching two good innings, which was a big thrill. Brooks Robinson made a couple of great plays, and I re-member thinking how nice it would be to have him playing behind me all the time.

Our defense had slipped noticeably since '64, and between that and my failed curveball experiment, I continued losing more than I was winning. By late September I was 12-19 with one scheduled start left, when Ralph called me into his office and told me he didn't want to see me lose twenty games. It was a stigma for any pitcher, so I agreed to give up my last start. Ralph put me in the bullpen, so there I was, on the second-to-last day of the season, in Chicago, watching the game without much thought of pitching when starter Hal Reniff let a lead get away in the eighth inning. The bullpen phone rang and bullpen coach Jim Hegan told me to start throwing. We didn't really have anything to play for, but Ralph played to win every game, and soon enough I found myself on the mound in a tie game with a couple of runners on base. I got a double-play ground ball to get out of the inning, pitched the ninth, and then gave up a run in the tenth on a single, a stolen base, and another single. Afterward Ralph sort of apologized, saying he'd tried to avoid it.

"It's the way our year has gone," he said. "I guess it was meant to be."

It was a real low point for me, but I bounced back to go 15-15 the next season, then 21-12 and 20-14 the next two seasons. As a team we started to show signs of turning things around, winning ninety-three games in 1970 but finishing a distant second to a dominant Orioles team. But we couldn't seem to sustain success from year to year, and the front office wasn't making moves to help. CBS owned the ball club at the time, and the feeling among the players, based on what we knew, was that there was no strong baseball presence in the front office. It was a true corporate ownership, with too many people involved in baseball decisions, and when we had opportunities to make trades, decisions were never made in a timely fashion.

So when a young businessman from Cleveland, one George Steinbrenner, bought the ball club in 1973 for $10 million, or about what the Yankees are now paying Carl Pavano per season, the players were excited. George promised to make the Yankees winners again. Of course, he also promised that he would be a silent partner. But in any case, we felt the club was headed in the right direction. Personally, I felt like I had another four or five good years left, and I remember thinking that maybe I would finally get that world championship ring I'd been chasing for ten years. Problem was, my shoulder had other ideas.

4

Promises, Promises

he sound is what I'll always remember. The pop in my shoulder sounded as loud as a gunshot, at least to me. In retrospect, I probably should have known my career was over right then and there, on June 4, 1974. I was pitching to Frank Robinson in a game against the California Angels at Shea Stadium—Yankee Stadium was being renovated that year—and I'd just gotten him to swing and miss at a curveball. I decided to throw another one, and as I tried to raise my arm a little higher than normal to get an extra-sharp break on the ball, the violent pop sent a lightning bolt of pain shooting through my shoulder. I bent over after throwing the pitch, grabbing my arm, as the trainer came running to the mound. The pain in my shoulder was so severe that I could barely move my arm at all, and when it didn't subside after a few minutes of hoping, I had no choice but to walk off the mound.

Even after the throbbing calmed down, the injury was unlike

anything I'd ever felt in my shoulder. I knew it had to be fairly seri-ous, but at worst I figured I'd be out a couple of weeks. All profes-sional athletes think they're indestructible, to some degree, and I had plenty of reason to believe I could overcome anything. In my eleven seasons in the majors I had never missed a start due to injury, while carrying a heavy workload every year. This was in the days before pitch counts, five-man rotations, ninth-inning closers, and multimillion-dollar investments in players, so starters piled up the innings and routinely pitched complete games. I threw 152 complete games and a total of 2,661 innings during what amounted to slightly less than ten full seasons, and since nobody worried about pitch counts in those days, I can't even begin to calculate the number of pitches I might have thrown during that time.

In those days, starters were expected to go the distance, or close to it anyway. If you went seven innings you felt like you hadn't done your job that day. There were no bullpen specialists, certainly no Mariano Riveras to lock up a win for you, as teams didn't groom closers at the time. For the most part, the guys in the bullpen were there because they weren't good enough to crack the starting rota-tion. And where most teams keep eleven or twelve pitchers on staff now, our staff at the time had nine or ten pitchers, with at least one or two of the relievers serving strictly as mop-up men to be used if the starter was knocked out early. I think starters these days come to rely so heavily on the bullpen that some of them never develop the toughness needed to pitch out of jams when they're a little tired. But then again, we took it to the other extreme when I was pitching. Looking back, it hurts just thinking about all those innings I racked up, and I guess it was no wonder that my arm finally gave out. Every-one in baseball has gotten smarter about protecting pitching arms since then, and though pitch counts don't always tell you how taxing a particular start may be, they do provide guidelines for injury pre-vention.

If coaching methods were less sophisticated in the 1960s, so was medical technology. Compared to the way injuries are treated today, those were still the Dark Ages in sports medicine, and we had a team doctor who wasn't exactly on the cutting edge at the time. After a few experiences with injuries, I didn't have much confidence in him. In 1967, for example, I had a foot injury that mystified him. In every start over the last few months of that season, my right foot would really bother me after about five or six innings on the mound. My toes would start to tingle and feel numb, and it was painful to push off the rubber. Our doctor (who has since passed away and I'd rather not name) said he didn't know what was causing it, so he tried taping my foot every way possible in an effort to relieve the pain. Nothing helped, so at the end of the season Ralph Houk made a call to the Mayo Clinic on my behalf, and I went to have my foot examined there. Within fifteen minutes, three doctors agreed that I had plantar neuroma, a condition in which a bone spur was irritating a nerve. They immediately did a surgical procedure, cutting between my toes to remove the bone spur, and within ten days I was at home hiking the hills in Yakima, doing all kinds of walking without any problem. I never had another problem with the foot.

It was about that time, in the late '60s, that my arm seemed to get sore in spring training every year, and our doctor treated it with x-ray therapy, a practice that was eventually stopped as the harmful effects of radiation became known. At the time it was used as a way to break up calcification in the shoulder. The doctor would have me rest my arm for about ten days, and during that time I'd go to the hospital to have my shoulder radiated. They would dial in the x-ray machine on my shoulder and shoot it with doses of radiation. It seemed to do the trick, too, because after a week or so my arm would feel better and I'd get through the season without any more problems.

I did that for three straight years in spring training, and when I developed the same soreness again the following spring, the doctor prescribed the same treatment. At the hospital, however, a radiolo-

gist who knew my case history told me I shouldn't get any more radiation, that any more would be dangerous. The medical field wasn't
as educated then about the dangers of radiation, but obviously the
amount to which I'd been exposed raised a red flag for this radiologist.

"And I'm not talking about just this year," he said. "In your lifetime you shouldn't have any more radiation."

That was all I needed to hear. Even though I had come to rely on
the treatment, I went back and told the team doctor what the radiologist had said, but, surprisingly, the doctor insisted there was no
cause for concern. He said the radiologist was mistaken, that I could
have another dose of the radiation, and there wouldn't be any problem. He tried to convince me to do it, but I told him I wouldn't, not
after the warning I'd received.

As it turned out, the warning may have come too late. I'll never
know for sure, but all of that radiation may have led to tragedy: My
youngest son, Jason, who died at age eleven from leukemia, was con-
ceived during one of those spring trainings when I was undergoing
the radiation treatment. It didn't cross my mind at the time Jason
became ill, but as doctors caring for him began to question me about
my medical history, they were very concerned when I told them
about the radiation treatment, and they gave me the impression they
thought it could have contaminated Jason's bone marrow. They
didn't say that definitively, and they told me there was no way to
prove it, but they seemed to believe it could have been a factor.

Years later when I was diagnosed with multiple myeloma, a bone
marrow cancer that is related in some ways to leukemia, doctors
again told me that all the radiation I'd been exposed to could have
been a factor. Over the years I've become convinced it played a role
in both of the diseases, and obviously it bothers me. I don't blame
anyone, but I have to say, based on a few examples, the medical care
the Yankees provided was not up to the standards you'd expect in
professional sports, and certainly not from the most successful sports

franchise in history. In fact, when our doctor said he thought I could continue the radiation treatments, I began to seek other medical opinions. I wound up being cared for by Dr. Dan Kanell, an orthopedist in Fort Lauderdale—and father of former NFL quarterback Danny Kanell—who was friendly with the Yankee training staff and hung around the team.

Strange as it sounds, Dr. Kanell even gave me a cortisone injection in the dugout after an exhibition game that year. I had explained my situation with the radiation treatments, and he suggested trying a cortisone shot to reduce the inflammation in the shoulder. I wanted to try it and didn't want to wait for the ball club to make an appointment for me. Besides, I knew that our team doctor wouldn't give his approval. He was very old-fashioned and my guess is that he was way behind in terms of newer medical procedures used for athletes, particularly pitchers. Cortisone shots were fairly new to baseball at the time, and I knew the doctor didn't believe in them, so I didn't broach the subject with him. I did tell my manager, Ralph Houk, and he approved it, so after an exhibition game one day, when everyone had cleared out of the dugout, I rolled up my sleeve and Dr. Kanell stuck a frighteningly long needle into my shoulder. Cortisone is no fun; it causes a burning sensation as it enters the body, but I'll tell you, it worked like magic. After a couple of days all the soreness in my shoulder was gone, and I didn't have any more problems the rest of the year.

I began to rely on cortisone over the next few years. The arthroscope hadn't been invented yet, so there was no such thing as arthroscopic surgery, which is so routine these days for repairing relatively minor shoulder damage with a minimum of invasiveness. Cortisone was not nearly as dangerous as those radiation treatments, but doctors say it can do damage, eating away at muscle tissue in shoulder or knee joints if used too often. I got one per year for a few years, and it was all I needed, until 1974 when that pop in my shoulder changed everything. Unfortunately, there was no such thing as a magnetic resonance imaging exam, or an MRI, in those days. Over the last ten years or so, the term MRI has become as common to baseball as RBI because it's an exam that gives doctors a picture of soft tissue injuries and shows the extent of damage to ligaments, tendons, and muscles. In the old days, X-rays detected broken bones, but otherwise, it was something of a guessing game to determine how badly a knee or a shoulder was injured.

If doctors suspected a tear in the rotator cuff, the only way to get a more definitive answer was to order an arthrogram, a procedure in which dye is injected into the shoulder capsule; if the dye leaks out, it means the ligaments and tendons inside the rotator cuff are torn. At the time I didn't know anything about such a test, and our team doctor didn't even offer it as an option. Instead he gave me the standard diagnosis at the time for any such injury, calling it tendinitis, or inflammation in the shoulder. After a couple of weeks of rest, he put me on a throwing program, thinking it would rebuild strength. When the pain persisted I stopped throwing, rested my shoulder, then followed his orders to try throwing again. I did that a few times, and even though the pain was still there, the doctor thought it was okay for me to try pitching out of the bullpen in September, when the Yankees were in a pennant race and hoping I could help them as a reliever. I made one appearance, allowed three runs in two innings, and I had so little zip on the ball that I'm not sure how I got six outs. My arm was killing me the whole time, and I knew I was done for the season.

I don't know if I ever would have made it back anyway, but when a specialist, Dr. Robert Kurland, diagnosed the injury in November as a completely torn rotator cuff, based on the results of an arthrogram, I couldn't help wondering how much more damage I'd done by continuing to try to throw that summer. The more I learned about such an injury over the years, as a coach working with other pitchers, the more I knew it was possible that I tore it more severely by throwing when I should have been allowing it to heal. Maybe it would have made a difference the next year, maybe it wouldn't have. But as I look back, it seems hard to believe how poorly the injury was handled by the Yankees.

When the pain from the injury lingered over a period of weeks and our team doctor didn't even suggest a cortisone shot, I began seeking help from other team doctors. We'd go to another city for a road game and I'd ask to see the team doctor for, say, the Baltimore Orioles or the Boston Red Sox. I wound up getting cortisone shots that way, injected a few times over a couple of months, as I kept hoping someone could find the exact spot that would give me relief. But as weeks went by, nothing helped, and I became desperate, willing to try just about anything. Whitey Ford recommended a doctor who had helped Giants football great Frank Gifford with a serious injury. To this day I can't tell you what kind of treatment I received. I sat in a chair with needles filled with some kind of liquid stuck in both nostrils. It wasn't acupuncture, but it seemed to work miracles. While I was there I saw people coming in bent over, unable to straighten up, only to walk out an hour later standing up straight as could be. But it didn't help me, so I kept looking for cures. I tried hypnotism but it didn't take. I even spent sessions with a priest who, at the time, was well known for doing psychological work with a lot of baseball players. Unfortunately, the injury wasn't in my head, but my shoulder, although one George Steinbrenner seemed to have his doubts about that.

At this point, I'd had virtually no contact with George since he bought the team from CBS in 1973. I don't think any of the players had. When he took over as owner, we didn't know much about him, but we thought it had to help us because CBS never seemed to want to spend money to improve the club, and no one in charge was willing to make timely decisions. Just about every year there had been trade rumors involving players who we felt could have improved the ball club, but the Yankees never pulled the trigger. As we understood it, a board of directors had to be consulted on every move and by the time everyone had their say, either they couldn't agree or another team had beaten us to the punch. We heard that George would be aggressive in trying to win, so we were all for him taking control. Word of his football mentality was already well known, but at the time we didn't know that he would expect us to win every game we played.

During his first couple of years, he didn't come into the clubhouse and mingle with the players as much as he would in later years. If he had something to say in those days, he would have a club executive read a letter to the players in the clubhouse. He did that a few times, usually involving rules he wanted to establish, such as a dress code for road trips or his policy on facial hair—mustaches only. In one of those letters he listed the numbers of certain players whose hair he thought was too long and ordered them to get it cut. Jim Mason and George "Doc" Medich were two of the players I remember being singled out, and, as a whole, this caused some grumbling among the guys, since long hair was in fashion at the time. Nobody made too much of an issue of it, but Graig Nettles always seemed to have a one-liner ready in those meetings. In this case, Medich was a highly respected pitcher we called Doc because he was going to medical school in the off-season. But he had a big head that was cause for clubhouse humor, and when his number was listed in George's letter, Nettles interrupted: "Tell George that's not all hair. That's Doc's head." That was Nettles. He was never afraid to needle someone, and over the years he would get in his digs at George.

I don't remember ever speaking much to our new owner before encountering him one day in the trainer's room after hurting my shoulder. This was a month or so after my injury, and I was lying on the table, getting some treatment on my shoulder from Gene Monahan, our trainer. George walked into the room, and I don't know if he came in because I was in there, but he didn't waste any time questioning my injured status.

"Stottlemyre," he said, "is your arm really hurting so bad that you can't pitch at all? You've been out over a month. It's got to be feeling better by now."

The insinuation that I was jaking it truly shocked me at first. How in the world could anyone question whether I wanted to pitch? I hadn't missed a start in ten years. I'd led the team in innings every one of those years. I realized that I'd done most of that before George was the owner, but he had to know my history. It was killing me to miss so much time. It really flabbergasted me that he could basically accuse me of not being tough enough to pitch through pain. My first thought was to get up and take a swing at him, but I resisted that urge. Instead, I convinced myself just to leave the room because I was afraid of what I might say if I answered him at all. So I didn't say a word to him, just shot him a hard stare as I got off the table and walked out. That little incident would add to my bitterness when the Yankees released me the following spring.

Actually, George's attitude toward injuries in those days wasn't all that unusual among baseball owners and executives. At the time they didn't have millions of dollars invested in players as they do now, and they weren't as patient or careful in dealing with injuries. The Yankees didn't have any answers for me regarding my shoulder, and after I threw those two painful relief innings in September, they practically ignored me.

It wasn't until I'd been home after the season for about three weeks that our GM, Gabe Paul, called me. He asked what I'd done about my shoulder and when I told him I hadn't done anything but rest it, he basically started chewing me out.

"Don't you think you should take your career seriously enough to look into what's wrong with your shoulder?" he said.

That was all I needed to set me off, after months of being told that I had a lingering case of tendinitis.

"Don't you think you should try to get me in to see somebody who can tell me what's wrong with my shoulder?" I yelled into the phone. "It's a two-way street, Gabe. I'm very serious about my career, you should know that better than anyone. But I haven't heard anything from you or anybody else with the Yankees telling me who I should see or what steps I should take to find some answers."

We went back and forth a little bit. It was kind of nasty. Finally, he said he'd look into having me see somebody, and soon I had an appointment with Dr. Kurland. Based in Los Angeles, he was the Dr. James Andrews of his day, a shoulder specialist to whom many major-league teams sent pitchers for diagnosis and treatment. He immediately gave me the arthrogram, and the dye leaked through the joint so quickly that he said there was no doubt I had a complete tear in my rotator cuff. That was basically a death sentence for pitchers in those days because the only way they could repair it surgically was to cut through layers of muscle in the shoulder.

"Your shoulder is a surgeon's dream," Dr. Kurland said.

"What do you mean by that?" I asked him.

"There are so many things I can correct surgically," he said, "but the bottom line is you'll have a frozen shoulder because the tear is deep inside the shoulder and I'll have to cut through everything to get to it. Your shoulder won't recover from that to allow you to pitch again."

He could see the news hit me hard, but he said all hope wasn't lost. He told me there was a chance the tear would heal itself if given enough time, and that I should rest it all winter, then proceed very slowly in spring training. Hearing all of this was hard for me to take, but I still didn't believe my career was over. I was young and strong, and I was still sure I could overcome the injury. That was my attitude all winter as I rested my shoulder and it began to feel better. Dr. Kurland had informed the Yankees of his diagnosis, and Gabe Paul and I came to an agreement that I would have until May 1 to decide if I could pitch again.

That was only after some heated contract discussion, however. At the time, players were still a couple of years away from being granted the right to free agency, but by then the players' union had already succeeded in gaining certain rights. Salaries could be cut a maximum of 20 percent from one year to the next, and contract arbitration was available to players who weren't willing to accept a club's offer. So Gabe called and told me the Yankees were cutting me the maximum 20 percent from the $90,000 I made in 1974. I told him I'd go to arbitration rather than sign the contract because what did I have to lose? I couldn't get cut more than 20 percent anyway.

Finally, we agreed on a split contract: I would be cut the full 20 percent if I was not able to pitch by May 1 of 1975. If I was able to pitch, I'd again be paid $90,000, the highest salary of my career. Gabe told me I'd be able to take my time in spring training with that May 1 date as my target. That seemed fair to me, and I went to spring training determined not to rush my arm. Because I didn't pitch in any exhibition games, I was more or less on my own program. I threw batting practice on the back field at times, but made a point of being careful. My arm continued to bother me, and I guess management was getting impatient because more than once, Whitey Ford, the pitching coach at the time, told me to watch my step.

"Some people are after you," he said.

He said he couldn't say more than that, but I knew it meant my status was being discussed in the meetings with coaches and the front office. Still, there wasn't much I could do about it until my arm felt better, and I continued to think I had until May 1 to decide if I could pitch. I assumed I would stay in Florida and continue to throw when the season began, but everything changed on the last day of March. It was an off-day for the players, and I had spent most of the day fishing with a teammate, Doc Medich. Late in the afternoon I had just returned to the apartment that I was renting when Bill Kane, our traveling secretary, knocked on the door. He said the ball club had been looking for me all day, and that Gabe Paul wanted to see me immediately. Because I had that May 1 date in mind, it never dawned on me that I was being released. I actually wondered if I was being traded, though I didn't see how, since I hadn't pitched in games that spring.

In any case, I drove to the ballpark and went to the trailer in the parking lot that served as the executive offices. Gabe and Bill Virdon, the manager that year, were waiting for me, and Gabe told me the club had decided to release me. There were no such things as guaranteed contracts in those days, and I found out later that by releasing me before April 1, the club was obligated to pay me for only thirty days of the season, or about one-sixth of my contract. I was stunned.

"You promised me I had until May 1," I said.

Gabe was obviously nervous and uncomfortable giving me the bad news. He sort of denied the May 1 date, insisting it was only a target for me to return, while explaining the club had decided not to wait. I asked him if he had tried to trade me at least, and he said no, he hadn't contacted any other clubs. He said maybe someone would be willing to give me a shot. I was becoming more upset by the minute, but there wasn't much else to say. I basically accused Gabe of lying to me, told him what I thought about it, and stormed out of the trailer.

I drove back to my apartment in a daze. I hadn't seen this coming at all, and suddenly I had to face the reality that I'd been fired, with only thirty days of severance pay before I'd be on the unemployment line if I couldn't find another job. I was thirty-three years old, with a wife and three kids to support. I'd made good money my last few years, but not the millions that players make today to set them up for life after retirement. My arm still hurt and, as I contemplated my future, I was scared.

When word got out that I'd been released, I received a call from Ralph Houk, my old skipper who was now managing the Detroit Tigers, saying they were interested in talking to me. So my wife and I packed up the kids and made the three-hour drive from Fort Lauderdale to the Tigers' camp in Lakeland. I told Ralph that I needed more time before I'd know if my arm was going to allow me to pitch again, and he said that was fine. He wanted to sign me and leave me in Florida when spring training ended in a few days, allow me to continue to throw on my own, and then add me to the roster if my arm responded. That night I was thinking over his offer when I received a surprise phone call from George Steinbrenner. He had tracked me down at the Holiday Inn, the Tigers' team hotel for spring training.

I wasn't too happy to hear from George, since I was convinced he was behind the decision to release me. But the first thing he told me on the phone was that he wasn't even supposed to be talking to me. He hadn't been around the club that spring, after being convicted in federal court of making illegal contributions to Richard Nixon's 1972 presidential campaign—and thus suspended from baseball for two years. I still found it hard to believe he didn't at least sign off on my release, but he insisted he wasn't happy about it and claimed to have nothing to do with it. He said that after all my years with the Yankees, he was concerned about my future and had a deal for me to consider. He wanted to put me on an arm-strengthening program with a guy named Charlie Beech, a kinesiology professor at Michigan State University whom George knew somehow. George said that he would pay me $40,000 to go and work with the guy, regardless of whether I came back to pitch for the Yankees or not. He said this wasn't a deal with the Yankees, but something he wanted to do on a personal level. And he said I wouldn't be committed to re-signing with the Yankees if my arm responded. It seemed fair to me, and after talking with Ralph Houk again, I decided to take George's offer. I didn't sign a contract, but I assumed that George would be good to his word.

I made the arrangements with Beech and flew to Michigan. Before he would start me on his workout program, he insisted that I attend classes for three days at Michigan State. In addition to sitting in on kinesiology classes, I went to three days of a relaxation class as mental preparation for his program. I stayed at Charlie's house, where he showed me films that demonstrated the inner workings of the shoulder during the act of pitching, how the muscles and tendons reacted to the stress of throwing a baseball 90 miles per hour. It was very educational, giving me a better idea of the extent of the damage in my shoulder. For three days he then put me through a series of exercises designed to rebuild my shoulder, doing high numbers of repetitions with light weights. I went home and did the exercises religiously for a few weeks, and though I wasn't doing any throwing, I could feel the shoulder getting stronger. At that point Charlie decided I was ready for the next phase of the program, what he called the power-training phase, and I flew to Los Angeles to work out with Dodgers pitcher Mike Marshall, who had worked with Beech for years. Marshall earned a measure of fame in the 1970s not only as one of the top relievers in the majors but for his own expertise in the mechanics of pitching. He had a doctorate degree from Michigan State in exercise physiology, specializing in motor development and biomechanics, and he could and would talk for hours about the relationship between pitching and the human body.

I didn't know Mike personally, but he was happy to demonstrate the exercises and work with me. My first day at Dodger Stadium I watched him go through his routine, doing things I'd never seen anyone do, like throwing a lead ball into a mattress. I found it amazing to watch the workout he put his shoulder through, knowing he might have to pitch out of the bullpen later that night. In fact, watching him work out kind of got me pumped up, and that turned out to be a terrible mistake. I'd been doing exercises with light weights, but rather than add weight gradually, I tried to keep up with what Marshall was doing. On one exercise I was lying on a bench, holding a barbell behind my head, arms bent at the elbow, then raising it by straightening my arms, when I felt something pop in my shoulder . . . again. It wasn't as loud or as violent as that first pop a year earlier, but I knew right away I'd hurt it again. I guess I was using too much weight too soon, and I could tell almost immediately that I'd undone all the progress I'd made since the original injury. The pain was back, and whatever strength I'd regained seemed to be gone. I wasn't as devastated this time as I was resigned to the fact that I was finished. I waited only a day, then went back home, figuring the comeback wasn't meant to be, and began looking to the future, uncertain of what I'd do next.

Meanwhile, I waited for the $40,000 that George had promised me. And I waited. And I waited. Weeks and months went by, and I didn't hear a word from him. I was too proud, I guess, to call him and ask about the money. It wasn't as if I had a contract or anything in writing. I just couldn't believe he wouldn't be good to his word, but he never came through with that money he'd promised. Well, at least not then. For a long time I thought I'd never see that $40,000, but I didn't forget. And when I got the chance, twenty years down the road, as I'll detail later, I made sure George settled up. With interest.

5

Jason

I have five world championship rings to show for my coaching career, and yet the best job of coaching I ever did might well have been in 1975 when I took a team of ragtag Little Leaguers in Grandview, Washington, whom nobody else wanted, and guided them to an undefeated season. Then again, my two oldest sons, Mel Jr. and Todd, had more to do with it than me, combining to pitch just about every game for that team and dominating most of them. I never expected to wind up coaching Little League that year, even after I accepted the reality of my shoulder injury and quietly retired from pitching. By the time I moved our family back to Washington that spring, it was a week or so into April and I wanted to get the boys involved in Little League. I was told the draft that divvied up players for teams had already been held, but the other managers in the league got together and said they would add an extra team if I was willing to coach it. I'd get my two sons, but the catch was that I had to take a bunch of kids who hadn't been selected in the draft because of their lack of ability.

I'm sure the other managers shared a few winks among themselves in giving me such a team, but the joke turned out to be on them. Being unemployed, as it were, I had a lot of time to work with those kids. We practiced every day after school, when the other dads were at work, and some of those kids whom nobody wanted turned out to be pretty good players. Mel Jr. and Todd did the rest. At ages eleven and ten, respectively, they had the kind of ability that made them stand out, and the fun I had coaching them was about the only thing that made the spring and summer bearable for me.

Though I knew my career was over, I was having a real hard time letting go of the game. At times I would think, *I'm thirty-three, still in my prime, for crying out loud. How can I be finished?* Of course, then I would try to lift my arm over my head and the pain would remind me I had no choice. Still, it didn't seem fair. It hurt to think about how quickly it had all ended. I couldn't even watch a big-league game on TV because it was too depressing, so the only baseball I watched that year was in the form of those Little League games.

The consolation was getting to spend that kind of time on the ballfield with my sons, which wouldn't have happened if not for my injury. They both had obvious talent, and though they were too young then for me to think seriously about whether they had a future in the game, I was impressed that each of them not only seemed to love playing, but had a real desire to excel. They worked hard in practice to get better, and they were so competitive with each other that I'm sure it gave them extra motivation to be the best.

As it turned out, they both made me proud as ballplayers. What father wouldn't love seeing two of his sons reach the major leagues, especially since, in my case, it meant following in their old man's footsteps. As it turned out, Todd, younger by eighteen months, had the more successful career, pitching fourteen seasons in the majors and playing on three world championship teams, two with the To-ronto Blue Jays in 1992 and 1993, and then with the Arizona Diamond-backs in 2001 (though he was inactive that year because of a shoulder injury). Mel Jr. might have had just as much success if he hadn't injured his shoulder, but several surgeries wound up limiting him to just one season in the majors, with the Kansas City Royals in 1990.

Yet even now I wonder if Jason, my youngest, would have been better than either of them. By the time he was ten years old, Jason was more advanced than his brothers had been at that age, at least partly because they had spent a lot of time working with him. His mechanics were so pure for his age, thanks greatly to the help of his brothers, that it looked as if Jason was born to pitch.

By then I had gone back to work in baseball, taking a job with the Seattle Mariners as a roving minor-league pitching instructor. During my two years at home I had opened a sporting goods store in Yakima, and that was paying the bills, but I missed being in base-ball. It's funny because I had always promised Jean that when I was through playing I'd walk away from the game for good. I didn't think I'd want to coach, but after a year at home my wife was pushing me to get back into the game because she saw how much I missed it. Or maybe I was just driving her crazy, being around the house more than usual. Anyway, the job with the Mariners was convenient be-cause, while I traveled some during the season, Jean didn't have to uproot the kids and bring them across the country for the summer, as she had for so many years when I was playing with the Yankees.

The job only paid $25,000 a year, but I still had the sporting goods store as well, and I was home enough to see my boys continue to progress as players themselves. Working with minor leaguers was giving me experience as a coach, allowing me to teach and begin to develop my own style and philosophy as a pitching coach. It wasn't anything like the thrill of pitching in Yankee Stadium, but I was happy being back in baseball, happy watching my sons play ball. Then life changed for all of us when Jason got sick.

My wife was the first to notice that something seemed different with Jason shortly before his seventh birthday. Until then he had been a normal, happy kid who loved to be outside. He was different from Mel Jr. and Todd in that he enjoyed chasing butterflies and catching frogs as much as he did playing baseball. He was fascinated with birds, too; he loved looking for birds when he was playing outside the house and would try to identify them from pictures in a book about birds that he looked at constantly.

I remember bringing Jason to the ballpark during spring training in 1975. I brought the boys around a lot that spring because I was rehabbing my shoulder and not making any of the trips for the exhibition games. One day when the club had a road game, I stayed back, as usual, and went through my own workout. Afterward I was taking a shower when I saw a little frog that had gotten into the shower room somehow. I scooped it up with a paper cup and gave it to Jason, who was in the clubhouse with me. He was delighted because he loved frogs. Then I saw Phil Rizzuto across the room, and anyone who ever listened to Phil broadcast Yankee games on TV for a couple of decades knows he's deathly afraid of everything from thunderstorms to anything that might crawl up his arm. So I pointed to Phil, who was sitting in a chair, and told Jason to go show him his frog. Jason, who was five years old at the time, ran across the room, tapped him on the leg, and as he showed Phil the cup, the frog jumped out onto the floor. Phil jumped out of the chair as if he'd seen a bolt of lightning and ran out of the room. Jason laughed and laughed over that. He couldn't believe a grown man was afraid of his frog, and he got a kick out of telling that story to people.

Jason loved playing ball, too, mainly because he wanted to be like his older brothers. He really idolized them, and they spent a lot of time with him in the backyard. Whatever he did, Jason was a happy kid who had an endearing way about him that made everyone smile. But then he came down with what we thought was a cold at first. When it lingered for more than a week, Jean became suspicious because Jason's equilibrium seemed to be off. He was stumbling at times, which was very strange for someone who, even at that age, was a natural athlete. He didn't have his usual energy, and he began complaining of chest pains. It seemed to pass at first, but when the same symptoms returned about ten days later, we took him to the doctor to be examined.

Jason had some blood work done and after we'd returned home, our doctor called to say we needed to bring him to the hospital right away so they could do some tests. This was alarming, obviously, but the doctor wouldn't tell us what he suspected, saying only that he needed to do more tests before he could make a diagnosis. Turned out he wanted to do a bone marrow test, which we were later told is necessary to definitively identify leukemia. The symptoms can be similar to that of mononucleosis, but when they found that Jason's bone marrow cells were contaminated, it removed all doubt. We were frightened when the doctor told us he had leukemia, but all of the doctors we dealt with reassured us that the odds were with him being cured. In fact, when he was first diagnosed, I remember being told that Jason had a 95 percent chance of surviving and living a long life.

The diagnosis started us on a five-year roller coaster of emotions. Twice we thought that Jason had beaten the disease, after chemotherapy treatments put it in remission, only to see it return. The first time it was in remission for two years, and that's when we were convinced he would be okay. When the symptoms returned, chemotherapy and then radiation treatments again put it in remission, this time for about a year. By this time Jason was going on ten years old, becoming more and more aware that his condition was serious. And yet he was remarkably strong during the ordeal. We had to make monthly trips from Yakima to the Children's Orthopedic Hospital in Seattle for his chemotherapy treatments, and the trips were exhausting for everyone, but especially for Jason.

During his visits there he would be injected with methotrexate, a medicine that had to be given to him through his spine. Jason had to get into a curled position and stay perfectly still, otherwise the drug wouldn't take. The doctors told us it was very painful for Jason, even though they numbed his spine, yet he never fussed, never threw a fit about having to get another injection. Even at a young age he understood it was necessary, to the point where Jean and I marveled at how well he handled it. Years later, in fact, when I was getting chemotherapy for my own cancer, I thought often of Jason and what a strong little guy he'd been during his treatment. It was a memory that constantly inspired me, helping me maintain my strength and determination.

Jason was so resilient throughout his treatment that his friends at school didn't even know he was sick. He played soccer, basketball, and baseball even during the times when he was receiving chemotherapy. More than once, after Jason received treatment, I remember racing home from Seattle to get him to a Little League game on time. He'd hop out of the car and go pitch or play shortstop, and usually he was the best player on the field. Nobody knew anything.

Still, it took quite a toll on our family. Fairly early during Jason's first round of chemotherapy, my wife told me that Mel Jr., who was about thirteen at the time, asked her point-blank: "Is Jason going to die?" Even during the good times, when the leukemia was in remission, life was never really normal. Everything revolved around Jason, naturally, because we wanted to make him happy. The two older boys were great about it. They had always looked out for Jason, but after he got sick they became more and more protective of him. Still, they had to feel a little neglected at times because we paid so much attention to Jason, and most of our family outings were usually to go places or do things that he liked. I even gave in and took him duck hunting because he kept asking. He was really too young for it, but after a while it was awfully hard to look at Jason and say no to anything.

Finally, when the leukemia returned for a third time, Jason's prognosis changed. The doctors told us they couldn't control the disease much longer with chemotherapy or radiation. They told us the best chance at that point to rid his body of the disease was by having a bone marrow transplant. They explained that it could be a dangerous procedure but said that, without it, Jason probably had only seven or eight months to live. The doctors again told us they were confident the transplant would be successful, but by now it was hard not to think the worst. To prepare Jason for the transplant they gave him more and more radiation, killing the contaminated cells so they could replace them with the transplanted cells. For the first time they radiated his head because they were worried about the disease spreading to his brain. That made Jason so tired that all he wanted to do was sleep in the hospital. By now he knew his condition was serious, but he continued to be unbelievably strong. As sick as he was, he seldom complained about anything. Most of the time he seemed more worried about how all of this was affecting his mom. Meanwhile, Jean and I, and the two older boys, talked to one another about trying not to let Jason see how worried we were about him. There were a lot of tears among the four of us, but we made sure not to let Jason see them. We tried to treat him as normally as we could because he was very good at picking up on our concerns.

Both of the older boys volunteered to be the donor for the bone marrow transplant, and the doctors decided that Todd was the best match. His blood type and his bone structure matched most closely to Jason's, which meant that Todd's bone marrow had the best chance of being accepted into Jason's body. It wasn't an easy procedure for Todd. He was hospitalized for a short time, during which they stuck him with an ungodly number of needles as they drew the marrow out of both of his hip bones. Afterward they said they stuck him a total of 260 times. Todd was given anesthesia so he slept through the procedure, and he wasn't in any danger, but it does leave the donor anemic, as well as sore. Mainly it just took a lot out of him, but he never complained. Both of the boys would have done anything for Jason.

Marrow is actually thick blood that they ran into Jason's veins through an IV. The danger in such a transplant, as the doctors explained it to us, is something called graft vs. host disease, a condition in which the body rejects someone else's marrow, and as a result, the transplant patient's own organs are affected. Ultimately, that's what happened to Jason. At first, however, the doctors were very encouraged after the transplant. For the first few days they said his body seemed to be accepting the new marrow, and he was doing well. Every day he seemed to be getting better, to the point where we were starting to think it was a sure thing that Jason would beat the disease. Once again our emotions soared, and then, suddenly, his condition took a drastic turn. From one day to the next, Jason's organs began to reject the marrow and they stopped functioning on their own. Within a matter of hours the doctors moved Jason into intensive care, as his condition was deteriorating rapidly.

He was in intensive care for a couple of days, and what I remember most is that all Jason wanted was to be moved back down to the floor where he'd been. He had pictures and letters from kids in his class hanging on his walls, and some stuffed animals. Though he never said it, I'll always be convinced that he knew he was close to dying and he wanted the comfort of familiar surroundings. The doctors agreed to it, I think because they knew they couldn't do much for him.

At that point, Jean and I realized he wasn't going to make it, and we wanted to spend as much time as possible with him. We had been staying with relatives about a forty-minute drive from the hospital, and leaving Mel Jr. and Todd there most of the time. But the day Jason was returned to his floor, all of us moved into the Ronald McDonald House across the street from the hospital, where housing was made available for the families of patients in grave condition.

The next day, Jason went into a coma, and from there either Jean or I made sure we were in his room at all times. Later that night, after the boys had gone to sleep across the street, we were both in his room, just sort of watching over Jason. It must have been about two in the morning, and Jean had gone for a walk to try to wake up. I was alone with Jason when his heart monitor started beeping, alerting his nurse that his heart rate was dropping rapidly. Within minutes his heart stopped beating, and when attempts at resuscitating him failed, Jason was gone. His organs had begun shutting down after rejecting the transplanted bone marrow, and finally his heart couldn't fight it any longer. It was such a horribly helpless feeling, watching it happen. One of the nurses went to find Jean, and she came running, getting back to the room just after he'd passed away.

We were both very emotional. Even though we knew it was coming, the reality of it left us numb with sorrow. The nurses let us sit in the room until nearly dawn, with Jason still in the hospital bed. We just sat there, as if waiting for him to wake up and tell us this was all some terrible nightmare. It was a way of saying good-bye to our beautiful boy, I guess, because we'd always been careful while he was conscious not to let him see how worried we were about him. Finally, as morning was coming, I knew we had to leave, but it was very difficult. I had a hard time convincing Jean it was time, but finally, we left the hospital, went across the street, and woke up the other boys to tell them. That only added to the heartbreak, because they had continued to hope and believe that somehow Jason would be okay.

The date was March 3, 1981, a few months after Jason's eleventh birthday, and I can't imagine a more painful moment for any parent. But in this case, it hit us that much harder because there was such hope after the transplant. The doctors were so happy with his progress that, just before his condition took a turn for the worse, they were talking about sending him home in a couple of days. When we lost him, there was such a blur of emotions that I don't remember much of anything the doctors or nurses said to us. I just remember having to tell the boys, hold them as they cried, and eventually drive home to Yakima later that day.

It was a week or so later that we received a copy of the autopsy confirming Jason had died from the graft vs. host disease. The doctors couldn't say for sure why it happened. They said they never know exactly why a patient's body either accepts or rejects a donor's marrow. In any case, I remember Jean sitting on the lawn reading those reports that day they came in the mail, and then tearing them up because we didn't want Todd to know. We feared he might blame himself because, as the donor, his bone marrow was rejected.

What we didn't know for years was that Todd didn't need to see those reports to blame himself. A year after Jason's death, Todd did a report on leukemia in high school, and the research told him that Jason's body had rejected his marrow. For years neither Jean nor I knew how devastated Todd was by that discovery. But obviously we were all shattered by Jason's death. The saying is that time heals all wounds, but I don't think the wound from this kind of tragedy ever completely heals, no matter how many years pass. Certainly the toughest time was immediately afterward. It's just so hard to comprehend that your son is gone. Jean said that she was so numb, she felt as if she were floating above the earth somehow, as if caught up in some out-of-body experience.

Maybe the hardest part was that none of us knew how to talk to the others about it. As a family we stayed close and tried to support one another, but we didn't talk about our feelings. Looking back, we probably should have, but it was the kind of thing where nobody wanted to bring up the subject because you were afraid you'd start somebody crying, or reliving the agony we went through. I know I felt that way, and Jean has told me the same thing. She couldn't talk to anybody in the family about it because it was so upsetting. She had one friend she'd go to lunch with once a week just so she could express some of her grief to somebody.

We never sought any counseling, and I know Jean thinks that was probably a mistake. She feels like it would have been healthy for all of us to talk to someone, either individually or as a group. I'm not so sure. I always thought that unless it was someone else who'd lost a child, nobody would understand what kind of emotions I was experiencing. So for a long time we tried to avoid the subject as a family because of the pain involved.

The first Christmas without Jason, Jean insisted that we go to the cemetery and visit his grave. That upset everyone terribly, and I know that Jean felt it was a mistake. I think she started to realize that everybody grieves in their own way, whether they show emotion or not, and it wasn't healthy to push anyone. Christmas was very hard because it's such a family time. The first two years after Jason's death, Mel Jr. and Todd had to talk Jean into getting a Christmas tree, and even then she couldn't bring herself to put it up until a day or two before Christmas. That first Christmas, especially, no one knew quite how to act. Nobody wanted to get out of bed and open presents.

For a long time Jean and I really didn't know how to talk to each other about what had happened. I was concerned about whether our relationship would survive, especially after I read a book on the subject that pointed out how losing a child often leads to divorce or alcoholism. I took those kind of warnings seriously, to the point where I didn't have so much as a beer for about two years. I had never been a heavy drinker, but I didn't want to start leaning on alcohol to ease my pain, or to somehow lead to an emotional argument with Jean. Eventually, as the years passed, it became a little easier to talk about Jason and recall the happy times we had with him. But you never knew when something might remind you of him. Each of us had certain things that reminded us of Jason. I know I didn't go duck hunting for nearly twenty years because it would bring back so many memories of the times I took him with me. Over the years I'd make arrangements to go with friends, and when it came down to it, I'd end up calling them to cancel because I just wasn't able to go through with it. Finally, I forced myself to go with Jean's brother one time, and I go occasionally now. But it always stirs some emotions, thinking about Jason.

We've tried to channel some of that emotion to help in the search for a cure for leukemia, by being active in raising money for research. For years I've lent my name to fund-raisers for leukemia, most notably a charity golf tournament in New Jersey every summer. When I was coaching we always held it on an off-day during the season, and the Yankee coaches and players were great about participating, which allowed us to raise tens of thousands of dollars. After my own illness I started the Mel Stottlemyre Myeloma Foundation, raising money to fight both leukemia and multiple myeloma, the cancer I had to battle. I guess it's only natural that it takes personal experience with a disease to motivate people like myself, because you see how it affects so many lives. When Jason was sick he was on a floor full of young leukemia patients, and I think all of them died. You see that and you feel the need to try and help in some way, especially in my case, as a public figure who can draw attention to a cause.

In any case, after Jason's death I went back to work with the Mariners within a few weeks and finished out that season, but then I told them I needed to take at least a year off from baseball. Rene Lachemann became the Mariners' manager for the 1982 season, and he wanted me to be his pitching coach, but I had to tell him no. I thought it was important to spend as much time as possible with Mel Jr. and Todd at that time, as they were in their final years of high school by then. I wound up staying out of baseball for two years, and it was the best decision I could have made. Jason's death had affected both of them in ways I probably didn't understand at the time, but I knew it had been as difficult for them as it had for Jean and me. I could see how it had changed their personalities, especially Todd.

Although Todd could be a little hyper at times, he had always basically been a very mellow kid; he was always very controlled, with no signs of a temper. After Jason died, however, it was almost like Todd wanted to lash out at the world, take out his anger on everybody else. Sports gave him that sort of outlet. He played basketball and baseball with reckless abandon, and he was ready to challenge anybody at any time. He seemed to be so fearless that I wouldn't let him play football because I was worried that he would injure himself. Junior had always been the one with the temper as a kid, but after Jason got sick it seemed he and Todd almost reversed roles. It may have been that Junior just began to mature with age and calm down a bit, but with Todd the change in personality definitely corresponded with Jason's death. It became something I had to talk to him about, tell him that he needed to control himself, especially in the way he went about playing sports.

Todd and Junior had always been close, but they were also extremely competitive, fighting with each other while playing sports, each of them always wanting to prove he was the better athlete. After Jason's death, however, they became very protective of each other, and less competitive. They really became a team, one doing anything to help the other. They roomed together at the University of Nevada–Las Vegas, where both of them played baseball before getting drafted as pitchers. It's funny, because Junior grew up as a catcher. He never really wanted to pitch when he was young, I think partly because of the expectations that came with his name. He pitched in high school when his team needed him to, but he went to UNLV as a catcher, and only switched to pitching when he hurt his knee and couldn't handle the squatting behind the plate. He had the arm to pitch, and there was a time when I honestly thought he was going to become the better pitcher of the two, partly because he had the experience of catching, which gave him a great perspective on the mental part of pitching.

Unfortunately, he wasn't blessed with the arm that Todd had, and it didn't hold up to the wear and tear of pitching. Junior was very driven to succeed, to the point where it may have hurt him, trying to come back too soon from his arm problems. He was the type of kid who thought he could cut his rehab time in half by doing ten times the work. But his body just wouldn't cooperate. He needed surgery after surgery—he had four on his shoulder and five on his knees over an eight-year period. I don't think anybody could have overcome the toll that took on his body. When Junior finally had to give up on his career, after that one year in the big leagues, I think it was hard for him, especially with his younger brother enjoying more success. But he's handled it well. He has stayed in baseball, working hard at becoming a good pitching coach. He coaches in the minor leagues for the Arizona Diamondbacks, and I think he'll be a major-league pitching coach pretty soon.

Todd's career ended because of a shoulder injury as well, but he had a nice, long run in the big leagues, pitching in the World Series in 1992 and 1993 with the Blue Jays, and eventually moving on to play for the Texas Rangers, the St. Louis Cardinals, and the Diamondbacks before retiring. It took Todd awhile to realize his potential, and I think a lot of the problems he had early in his career were the result of that personal burden he carried after Jason died. He competed so hard that he was always at full throttle, and you can't pitch that way all the time. He was fearless on the mound, which is important, but he was also pretty high-strung, always ready to fight, figuratively, if not literally.

It took Todd a long time to come to terms with Jason's death. For years he talked less than anybody else in the family about Jason, and that was quite a change. My wife used to say that Todd was the one she could talk to about anything. He just had a real hard time accepting the fact that it wasn't his fault that Jason's body rejected his bone marrow. It wasn't something that he felt comfortable talking about with friends or teammates. He told me that what really helped him was meeting with Harvey Dorfman, a noted sports psychologist who works with a number of major leaguers. Todd said the first time he met Harvey, he spent twelve hours talking to him in a hotel room, unleashing, as he put it, the storm that he'd kept inside of him for years. He said he needed to let it out, and when he did, it was a way for him to begin to heal.

I know it's something that never goes away for Todd, and though he admits he had trouble channeling his emotion for years, he also used it to continue to fight Jason's fight, in a way, by committing time and money to charities involved in fund-raising for cancer research. Junior has done much the same thing, recruiting me to help with fund-raising efforts in which he became involved. It's just that Todd, as a public figure, had a bigger platform to help. In 2000 he was named by Major League Baseball as the winner of the Branch Rickey Award for outstanding community service. Among other things, while playing for the Diamondbacks, Todd donated $1 million to the Valley of the Sun United Way in 1999 for cancer research, specifically leukemia. One year while he was playing for Arizona he led a fund-raising effort for a nine-year-old girl who needed a rare bone marrow transplant.

Jean and I have both seen a difference in Todd in the last few years, as he has retired from baseball and devoted time to his four kids, while going to work as a stockbroker. I know he has talked to a minister about Jason, and that may have helped. His wife has been good for him in that regard, too. Both of the boys have wives who have been great for them, and each of them has kids they really enjoy.

Considering what we went through with Jason, I'm grateful that both boys have loving families and seem to be happy with their lives. In the long run, Jason's death brought us all closer together as a family, as difficult as it was for so many years. I know it gave me a perspective on life that I've carried with me since that time. Not that I wasn't as competitive in my job as ever after he died, but I didn't let little things bother me as much. Jason's courage gave me strength during my own cancer ordeal, but it also gave me patience to deal with so many things that come with being in such a high-profile job.

Without that perspective, I might not have been able to handle some of the verbal jabs from George Steinbrenner, for example, in my last few years as pitching coach. But after what we went through as a family, I just didn't sweat the small stuff as much. Jason taught us all about what's important in life.

6

Doc and Darryl

was sitting on my couch in September of 1983 when a vision appeared before me, in the form of an eighteen-year-old pitcher
named Dwight Gooden. I was still out of baseball at the time,
running my sporting goods store in Yakima, but as fate would have
it, I happened to be flipping the TV channels one night when I came
upon a minor-league playoff game on ESPN. I had never heard of
Gooden, and I had no intention of watching him for long on this
night, but after a few pitches I was mesmerized. He was barely a
year out of high school and he was blowing the ball by Triple-A hitters with astonishing ease, or occasionally locking them up with an
overhand curveball that he seemed to throw for a strike any time he
wanted. Who was this kid, anyway? That's what I remember thinking as I sat there, watching him pitch with the polish of a ten-year
veteran. By the time he'd finished a complete-game, 2–1 victory for
the Tidewater Tides, I knew one thing for sure: The Mets might have

been the dregs of the National League at the time, but they had a star in the making who just might change everything.

Six weeks later I got a phone call from Lou Gorman, the Mets' assistant GM, asking me if I'd be interested in the job as their pitching coach. The phone call was so out of the blue that I didn't make the connection immediately, but at some point after I hung up with Lou and began to consider the prospect of returning to New York, of all places, I remembered the kid I'd seen on TV. At that point I thought, *where do I sign?*

It wasn't quite that simple, of course. It had been two years since I resigned from my position as the Mariners' roving pitching instructor following Jason's death, and during that time my life had changed considerably. Staying home, I had seen just about every one of Mel Jr. and Todd's baseball and basketball games in high school in those two years. It gave me the opportunity to reconnect with them, as well as my wife, Jean, after the five-year ordeal we'd all been through during Jason's sickness, and the time together gradually helped us heal as a family and become closer than ever.

Now both of the boys were out of the house, as Todd had graduated from high school that spring and joined Junior at the University of Nevada-Las Vegas. In that sense, the timing was right to return to baseball, but it wasn't easy for Jean, suddenly having so much quiet in the house. It was one more reminder that Jason had been taken from us, since Jean was only thirty-seven years old and feeling much too young to have an empty nest. If I returned to baseball, she would have more flexibility to travel, but there would still be a lot of lonely nights while I was on road trips. Jean knew I was itching to get back into baseball by then, and we both recognized that it would be a good move financially. We were making money with the sporting goods store, but I was putting in long hours there. The Mets job paid $40,000 and, since we had a partner in the store, we could hire people to run it while continuing to own it.

So while Jean was all for me taking the job, she was hesitant about committing to a life of baseball herself. In fact, she tried to talk me into adopting another child, preferably a little girl, but if I was going to take the Mets job, I didn't think it was a good idea. After all those years when baseball had made life difficult on her and the kids, with them joining me in New York only when school was out for the summer, I saw this as an opportunity for Jean to enjoy such a life. She could join me for spring training in Florida, parts of the season in New York, and even on road trips in shopping-friendly cities such as Chicago, Montreal, and San Francisco, depending on how much time the boys would be spending at home in the summer. Finally, she agreed it was worth a try.

The connection to the Mets was Gorman and Steve Schryver, their director of minor-league operations at the time. Both of them had worked for the Mariners during my time in Seattle as a roving pitching instructor, and they had convinced the Mets' GM, Frank Cashen, that I was a good choice. They were overhauling their major-league coaching staff, while bringing in Davey Johnson from their Triple-A team to take over as the manager. I knew Davey only as an opponent, having played against him when he was with the Baltimore Orioles, and I respected him as a fierce competitor. I don't know if he had much say in my hiring, but he was receptive from the first time we began talking that winter. And one of the first conversations we had was about Gooden.

Davey didn't know I'd seen Gooden pitch in that playoff game, which he had managed for Tidewater, and right away he asked me to keep an open mind about him when spring training began. Davey was already convinced that Doc, as I quickly came to know him, could make the jump to the big leagues. Gooden had turned nineteen in November and had pitched only a couple of games in Triple-A after spending most of the season in the Class A minors, yet Davey was sold on his precocious poise and presence, as well as his explosive fastball. Basically Davey wanted an ally in me because he knew he was in for a fight with Cashen, an old-school GM who would sooner be seen in public without one of his trademark bow ties than rush a pitcher to the big leagues. In fact, more than once during spring training, Davey and I had dinner with Cashen, as well as our wives, and anytime we even broached the subject of Doc starting the season with us, he would grab his glass of whatever he was drinking, raise it, and say, "Here's to the ladies." Anything to change the subject. He wouldn't even engage in such a conversation.

I could understand his thinking. Before spring training began, my own instinct was to say that, at nineteen, Doc was too young to start the season in the big leagues, no matter how good he had looked to me on TV. Meanwhile, Davey had been in my ear about Doc throughout the winter, saying, "We've gotta push for this kid. He can help us." It reached the point where I started thinking it was going to be a letdown when I finally saw him in person, because he couldn't be this good. But the first time I saw him up close, early in spring training, he just popped my eyes out. He was even more impressive in person than I expected, as far as the way he unloaded the baseball, out in front on his delivery to maximize the power and movement, and the way the ball came out of his hand, with such life.

Radar guns are all the rage in baseball now, with just about every ballpark flashing the speed of every pitch somewhere on the scoreboard. But two pitchers clocked at the same speed can have very different fastballs because the gun can't measure a pitch's explosiveness, or what we call late life. With some guys the ball just seems to take off, especially up in the zone, as it nears the plate, which makes them very difficult to hit, while others with the same velocity get smacked around because their fastballs straighten out and lack that last-second pop. Doc looked like he had patented the late life, but what made him even more impressive was both his poise on the mound and the confidence that allowed him to throw his big-breaking curveball for a strike on any count. Even in exhibition games that first spring he was making hitters look silly by throwing his curveball on 3-2 counts, usually striking them out and leaving them shaking their heads in disbelief.

So it didn't take long for Doc to convince me that Davey was right, that the kid could go to the big leagues and win right away. Cashen and other executives in the organization remained against it even as Gooden was dominating hitters in spring training, but at the time Davey wielded a lot of influence. He had played with the Baltimore Orioles when Cashen was the GM there, and Frank considered him one of the brightest minds in the game. Of course, he sometimes wished Davey didn't speak his mind as often as he did, revealing his forthright, even brash manner. Cashen was conservative by nature, and he cringed when Davey would display his bravado publicly, as in the spring of 1986 when he declared that he expected the Mets to not only win but dominate the National League. Nevertheless, Cashen had a strong belief that Davey would develop into a great manager, and though their personalities eventually would clash, Cashen at the time was willing to listen to Davey on personnel matters. In this case, he finally gave in on Gooden late in spring training and agreed that Doc could open the season in the big leagues as one of our five starters.

As part of the deal, however, I was under strict orders not to mess with him. Cashen didn't want me tinkering with Doc's delivery, or changing anything that might affect his long-term growth. Not that Doc needed any real help. His one weakness was holding runners on base, as he had a long delivery from the stretch position that made him vulnerable to stolen bases. But the organization didn't want us trying to speed him up for fear it would affect his pitching, and it didn't matter much anyway because he could get an out just about any time he needed it. At the time Doc was strictly a two-pitch pitcher, throwing his four-seam fastball and that wicked overhand, 12-to-6 curveball. He didn't need another pitch then because he had such great command of both the fastball and the curve. I knew at some point he'd need something off-speed, either a splitter or a changeup, and we talked about that. He even worked on the change-up during bullpen sessions, but never to the point where he thought about throwing it in a game. Mostly we just talked a lot about pitching, about the mental part of it, paying attention to hitters' swings and making adjustments based on how hitters were approaching him. He was a great student, really studied hitters during games. He had a knack for knowing when to throw his curve, especially when he saw hitters cheating to catch up to his fastball. Still, he probably threw 70 to 75 percent fastballs that first year.

From the start we were careful not to overload Doc. We put him at the back end of the rotation, so that his first start would be in Houston, rather than New York, and we were careful to limit his innings. Davey was great about bringing young pitchers along, getting them out of the game at a point where they could feel good about their outing and constantly build on positive starts. He might leave a veteran starter in to pitch his way out of a jam in, say, the seventh inning, but almost always he'd take a young guy out, even if his pitch count was good. He just believed that by leaving the young guy in there, he ran the risk of changing the way the pitcher felt about his start, and Davey thought it was vital for young pitchers to build confidence. That's a philosophy I adopted as a pitching coach over the years, trying not to put young pitchers in situations where a strong start could blow up on them and leave them second-guessing themselves.

Initially Davey was not the easiest guy for me, or any of the coaches, to work with. He demanded that we tell him absolutely everything we did, with each hitter or each pitcher. Any time I worked with a pitcher on the side, between starts, he wanted to know everything we did, down to the last detail. I didn't have a big problem with it, but Davey wanted to be in control. It probably took a couple of months for us to trust each other, but eventually he stopped interrogating me after every side session, and we developed a good working relationship. He became comfortable with the work I did with my pitchers, knowing I'd tell him if I did anything significant in terms of changing somebody's mechanics or something like that. At times we had lengthy discussions about individual pitchers, how to get the best out of each of them, and we never really clashed in terms of philosophy. We both had the same ideas about how to build confidence in a young pitching staff, and eventually that became the foundation for a championship.

From the start in 1984 we both saw Doc as the centerpiece to building a contender. And he bore out our belief that he was ready for the big leagues, earning Rookie of the Year honors in '84, winning 17 games, and leading the NL in strikeouts, posting what turned out to be a career-high 276 Ks in 217 innings. In terms of sheer overpowering pitching, he was probably the closest thing anyone had seen to Nolan Ryan at that time. And he was even more dominant in '85, winning the Cy Young Award with a truly remarkable season, as he posted a record of 24-4 with a 1.53 ERA. It was just something magical, being along for that ride.

He did practically anything he wanted on the mound that second year. I remember him getting into bases-loaded, no-out jams a couple of times, and it was as if he could shift to a higher gear at will, throwing unhittable fastballs and occasionally finishing someone off with that knee-buckling curve as he escaped unscathed. His starts in those first couple of years became happenings at Shea Stadium, with fans flocking to see him and starting the now-common practice of hanging K signs for every strikeout. The electricity for every one of his home starts was something you had to experience to believe. It gave you goose bumps sometimes, the way the place would explode with noise when he rang up another punch-out. Doc was so untouchable in those days that Davey would kid me on the nights he was pitching, saying, "Enjoy your night off." And most times he was right; I just wound up enjoying the show like everybody else.

Even off the field, Doc was low-maintenance. In fact, to me the best part about coaching him then was that he was such a great kid.

He loved to compete. He had a real passion for the game. At that time I never could have imagined what would become of his life, how he would eventually destroy his career with drugs, because he didn't offer even the slightest indication. And I felt like I came to know him well. Then again, every time he'd get into trouble over the years, right up until he went to jail in 2006, I'd always have to remind myself that I didn't really know him like I thought I did. To me it just tells you how terribly addicting those drugs can be, because Doc seemed so grounded as a young guy, handling his success with a humble nature that made him very popular with his teammates. Unlike Darryl Strawberry, whose immaturity occasionally rubbed guys in his own clubhouse the wrong way, Doc seemed mature beyond his years.

During those first couple of years I felt it was part of my job to watch out for him because he was so young and already a huge star. He was close to the same age as my sons, and after a while I felt somewhat like a father to Doc as well. We talked a lot, about baseball, about life, sometimes over dinner on the road, and we quickly became very close. I felt like he had a lot of trust in me, which made for a good working relationship. In those first couple of years the club had no reason to suspect that Doc had any problems, but the Mets were careful just the same to try to keep him in a cocoon. Jay Horwitz, our PR guy, was always taking Doc out to dinner on the road, as per instructions from Cashen, doing his best to shield him from the usual late-night temptations.

Doc experienced frustration for the first time when he failed to earn a win in four October starts during our victorious postseason in 1986. He pitched brilliantly in the NLCS against the Astros, allowing just two runs in seventeen innings over two starts, but ran into hot pitchers on the other side in Mike Scott and Nolan Ryan. In the World Series, however, he just didn't pitch well, failing to get past the fifth inning in either of two starts against the Red Sox. Though we won the championship, I know it bothered Doc that he wasn't able to win a game. Still, I didn't think much of it when he missed our victory parade, explaining that he'd overslept, and it never crossed my mind that he could be heading for big trouble.

By spring training the next year, 1987, I'd heard talk that Doc was running with a bad group of friends in his hometown of Tampa during the off-season. But I didn't pay much attention because I saw no signs of a problem. He was the same happy-go-lucky Doc, always upbeat at the ballpark, excited to be doing his thing on the mound. Then, on April 1, just before the end of spring training, Cashen gave Davey the news that Doc had tested positive for cocaine. Davey found me immediately that morning and told me we needed to talk. Instead of going into his office, he walked me out onto the field, I guess because he didn't want anybody else to hear the news just yet. When he told me, I literally almost fell over. I didn't know what to say. My first thought was that Davey was playing some cruel joke on me.

"Davey, it's April Fools' Day," I said. "You're not kidding me, are you?"

Davey said he only wished it were so. I felt like an unsuspecting parent, in denial after being told his kid had a drug problem. What signs had I missed? What could I have done to prevent it? Those questions would tug at me for weeks. I wanted to see Doc that day, as if looking him in the eye somehow would provide some answers, but he'd been told not to show up at camp. And he went right into rehab at Smithers Institute in New York, so I didn't see him until he completed his rehab program some six weeks later. When he returned to the team, it was emotional and a little awkward at first for me. I didn't really know what to say about failing the drug test, or whether he would want to talk about it, so I kind of avoided the subject. I just welcomed him back, made sure he knew how much we missed him on a personal level, and tried to make him feel comfortable in getting back to pitching.

I guess we were all naïve about it, but I assumed Doc would learn his lesson from the episode and never make the same mistake again. He seemed genuinely ashamed about it, concerned above all about what his mother and father would think of him. Remember, he was just twenty-two years old at the time, and he thought the world of his parents. Also, you could tell by his demeanor that he felt he'd let the ball club down. He was a little more subdued than usual for a while, as if he understood he needed to earn the trust of his team-mates again. But everybody seemed very accepting of him right away. It was just impossible not to like Doc. I know I supported him 100 percent when he came back, and our relationship remained strong.

Looking back, I just wish I would have done more to address his problems with drugs. I guess it was easier not to talk about it, and I know I consciously avoided the subject with him for the most part. I did try to become more attuned to his moods and even his behavior, but it wasn't long before he seemed like the old Doc. It helped that Mets fans were quick to welcome him back, giving him ovations at Shea Stadium as if nothing had happened. Once again he seemed to have a perfect temperament around the ballpark. He was upbeat, friendly with teammates, always ready to do his work between starts, and more than ready on his day to pitch. He always seemed to be having fun. He was great with fans, especially signing autographs for kids. Even after he went through rehab, I just never saw signs of a guy who had problems, and as time passed I became more and more convinced that, if anything, he just needed to stay away from his old circle of friends in Tampa, where trouble always seemed to find him.

Doc pitched pretty well that 1987 season, going 15-7 with a 3.21 ERA, not bad for missing the first month of the season. Still, there was no denying that his fastball was not as explosive as it had been his first couple of years. At the time I thought it was just a product of his body beginning to fill out, making him a little less supple, taking a little of the snap out of his delivery. He still had a very good fast-ball, but it just didn't have the same takeoff high in the strike zone as it neared the plate that had made it impossible for hitters to either catch up with or lay off entirely. Hitters were definitely doing a better job of staying off his high fastball in '87, and some of that may have been because they'd seen him for a few years. In some cases, entire clubs were taking a different approach against Doc, cutting down their swings, just looking to make contact at anything down in the strike zone. Doc was still overpowering at times, still had days when he looked untouchable, but he would also get smacked around a little if he didn't locate his pitches with good command. During that 1987 season the Pittsburgh Pirates were one of the first to rough him up.

The Pirates had been a weak team for years but they had some good young players, including Barry Bonds, who would turn them into a playoff team in the near future. Doc had really dominated them in previous years, and before the start of a series with them he made the mistake of telling a New York reporter that pitching against the Pirates reminded him of his Little League days, when he could strike everybody out. The Pittsburgh players saw those comments, and one of their guys told me they were upset about it. They posted the newspaper story in their locker room and went out and lit up Doc, knocked him out of the game early en route to beating us 9–3. It was Doc's first real ass-kicking, and I think he learned a lesson as far as dealing with the media. Still, I couldn't have imagined the Pirates or anyone else doing that to him a couple of years earlier, no matter how fired up they might have been.

It was only years later, after repeated incidents, that I started to think his use of drugs had a significant effect on his pitching. I still can't say for sure where and when that effect showed up, but Doc never did regain that explosiveness in his fastball, at least not on a consistent basis. At that time, I didn't really give it much thought. Even if he wasn't quite as unhittable as he'd been at nineteen and twenty, I was sure that Doc was going to have the Hall of Fame career that everybody was predicting for him. As a coach you try to stay away from thinking like that, but Doc was so dominant that I was never afraid to say he was headed for Cooperstown.

Whatever it was that began to steal the life from his fastball, Doc couldn't make the adjustments to remain on an elite level as he got into his late twenties and beyond. Even with all of his off-the-field problems, I think he could have continued to dominate if he could have developed another pitch, the way Roger Clemens did as he got older. Clemens was just like Doc, a two-pitch power pitcher, and he was starting to have some ordinary years until he came up with his splitter, his late-sinking pitch that changed his entire career. The splitter kept hitters from cheating on his fastball, or even looking for it, and suddenly his fastball was overpowering again. I think it would have been the same for Doc, but he could never master an off-speed pitch like that. We used to work on it during his bullpen sessions between starts, and as long as his fingers were, he should have been able to develop a nasty splitter that would sink hard and late. But he couldn't seem to get the feel for it at first, at least not to where he was comfortable throwing it in games, and then his career kept getting interrupted by his problems with drugs, to the point where he was having to devote all of his time toward retaining command of his primary pitches. He knew he needed another pitch as he got older, but he was just never able to perfect anything.

It was a shame because his problems seemed to catch up with him all of a sudden. After his drug-shortened season in '87, he won 18 games in 1988 and was having a strong year in '89 until a shoulder injury sidelined him for a couple of months. Even so, after he won 19 games in 1990, he had a remarkable career record of 109-46, and he was still a couple of months shy of his twenty-sixth birthday. The Hall of Fame still looked like a lock for him, but from there he earned only 85 more wins, against 66 losses the rest of his career. He missed most of 1994 and all of 1995 when he was suspended for drug use, and he finished his career as a journeyman, pitching for a handful of teams, including the Yankees, before retiring at age thirty-six after being released by the Yankees in the spring of 2001.

So 1990 was his last big year, and the shame of it was that he had a shot at a twenty-win season. We were in Pittsburgh for the final weekend of the season, and though the division-winning Pirates had eliminated us from the race, Doc was pitching the final game of the season with a chance to win his twentieth. I remember it well, partly because Darryl Strawberry didn't play. Mets fans probably always will remember Doc and Darryl as a tandem, both superstar talents who helped revive the franchise and created tremendous excitement at Shea Stadium but failed to realize their potential. To me, however, they were two distinctly different guys, at least during their younger days as Mets. As much as everybody loved Doc, Darryl was more of a self-centered guy who had a tendency to drag the team down with some immature behavior. I thought he was a good kid at heart, but the team relied heavily on him and he didn't always come prepared to give you his best effort, especially when he got caught up in personality clashes or contract issues.

Still, Darryl did some great things for the Mets, and he was one of the most electrifying talents I've ever seen. You never wanted to miss one of his at bats because you never knew when he was going to hit a ball to the moon. There were times when he carried the club offensively in a way that only a few players in the game can. When he was hot he could do for the Mets what a guy like Barry Bonds did for the Giants during his best years. I'm not saying Darryl compared to Bonds as a pure hitter, but he could have the same effect on a club, or an individual game. His power always made him the most imposing presence in the lineup.

Unfortunately there were times when the club felt it couldn't count on Darryl. He had back problems or other little ailments that would occasionally keep him out of games, but sometimes his teammates noted that such ailments seemed to flare up when he was unhappy about contract negotiations or perhaps not feeling so great after a late night somewhere. Once when Darryl missed a game with "flulike symptoms," Wally Backman publicly accused Darryl of dogging it, telling reporters "nobody gets sick 20 times a year like he does." Darryl responded by calling Backman "a little redneck" in the newspapers, and that led to words in the clubhouse between Wally, who is five foot eight, and Darryl, who is six foot six. Scrappy as he is, Wally wouldn't back down from Muhammad Ali in his prime, but fortunately teammates intervened before the situation got physical. Another incident did lead to punches being thrown, when Darryl took a swing at Keith Hernandez on picture day in spring training of 1989. By then Darryl was two seasons away from free agency and upset that the Mets wouldn't give him a long-term contract. He wasn't handling it well, and as they lined up for the team picture, Keith basically told him to grow up, and that led to swings being taken.

The funny thing was the Yankees had been associated with chaos for years, from the time their former Cy Young winner, Sparky Lyle, had labeled them "The Bronx Zoo" in the title of his book chronicling the Billy Martin–Reggie Jackson–George Steinbrenner era. But with Darryl's habit for inciting controversy, it often seemed the zoo was in Queens by the late '80s. Davey didn't call many meetings, but when he did they often involved Darryl. Davey didn't mind players criticizing the manager in the newspapers, but he gave the guys hell when they started sniping at one another publicly, as in the case of Darryl and Wally.

On one occasion late in the 1989 season, Darryl pushed Davey to the limit. That was the year that began with Darryl taking a swing at Hernandez, and he let his contract situation affect him all season. He hit just .225 that year, with 29 home runs and 77 RBIs, and his decline in production from previous years was a big factor in us winning only 87 games, as we finished second to the Chicago Cubs in the NL East. We were in Chicago in mid-September, trailing the

Cubs by five and a half games, so this was our last-gasp attempt to stay in the race, and we were losing 10–4 as we came in for the top of the ninth inning. Darryl had just hit in the eighth, and I guess he'd seen enough because he left the dugout as we were batting, went back to the clubhouse, and began getting undressed to take a shower. Nobody really noticed immediately, but suddenly we were rallying against their closer, Mitch Williams, and we were getting close to Darryl's spot when someone sent word to Davey that his right fielder was nowhere to be found. Neither was Kevin McReynolds, who batted behind Darryl in the lineup. Davey sent someone up the tunnel to the clubhouse to get the two players, and a couple of minutes later they came hurrying into the dugout. It was obvious they'd thrown their uniforms back on in a panic. McReynolds didn't have anything on under his pants and jersey.

We ended up getting Darryl to the plate as the potential tying run, but he struck out swinging, chasing two bad pitches against Williams to end the game and leave the bases loaded. Davey was furious, as mad as I've ever seen him, but he handled the situation smartly. He didn't say a word to those guys that night, but checked with some of our support people to make sure it was true, that indeed they'd been getting undressed while the game was still going on. The next morning, before a day game against the Cubs, Davey called both players in to tell them they were being fined $500 each and that he expected each of them to stand up and apologize to the team in the clubhouse before the game. McReynolds, who was quiet and one of the last guys you'd ever expect to pull a stunt like that, accepted the punishment without a word, but Darryl said he didn't see why he should apologize. He and Davey wound up screaming at each other, until Darryl finally backed down and agreed to apologize to the team. The amazing thing was that Darryl didn't understand why getting undressed during the ninth inning was such an issue, and he told reporters he felt he was being picked on.

There was just no reasoning with Darryl when his anger over his contract situation dictated his behavior in '89 and again the next year. His status as a pending free agent in 1990 motivated him to put up big numbers, and indeed he hit .277 with 37 home runs and 108 RBIs, which earned him the respect he sought in the form of a $20 million contract with the Los Angeles Dodgers. Off the field, however, Darryl wasn't easy to handle, especially as the season went along and it seemed more and more likely that he would leave the Mets.

On that final weekend in Pittsburgh, we were out of the race and Darryl had been in and out of the lineup over the last couple of weeks of the season because of back pain. By then some of the players questioned the severity of his injury, knowing that Darryl was all but out the door as a free agent. On the last day of the season a bunch of the regulars didn't play, as the game didn't matter, but Doc was going for his twentieth win and I thought Darryl would make the effort to help him get it. When he said he wasn't playing, I remember that I was upset with him. Doc was pitching on three days' rest just to take a shot at twenty, and Darryl had to know what the win would mean to him. I'm not saying his back wasn't bothering him, but out of his friendship to Doc, I think he could have sucked it up one last time. Doc and Darryl were never as close as it was portrayed publicly; they were friendly but each tended to hang out with other guys on the team. Still, they'd been through a lot as teammates for seven years, and I know Doc was hurt and angry that Darryl sat it out. As it turned out, it may not have mattered, as Doc lasted only four and a third innings in a 9–4 loss, but that wasn't the point.

It was six years later before the two of them played together again, this time as Yankees in 1996, and I'm sure Doc had forgiven Darryl by then. He wasn't the type to hold a grudge, and besides, he was happy just to be back in baseball. It was kind of strange, being together with Doc and Darryl again on the other side of town, and the other side of their careers as well. Another positive drug test during the 1994 season had caused Doc to be suspended for the remainder of '94 and the entire '95 season. Darryl too had hit bottom, released by the Dodgers in May of 1994 after spending time in rehab for an admitted drug problem, then released the next spring by the San Francisco Giants after being suspended sixty days for a positive drug test. Despite their problems, George Steinbrenner loved the idea of bringing over a couple of big-name former Mets, and he was quick to take a chance on them. Both paid dividends in part-time roles. Darryl delivered some big hits in '96, in the postseason, too, and Doc not only won nine games filling in while David Cone missed three months with an aneurysm in his shoulder, but also pitched his first no-hitter.

It was fun having them around because by this point, Darryl was as easy to like as Doc. After all of his problems, he had matured a great deal. He was grateful to the Yankees for taking a chance on him, and he became a guy who fit in beautifully to Joe Torre's team-first concept. The change was dramatic. Darryl just enjoyed being at the ballpark every day, and everyone loved having him around.

Doc had been through so much, but he was still the same at the ballpark, upbeat, happy to be pitching. From a pitching standpoint, however, it was entirely different working with him as a Yankee. The Mets had that hands-off policy regarding Doc, so I never did much tinkering with his mechanics, his way of pitching, in those early years. With the Yankees it was entirely different. Under Joe Torre I had carte blanche in working with pitchers, and in Doc's case, obviously he wasn't the overpowering young kid from a decade earlier. He hadn't pitched in nearly two years because of his drug suspension, and even though he was only thirty-one years old, he couldn't do the things he'd done in his early twenties.

By this point he had only an average major-league fastball, and he had kind of lost his feel for his curveball. He realized he had to adjust now to stay in the big leagues, and we worked at it that spring. I taught him to use the sinking, two-seam fastball that I always thought he should have developed as a complement to his high-riser.

The two-seamer sank down and in on right-handed hitters, and he began using it effectively. He developed a slider to replace his old overhand curveball, and though he never developed the feel for the splitter, he did begin using a changeup occasionally with some success. In fact, I remember him getting Ken Griffey Jr. out twice with it when he threw his no-hitter against the Seattle Mariners in May of '96. It was a nice moment for Doc, especially because his father was undergoing heart surgery the next day, and when he flew to Tampa to see him, he gave him the game ball from the no-hitter.

Doc went 11-7 with a 5.01 ERA for us that year, making twenty-nine starts because of injuries to Cone and others, before tiring so much in September that we didn't use him in the postseason. Overall Doc was a smarter pitcher, better at some things than he'd been as a phenom. But he'd lost a good 5 miles per hour off his fastball, and that's the difference between overpowering and ordinary against major-league hitters. He was probably twenty pounds heavier than he'd been when he was striking out the world at age nineteen, and that may have cost him some explosiveness, but he'd never had surgery on his pitching arm, and I have to think his use of drugs was at least partly to blame for losing so much off his fastball. You see a lot of pitchers get better as they get into their thirties because they understand their craft and learn how to get outs without being at full-throttle all the time. But Doc never found that lower gear where he could win consistently without his overpowering heater. He didn't pitch with the same confidence, and his body just wasn't as strong. Sometimes he looked a lot older than thirty-one.

It was nice to see both Doc and Darryl enjoy some success with the Yankees before each of them retired in the next few years, but it was also sad in a way because it was a reminder of how far they'd fallen in just ten years. From a baseball standpoint it really bothered me to see what happened to them, because you hate to see anyone blessed with such talent cheat themselves of greatness. From a personal standpoint, it pains me to see how they've both continued to struggle with drug problems. It's a deeper hurt with Doc because of how close we were for years and years. But as much as I want to believe I know the real Doc, he's obviously not the same guy. I'm convinced someone else jumps into his body when he does those drugs, but I still love the guy and I'd do anything for him. I still believe that he's a tremendous human being who just needs a great deal of help. The real tragedy isn't what he did to his career but what he's done now to make such a mess of his life. It haunts me at times because of all those memories with him. I still think back to those early days, how he was at his best when he was in trouble on the mound, turning up his fastball a notch and usually escaping unharmed. If only he could do the same now in his real life.

7

The '86 Mets and the Dynasty That Wasn't

In the twelfth inning of Game 6 of the 1986 NLCS against the
Houston Astros, the most emotionally draining game in which
I'd ever been involved, Davey Johnson leaned over to me in the
dugout as though he were going to ask something important, like
exactly what my plan might be if we ran out of pitchers. Instead he
somehow decided it was the right time to announce that he was having a zen moment.

"You know, you just gotta take in every minute of this," he said,
gazing across the Astrodome ballfield. "You really gotta smell the
roses and enjoy all of this."

I remember thinking, *Man, this guy's crazy. I'm a nervous wreck
here, living and dying with every pitch, and he's talking about smell-
ing the roses.*

But that was Davey. He had a definite calmness about him in
those situations. The stage was never too big for him, the lights were

never too bright, which is why he was the perfect manager for the 1986 Mets. It's a team whose reputation for partying became so notorious that over the years it has almost overshadowed the championship we won. And that's crazy. They were a wild bunch, no doubt, but they were also one of the toughest-minded, hardest-playing, go-for-the-throat ball clubs I've ever seen.

Davey set the tone, saying publicly in the spring that he expected his team to dominate the National League. The players took it from there, playing with a swagger that rubbed some people the wrong way, making us a hated club as the wins began to pile up, but we weren't interested in making friends that year. In fact, our guys were more than happy to brawl if somebody wanted to play macho, and we didn't lose many fights or ball games that season. We were an imposing club that made a habit of scoring runs early in games, putting pressure on the opposition that made our strong pitching even better. We thrived on being the bullies, beating up on teams with our bats, and we had a physical presence that added to our intimidation factor. We took guys out at second base on double plays with hard slides better than anyone in the league. And if other teams wanted to play rough, we had guys who were more than willing.

Ray Knight was a hard-nosed veteran who played the game all out, but he also had a background in boxing, and he didn't back down from anybody. When he famously popped the Cincinnati Reds' Eric Davis in the jaw with a right cross after a hard slide by Davis at third base one night, and then challenged big Dave Parker verbally in the scrum that followed, it sent a message that we were not a team you wanted to mess with. Guys like Kevin Mitchell and Darryl Strawberry could really handle themselves, and they were always ready to fight. Then there were the little scrappers, Wally Backman and Lenny Dykstra, who loved agitating the other team almost as much as they loved getting their uniforms dirty.

It was really a fun year. The guys developed a real closeness, maybe because they spent so much time together off the field. It was a loose team, no question about that. They liked to have fun at night, and in the years to come that would take a toll on certain guys. But not that year. Davey gave them a pretty loose rein, but players knew they'd hear about it if they didn't play hard. It was never an issue in '86. However hard some guys may have run at night, they were always ready to play when they came to the ballpark. And they took a high level of intensity onto the field every day, no matter who we were playing, even as we were running away with our division. Basically everybody was hungry for a championship, after finishing close behind the St. Louis Cardinals in 1985, and the players wanted to prove they were the best.

We had a team full of gamers, but the guy who established the standard was Keith Hernandez. He was into every pitch, every at bat, always talking, and his intensity became contagious. He was a tremendous help to me because he was almost like a pitching coach on the field. He was always talking to the pitcher, pumping him up, reminding him he couldn't make a mistake down and in to a certain hitter, or not to groove one here because this next guy was a first-pitch fastball hitter. He wore out a path between first base and the pitcher's mound, jogging in there to make a point in a big spot, but usually it was just what the pitcher needed to hear at the time. The pitchers had tremendous respect for him and his knowledge of the game, and most of the time they welcomed his input. It got interesting at times because Gary Carter was an All-Star catcher who wanted to have his own input. In truth, both of them wanted to be the guy controlling the game as much as possible, and sometimes the pitcher got caught in the middle. Usually it seemed as if Keith won most of those little power struggles, maybe because he was always in the pitcher's ear from his position at first base.

I guess the most famous one was in that sixteen-inning game in Houston. By the time we finally got to the sixteenth, Jesse Orosco was struggling to hold a three-run lead. He'd given up two runs, and when he then put the tying and winning runs on base, Hernandez went to the mound and Carter came jogging out to meet him.

"Jesse," Hernandez said, "if you keep throwing fastballs instead of sliders, you and I are going to fight."

Keith said later that he meant it more as comic relief than anything, hoping it would ease the tension for Orosco. But Carter, who had been calling the fastballs, took it kind of personally and told Keith he'd handle the pitch selection.

Then he went back, called four straight sliders, and Kevin Bass struck out swinging.

That final game of the NLCS was unlike any game I can remember. The famous Game 6 comeback against the Red Sox in the World Series, which made Bill Buckner such a villain in Boston, is widely regarded as the most spellbinding finish in Mets history. But those sixteen innings against the Astros were murder on the nerves because it seemed the game would never end. And though we were leading the series 3–2, it felt like an elimination game because we knew that waiting for us in Game 7 was Mike Scott, the Cy Young winner that year who had already beaten us twice in the series, dominating us with his hard splitter that we couldn't seem to touch. Some guys were completely psyched out by him because they were convinced Scott was cheating, getting his fastball to sink or sail by scuffing the baseball.

That entire series had the feeling of Scuff-gate. We were convinced that both Scott and Nolan Ryan were scuffing the ball in that series, and we collected balls as they were thrown out of the game and found evidence of scuffing. They were roughed up in the same spot, so it seemed logical that both of the pitchers were using a piece of sandpaper or something else kept in the glove to deface the baseball, which made it easier to create movement on a pitch. Actually, some of our guys were convinced that their catchers were doing the scuffing. In any case, we collected eight or nine balls from one of

Nolan Ryan's starts, and I took them and put them in the bottom of my locker. Doug Harvey, the umpire-in-chief for that World Series, must have heard that we'd been collecting them, and before the next game he came and knocked on the door to the coaches' dressing room. He wanted to see the balls, but I told him I'd already returned them to our bucket of balls for batting practice.

Because it was Nolan Ryan, I didn't think it was right to start a big controversy with the balls. I didn't really think Harvey would do anything anyway. Ryan was a future Hall of Famer, and I couldn't see Harvey going to the mound during the game to check his glove. I'm not saying he was definitely using anything to doctor the ball, because I have all the respect in the world for Ryan. But it just seemed funny how that year, and especially in that series, at age thirty-nine, he came up with a nasty sinker at 92–93 miles per hour that he'd never had in his arsenal.

We tried to make our case more with Scott. Scuffing his fastball made his split-finger pitch all the more deceptive, and, as it was, he had one of the best I've ever seen. At the time the splitter wasn't as prevalent as it has become in the last twenty years. It's effective because it tumbles as it nears the hitter, but the rotation makes it look like a fastball, so it's difficult to detect. The harder a pitcher can throw such a pitch, the more devastating it is because the hitter has less time to recognize and react to the late sinking movement. Some guys use it as an off-speed pitch, but even the pitchers who throw more of a power splitter usually throw it 5 to 7 miles per hour slower than their fastball, somewhere around 85 miles per hour. Somehow, Scott could throw his in the low 90s, about as hard as his fastball, and that's what made it so difficult to hit. Whatever he may have been doing, he had a phenomenal year, and he was at his best against us in that playoff series. The scuffing just made him a little better.

We tried to show the umpires evidence that Scott was scuffing during Game 1, but they didn't want to hear it. Harvey was behind the plate, and I know for a fact that he looked at one ball that was scuffed, when our hitter asked for it to be examined, and he threw it back to him anyway. I know because Scott threw two more pitches with the ball, and neither one hit the dirt or anything, and then Harvey threw it out of play. I took it from the batboy to look at, and the scuff mark was plain as day. At some point Davey tried to show Harvey a couple of the scuffed balls, but he would have nothing to do with it. He was such a righteous presence as an umpire that his nickname around the game was God, and it was obvious that he didn't want to give any impression that someone might have the audacity to be cheating with him behind the plate. So he ignored our complaints, and we couldn't touch Scott. The right-hander threw a shutout in Game 1, outdueling Doc Gooden 1–0, and then dominated us again in Game 4, going the distance again in a 3–1 victory. In eighteen innings against him we'd managed a total of eight hits, all of them singles. So by then we knew we better win the series in six games or we were in big trouble.

That thought was hanging over our heads for all four hours and forty-two minutes of Game 6, which is what made it so nerve-racking. People tend to forget the comeback in that game was every bit as remarkable as the one nearly two weeks later against the Red Sox. We were down 3–0 going to the ninth inning and rallied to tie the game against left-hander Bob Knepper and reliever Dave Smith. After Roger McDowell pitched five scoreless innings of relief, in one of the great unheralded performances of that postseason, we thought we'd won the game with a run in the fourteenth, only to have Billy Hatcher tie it in the bottom of the inning with a home run off Orosco. Finally, we scored three in the sixteenth to take a 7–4 lead, and then still had to hang on for dear life when the Astros scored two runs and put two runners on before Orosco finally struck out Bass with the slider that Hernandez wanted him to throw.

The win uncorked one of the most emotional celebrations I've ever seen. It started in the locker room and carried onto the plane for the flight home that night. That flight became part of the partying legacy of the '86 Mets, after word leaked out that the team had torn up the back of the plane, doing thousands of dollars worth of damage with some excessive celebrating. I don't know what was going on back there because I was sitting in front with Davey, some of the other coaches, and our wives. I know there was a lot of noise in the back, but we didn't really think anything of it. It's not like our flights during the season had been quiet. Davey permitted players to drink on the team flights, and though they were fairly well-behaved most of the time, we'd become accustomed to commotion at times, with some guys having a few too many drinks, getting a little carried away.

Because it was the playoffs, the players' wives were on the flight for the first time all year and apparently that raised the raucousness to a different level. From everything I heard, some of the wives were out of control. All I know for sure is that Frank Cashen was one angry man when Trans World Airlines sent him a letter a couple of days later demanding compensation for $10,000 worth of damages to the plane. Cashen brought the letter to Davey and said he expected the players to make good on it. Davey then called a meeting before the World Series to tell the players that he didn't approve of their behavior, but he made it clear he was on their side. "You guys have made them plenty of money this year, so they can pay for it," he told them. Davey wasn't about to let such a relatively small matter interfere with the chance to win the world championship. And indeed, the club wound up paying the tab.

When the World Series with the Red Sox opened at Shea Stadium, we found out just how emotionally drained the battle with the Astros had left us. Our dugout had all the energy of a day game in August against the Montreal Expos. Bruce Hurst shut us out on four hits as we lost 1–0, and the malaise carried over to the next night when we lost 9–3, playing as if we were in a fog. Suddenly history was telling us we were dead: Only once before had a team ever lost the first two games of the World Series at home and come back to win the championship. We flew to Boston after Game 2, and Davey made a decision that turned out to be a touch of genius: He canceled the off-day workout. Davey was upset about the way we'd played, but nobody had a better feel for the pulse of our club, and he understood that the players needed to recharge mentally more than they needed to take some swings in the batting cage.

So he called a meeting immediately after Game 2 and told them he didn't want anybody showing up at Fenway Park the next day. He said he didn't care what they did or where they went on the off-day in Boston, only that they thought long and hard about how we'd played as a team in Games 1 and 2, and prepared themselves to come ready to play Game 3 the way we'd played all year. Part of Davey's motivation was shielding the players from the interrogation that awaited us on that off-day from the national media. He didn't want his players to have to answer questions about how poorly they'd played the first two games, and he knew there would be no avoiding it if they showed up at Fenway Park. Davey himself didn't even show up, and the media took him to task for it. Outside of New York we were already perceived as the most arrogant team ever to put on spikes, criticized for taking too many curtain calls after home runs and generally basking in self-congratulation, so now our no-show was seen as just another example of arrogance. Suffice to say we took a beating for it in the newspapers.

Unfortunately for me, somebody had to be at Fenway that day. At the threat of a fine to the ball club, Major League Baseball demanded that at least one player be there to provide an off-day story for the hundreds of reporters covering the Series. Usually the obvious choice is the next day's pitcher, Bob Ojeda in this case. Usually the manager is expected to make an appearance as well, but Davey being Davey, he didn't care much what the suits at MLB thought. So that left me to accompany Bobby O to Fenway and together we took questions at a press conference. Ojeda made for a juicy story, since he'd been traded from the Red Sox the previous winter and now was coming back to pitch a must-win game in a ballpark that is generally considered death to left-handers because of the famed Green Monster in left field. In keeping with his personality, Ojeda handled the questions with poise and candor, and I left Fenway that day feeling that Bobby O was the best suited of our five starters to handle the pressure of trying to pitch us back into the Series.

Four runs in the top of the first inning helped relieve some of that pressure, but as it turned out, I was right about Ojeda. He was a tough-minded guy who never seemed to get rattled, and he had learned how to pitch in Fenway with the Red Sox. His best pitch was his changeup, which died down and away from right-handed hitters and made it tough for them to pull. He pitched beautifully that night, changing speeds, keeping the ball down, getting the Sox hitters to chase his changeup and hit a lot of routine ground balls. Ojeda wound up pitching seven innings, surrendering only one run on five hits, as we won a 7–1 laugher. Considering the circumstances, it was one of the gutsiest games I've ever seen anyone pitch, and it changed the entire feel of the Series. Suddenly we had some momentum and a little of our swagger back. Ron Darling delivered another gem the next night, pitching seven shutout innings as we won 6–2 to tie the Series at 2–2 and ensure a return to Shea.

In fact, we loved our chances at that point, with Gooden pitching Game 5, but for the second time in the Series, Doc was surprisingly hittable. Looking back, I wonder if he paid a price for pitching ten innings in Game 5 against the Astros. Doc was brilliant that day, giving up just one run in dueling with Nolan Ryan, giving us a chance to win a crucial game in the twelfth inning. But five days later the Red Sox had scored six runs against him in five innings in Game 2, and this time, pitching on three days' rest, he lasted only four innings, giving up four runs on nine hits. Doc didn't show any signs of fatigue at the time, and at that point I guess we thought he was Superman, but maybe we were a little too cavalier in the way we used him. In any case, Sid Fernandez kept us in that game by pitching four shutout innings in relief, but we lost 4–2 as Hurst shut us down again.

So we came back to Shea for what is surely one of the most famous World Series games in history. Once again Ojeda delivered under pressure, giving us six solid innings, allowing only two runs while pitching on three days' rest, instead of his normal four. Roger Clemens was equally solid, giving up two runs in seven innings, and after each team scratched out another run, the game went to extra innings at 3–3. Then the Sox went ahead 5–3 in the top of the tenth, and when we made the first two outs in the bottom of the tenth, I was like every Met fan in New York City's five boroughs: I thought we were finished. Even Davey looked pale at that point. I don't think he could smell the roses just then.

Shea Stadium, so loud all season, was now so quiet that Tom Seaver, the ex-Met star who was finishing out his career that year with the Red Sox, had no trouble getting third-base coach Buddy Harrelson's attention from the dugout.

"Buddy," Seaver called out to his old pal, "I'll call you soon, and we'll get together."

Buddy told me he just nodded, trying not to think about the long, cold winter that was suddenly staring us in the face. But I'll tell you, not everyone was giving in to the inevitable. I remember Gary Carter looking at us from the on-deck circle, just as Keith Hernandez was flying to center for the second out, and voicing what sounded like a guarantee:

"*I'm* not making the last out," he said emphatically.

Sure enough, he singled to left, and I'm sure Mets fans remember the sequence of events that followed much the way they remember the dates of family birthdays: Kevin Mitchell single to center; Ray Knight single to center; Bob Stanley wild pitch to Mookie Wilson; and finally, the play that eventually forced Buckner to move to Idaho to escape the wackos in Boston who wouldn't let him forget. I always felt sorry for Buckner after that ground ball went through his legs. By that time the game was already tied, we had all the momentum, and I felt like we were going to win it one way or another. And I don't know if Buckner could have beaten Mookie to the bag even if he had fielded the ball, as slowly as it was hit. Mookie could fly, and he'd gotten a good jump out of the batter's box, pulling the ball as a left-handed hitter. Stanley was a little slow getting off the mound, and I know Mookie has always thought he would have beaten Buckner to first.

We'll never know, of course, because the ball wound up in right field, and Knight came around to score easily for a 6–5 victory as we all flew out of the dugout in wild celebration, feeling as if we'd gotten one of those calls from the governor to save us from the electric chair. Buddy was one step behind Knight, following him down the third-base line. And after jumping on the celebration pile, he somehow thought to look over to the other dugout and catch Seaver's eye, as the Sox players stood dumbfounded, watching in disbelief. The two of them are the closest of friends, but Buddy couldn't resist a dig:

"How's tomorrow, Tom?" he called out.

In the clubhouse, we kept looking at one another and saying, "How did we do that?" Yet it seemed fitting for a team that all year long believed it couldn't be beaten. For most of the year it felt like we were destined to win a championship, and now it was clear that destiny was riding shotgun in our dugout. Until it rained the next day, anyway, forcing a postponement of Game 7. We hated the idea of sitting around for a day, and perhaps losing some of the momentum of our Game 6 miracle. But the rainout had a more tangible effect as well, allowing the Sox to substitute Hurst, a Met killer in this series who now had three days' rest, for Oil Can Boyd, who we'd hammered in Game 3.

Hurst wasn't quite Mike Scott in our eyes, but he'd been just as effective, allowing a total of two runs in seventeen innings while beating us in Game 1 and Game 5. Unlike Scott, Hurst wasn't overpowering, but he was a talented lefty who had kept us off balance with his fastball and curve, and when he shut us out over the first five innings in Game 7, we were losing 3–0 and wondering how many comebacks the baseball gods would grant us in one postseason. But then we broke through against him in the sixth, tying the game 3–3. Hurst was probably tired, pitching on short rest, and Red Sox manager John McNamara pulled him after the sixth. He then did us a favor by bringing in Calvin Schiraldi, a hard-throwing right-hander who had come up through our minor-league system before being traded as part of the Ojeda deal the previous winter. His fastball was pretty straight, and he liked to challenge hitters, so let's just say that our eyes lit up when he came in the game. In addition, Schiraldi may have been a bit scarred from Game 6, since he was the one who couldn't get that final out in the tenth and suffered the loss after Stanley came on to give up the wild pitch and the Buckner ground ball.

Sure enough, we pounced on him, scoring three quick runs, including the go-ahead run on a home run by Knight. Schiraldi lasted only a third of an inning, and we went on to win 8–5 as Orosco pitched the final two innings, finally flinging his glove in the air after the last out to start another wild celebration. I enjoyed it as much as anybody, finally getting the championship ring that had eluded me during my playing career with the Yankees. It was quite a thrill, and I was sure there would be more with the Mets. That team was loaded with talent, much of it young talent, and the pitching staff was strong enough to practically ensure years of contention ahead.

But things happened. Sad things. Weird things. Bad things. So many things that sometimes it seemed the baseball gods were making us pay for the Game 6 miracle they'd granted us against the Red Sox. It started the very next spring, when Doc tested positive for cocaine and missed the first month of the season while in rehab. That and a rash of pitching injuries caused us to come up short in chasing the St. Louis Cardinals in 1987, but then we put it all back together in '88 with a team that was just as strong as the '86 champs. We were so much better than the Los Angeles Dodgers, our opponents in the NLCS, we should have cruised into the World Series. We'd beaten them ten of eleven times during the regular season, and when we survived Orel Hershiser, who'd thrown a major-league record fifty-nine consecutive scoreless innings that season, to win Game 1 in Los Angeles, I thought we might sweep them.

But then David Cone paid for the mistake of writing a column in the *New York Daily News* during playoffs. He was horrified to learn that some derisive comments he made about the Dodgers to *News* sportswriter Bob Klapisch, Cone's ghostwriter for the column, which he thought were off the record, showed up in print on the day he was scheduled to pitch Game 2. When word spread to our side before the game that the Dodgers were furious about the story, Cone was visibly shaken and lasted just two innings in a 6–3 loss. Still, after an off-day and a rainout, we survived Hershiser again to win Game 3, and seemed to be on our way to putting a choke hold on the Series until Doc Gooden gave up that infamous ninth-inning home run to Mike Scioscia in Game 4, and we never fully recovered.

Doc was cruising at the time, winning 4–2, and hadn't allowed a run since the first inning. Even so, it was a different era. It doesn't seem that long ago, but managers didn't rely on the bullpen then nearly as heavily as they do now. Given the same situation twenty years later, Doc may have started the ninth, but when he walked John Shelby, there's probably not a manager in the game who would have allowed him to pitch to a left-handed hitter as the tying run. However, it doesn't mean our thinking was wrong at the time. Doc had pitched ten complete games during the season and he still looked like he was in complete control. In addition, we didn't consider Scioscia a power threat, since he'd hit only three home runs that season. But somehow Scioscia caught up with a fastball, pulled it over the wall in right to tie the game, and we lost it in twelve innings. Davey was second-guessed in the newspapers for not going to the bullpen, and even then you can argue that would have been the book move, bringing in Randy Myers to create a lefty-lefty matchup. But Davey didn't always go by the book, and he certainly never worried about being second-guessed. He was a smart guy who was one of the first managers to utilize statistics of individual matchups, but he wasn't a slave to numbers, relying strongly on gut feelings at times about who he could and couldn't count on in big situations.

Davey had just enough ego, in tandem with his intelligence, to be absolutely convinced that he was right in any decision he made. It was a necessary quality for a manager in New York, where the media scrutiny can eat guys alive. That's partly what made Davey so good at the job. He'd get mad if he was second-guessed, but he didn't let it bother him because he was sure he was smarter than everybody else. He might blow up at a writer, call him a few names, but then he'd laugh about it with the same guy the next day. He was that way with the players, too. He'd criticize them publicly from time to time as a way of sending a message, something Joe Torre never does. It can be a dangerous strategy because if players think you're selling them out in the newspapers, they can turn on you. But Davey kind of liked creating a little tension at times. He thought it kept players from losing their edge. So he might tell reporters that he was tired of Ron Darling nibbling with his pitches rather than challenging hitters, or he might slam Lenny Dykstra for trying to hit home runs rather than singles at times. And he didn't mind if they fired back at him in the newspapers, which those guys often did. He figured they'd try hard to prove him wrong, and usually they did.

In any case, Scioscia's home run changed everything in that Series. The shock of losing that game was compounded by a quick turnaround for a day game the next afternoon—and the way our pitching rotation fell at the time. Sid Fernandez, who was rather fragile emotionally, was the wrong pitcher to be taking the mound with all of the momentum on the Dodgers' side, and sure enough, he was knocked out early in a 7–4 loss. Coney made up for his Game 2 debacle by showing some real guts in Game 6, throwing a complete-game five-hitter in a 5–1 victory. But finally Hershiser got us in Game 7, throwing a five-hit shutout to beat us 6–0, and we flew back to New York in utter disbelief that we'd blown the Series.

Still, the future seemed so bright for that team, but from that point, things never felt quite the same. Players grew apart, more concerned with achieving individual goals in search of big contracts than winning as a team. And Davey Johnson's relationship with Frank Cashen and the front office seemed to change drastically. Suddenly there was friction, largely because Cashen thought Davey's loose rein had created a lack of discipline in the ball club, especially when we won only eighty-seven games in 1989, finishing second to the upstart Chicago Cubs in the NL East. Davey disagreed, but the front office began ignoring his input on personnel decisions, more so when Cashen decided to step back from the day-to-day duties as GM and become an adviser as Joe McIlvaine took over as the primary decision maker. I don't think Davey had nearly as much respect for McIlvaine as he'd had for Cashen, and there was more tension between them than most people knew. Hard feelings were cemented on both sides when McIlvaine's first big trade, Lenny Dykstra and Roger McDowell to the Philadelphia Phillies for Juan Samuel, proved disastrous and he publicly put some of the blame on Davey. Samuel was a bust in New York, and McIlvaine responded by telling the press that Davey had pushed hard for him to trade Dykstra because he'd grown tired of Lenny complaining about being platooned with Mookie Wilson.

I know that Dykstra had been complaining a lot, and I remember Davey telling me that he was tired of Lenny's bellyaching. But I don't think he appreciated McIlvaine pointing the finger at him, and their relationship only soured more from that point. McIlvaine seemed to want to reshape the team as he saw fit, trading guys like Wally Backman, whose scrappy style and day-to-day energy was a key to that ball club, to make room for the pride and joy of the farm system,

Gregg Jefferies. The front office loved Jefferies, and that became a sore point in the clubhouse, especially after Backman was traded. Jefferies wasn't real popular in the clubhouse. The veterans perceived him as kind of selfish, just interested in getting his hits, and immature as well. He wasn't good defensively, and the players made jokes about him, saying that, yeah, his dad may have built him a batting cage in his backyard as a kid, but he forgot to buy him a glove. I don't know how many times I heard that one. He was obsessed with working on his hitting, but he didn't seem to want to work on his defense, especially when Davey moved him from third to second base. He shied away from contact making the pivot on the double play, and that was a no-no on a team full of playoff-tested veterans, especially since Jefferies was replacing Backman, who had been fearless turning the double play.

Such clubhouse issues began to tear away at what had been a championship chemistry. Darryl Strawberry and Keith Hernandez engaged in their famous exchange of punches on picture day in the spring of '89, and tension lingered between them. They'd had something of a little brother–big brother relationship, but Darryl eventually grew tired of Keith poking and prodding him to play to his potential. Problems like these, as well as a shoulder injury to Doc Gooden that forced him to miss the second half of the season, contributed to a disappointing '89 season, and when we started slowly the next year, the club was quick to fire Davey. The ax fell on May 29, when we were 20-22 and playing lethargically, and third-base coach Buddy Harrelson took over as manager.

Davey wasn't surprised when it happened. He'd been telling us for a couple of weeks that he thought he was going to get fired. As his coaches, we'd heard rumors that McIlvaine, in particular, thought Davey had lost control of the club. McIlvaine thought Davey wasn't communicating with players, and he was convinced that a lack of discipline was showing on the field. Personally, I never agreed with any of that. I thought Davey handled the players the same as always.

He did have a loose style, but he came down hard on guys if they tried to take advantage of it. He had a lot of closed-door meetings that I don't think management knew about, and to me he handled situations just as he'd done in '85 and '86 when we were on the rise. I think it was really more of a personality clash between McIlvaine and Davey. McIlvaine thought the team had stopped playing hard for Davey, but as it turned out, firing him wasn't the answer to our problems. The club did play better for Buddy that year, going 71-49 to finish with ninety-one wins, but we finished four games behind the Pittsburgh Pirates.

By then Carter and Hernandez, the linchpins in the glory days, but now in the twilight of their careers, had moved on to other clubs. That winter, Cashen and McIlvaine, tired of dealing with Strawberry, allowed Darryl to leave as a free agent, signing speedster Vince Coleman as a replacement. Suddenly we were a team searching for a new identity, one in need of a strong managerial presence. Maybe it wouldn't have mattered who managed in 1991, as neither of our aces, Doc or Frank Viola, had dominant seasons, and we went 77-84, the first losing season since I'd been there. But the weight of such disappointment fell heavily on Buddy Harrelson's shoulders.

Buddy was a great guy and a solid baseball man, but he didn't have Davey's ego, and he worried constantly about how he was perceived by his own players and the press. It affected his decision making, and he had trouble dealing with the stress of the job. He didn't sleep well at night, and I saw him age considerably before my eyes. Until then I had thought I might want to manage someday, but Buddy was a good friend, and I lost any taste for managing after I saw what it did to him. He was fired with a week remaining in that '91 season, and he never even worked as a coach in the big leagues again. It was tempting financially to think about managing, but I don't know if I was suited for it. Over the years managers have had to devote more and more time to the media, meeting with the press before games as well as afterward, and it takes a certain temperament to handle that every day, especially when the team isn't doing well. I think I could have been good at dealing with players, even being a tough guy if necessary—I'm not always as easygoing as people think. But I'm not sure I would have had the patience to cope with answering questions day after day after day.

In any case, the Mets didn't ask me at the time, hiring Jeff Torborg instead. Allowed to leave the Chicago White Sox as manager for the Mets job, Torborg was a rah-rah guy who had too many meetings and too many rules for a group of veterans accustomed to doing things their way, and they just didn't respond to him, losing ninety games in 1992. Suddenly a franchise seemingly on the verge of a dynasty was deteriorating as quickly as my old Yankee club had in the mid-1960s. Looking back, regardless of who was managing in the dugout, upper management may have been too quick to break up that '86 team out of concern for players' off-the-field carousing. I couldn't have imagined it all falling apart the way it did, but a combination of bad trades, bad free-agent signings, and bad luck with injuries turned the Mets into a state of disaster, winning only fifty-nine games by 1993.

Despite the losing, I enjoyed my time with the Mets, even the bad years—until that '93 season, when Dallas Green replaced Torborg as manager thirty-eight games into the season. Dallas is the only manager I've ever truly clashed with, and it only took a few weeks with him for me to know I was working my last season for the Mets. One incident in particular gave me all the indication I needed.

We were in Miami, playing the Marlins on an extremely hot Sunday afternoon. Doc was pitching, and we were leading by three runs after seven innings. Doc had thrown about a hundred pitches as he came into the dugout after the seventh, and as I always do with my pitchers at that point in the game, I went to see how much he had left. He told me he was out of gas, so I walked back to where Dallas was sitting in the dugout to relay the message.

"Doc says he's out of gas," I said. "We probably should get somebody else in there."

"You gotta be shitting me," Dallas said.

"No, that's what he told me," I said.

"Well, you go back and tell Doc that we need him to go and pitch some more," Dallas said, his voice growing louder now. "That's ridiculous. We've got a three-run lead and we need him. Tell him I said that."

So I went back and told Doc, "He wants you back out there. He's not going to get anybody up in the bullpen."

Doc looked at me in disbelief.

"I'll try, Mel," he said, "but I'm done, man. The heat's brutal. I'm wasted."

So I went back to Dallas and told him that Doc would give it a go, but I repeated that Doc didn't think he had anything left.

Now Dallas got even louder.

"That's just ridiculous," he said, loud enough for Doc to hear at the other end of the dugout. "These goddamn guys, they just want to pitch their seven innings and get their ass out of there. They don't know how to pitch late in games. They don't know how to suck it up and finish the job."

I got the feeling Dallas was putting on a show for the players in the dugout. He wanted to let them know who was boss, that he could be a tough guy. He was an old-school manager who longed for the days when pitchers went the distance, when nobody was counting pitches or applying ice to their arms after every start. I thought it was kind of funny, because I saw Dallas Green pitch, and I don't exactly remember him being a guy who toughed it out in the late innings. Still, there was something to be said for the idea that the modern-day pitcher is babied at times, but in this case, I totally disagreed with him. For one thing, Doc was a guy who always gave you everything he had, and when he said he was done, it wasn't because he wanted to bail out with a lead and leave it up to the bullpen. And by this point, Doc had incurred a couple of shoulder injuries. He wasn't a kid anymore, and I felt like Dallas was flirting with a chance for injury by pushing him to keep pitching when he said he was gassed. Doc wasn't a sinkerballer who could get by on fumes. He was a power pitcher who needed to throw the high fastball at maximum effort to be effective. Dallas knew that but he was obviously trying to use Doc as an example for the other guys.

Anyway, Doc went back out there and never got out of the inning. He got hit pretty hard and lost the lead before Dallas finally took him out, and we ended up losing the game. Dallas knew I didn't approve of the way he handled the situation, but I don't think he cared. He did things his way. We had other disagreements, but that was probably the most extreme. Dallas decided to make a point with it afterward. When we got back to New York, he announced that he was putting Darrell Johnson, a buddy of his who he'd added to the coaching staff, in charge of the pitchers' conditioning. The message was that I didn't have the pitchers in good enough shape, so Johnson oversaw their running between starts. It was kind of a farce, really, because the pitchers realized what was going on, and they had no respect for Johnson. If anything, they ran less than they had for me. But it gave him something to do, and I guess Dallas was happy.

That year really became miserable for me, but I was going to stick it out until the end of the season. There was no way I would have come back the next year, but as it turned out, I was fired on the last day of the season. We were in Miami that Sunday, and Dallas called me in the hotel that morning to tell me the club wanted to make a change at pitching coach. I told him that was fine, but I also told him I found it strange that he was the one telling me I was fired because that's usually the job of the GM. Dallas let that pass and said I didn't have to go to the ballpark if I didn't want to, but I went anyway. I didn't put my uniform on that day, and it was really strange. I tried to find things to do to keep myself busy. I'd been there for a couple of hours when Joe McIlvaine walked in. He looked surprised to see me.

"Oh, you're just the person I'm looking for," McIlvaine said.

"You couldn't have been looking very hard," I said. "I've been here all morning."

McIlvaine then told me he hated the idea of letting me go but said it was Dallas's decision. Of course, Dallas had told me it was management's decision, but whatever. I told Joe that, after my ten years with the Mets, I thought he should have been the one to tell me I was being fired. I told him I didn't think he should have left it up to Dallas. He just sort of hemmed and hawed. Joe and I didn't have a great relationship anyway. We seemed to argue every year, either over contract negotiations or something else. But anyway, I said my goodbyes that day and went quietly. A lot of people thought I left on my own, but I was fired. I hated to see it end that way with the Mets, but it's the nature of baseball. You rarely get to leave a job the way you'd like to. In this case, however, it worked out for the best. Had the Mets not fallen into a state of chaos in the early '90s, I may have never found my way back across town for the ride of my life.

8

Return to Pinstripes

The phone call came one afternoon in the middle of October 1995. Arthur Richman, an old friend working for the Yankees as a senior media adviser, said a friendly hello and asked how I was doing, but quickly made it clear this wasn't a social call.

"George wants to talk to you," Arthur said.

George? George Steinbrenner? I hadn't spoken to him since 1975, and the only contact I'd had with the Yankees during that time was turning down the annual invitation to Old-Timers Day that I received in the mail. So I was more than a little suspicious.

"Arthur," I said, "have you been drinking?"

By then Arthur was about sixty-five years old. He has been around the game forever, as a sportswriter, traveling secretary, and confidant to dozens of star players, going all the way back to Joe DiMaggio. Arthur is quite a character. I'd gotten to know him pretty well with the Mets, when he was the traveling secretary, and I knew he liked an occasional cocktail. One spring training I had the room next to his in the team hotel, and every night Arthur would knock on my door and ask, "Stot, you want a toddie?"

But on this day Arthur assured me this was no happy hour prank. He told me the Yankees were making big changes, from the manager to the coaching staff, and that he'd recommended me to George as the pitching coach. He knew all about my bitterness over the way I was released from the Yankees, but he said that George wanted the chance to explain his side of the story after all these years.

From a distance I was aware that Buck Showalter had either resigned or been fired as manager, depending on which story you believed. And as fate would have it, I was a free agent at the time. After leaving the Mets, I'd spent two years with the Houston Astros as their pitching coach, but at the end of the '95 season I had decided to leave that job because my wife's allergies were so bad in Houston. The tropical climate made it hard for Jean to breathe there, to the point where her doctor told her she could not spend any more summers in Houston. The Astros tried to talk me into staying, but Jean had always been with me, wherever I went, and I wasn't going to leave her at home. So I left the Astros job with every intention of sitting out for at least a year, seeing what life was like without baseball.

I'd only been home in Yakima for a couple of weeks when Arthur Richman called. He finally convinced me that George really wanted to talk to me, so I said I was willing to listen. It was early in the afternoon on the West Coast, and Arthur said that George was going to call me at 2 o'clock, my time. I waited until almost 2:30 but had to leave for a dentist appointment. George called shortly after I left and told Jean that he'd try again the next morning. I was shocked that he'd actually called, and, as promised, he did call back the next morning.

Our conversation went better than I expected. From the start George was pouring on the charm, complimenting my work as a pitching coach, then explaining that he'd always felt terrible about the way my career as a player had ended. He told me that, because of his suspension from baseball at the time, he truly was not involved in the day-to-day operations of the ball club that spring. He blamed everything on then-GM Gabe Paul, and though it's still hard to believe he didn't at least sign off on my release, I guess down deep I kind of wanted to put my long-standing grudge to rest. Although I'd remained stubborn about my stance publicly, my feelings had begun to thaw after my son Jason's death in 1981. Who knows, maybe if George had reached out to me years earlier, I would have been just as willing to forgive and forget. The more time I spent in baseball as a coach, the more I understood how things worked in the front office, how finances often dictated decisions involving players. Not that any of it made me feel any different about what happened to me, mainly because Gabe Paul had broken a promise, but being around the game for so long made it a little easier to swallow. So now that George was essentially asking me to accept his explanation—he never actually apologized, but I got the feeling that he was trying—I found my bitterness dissolving.

During that first conversation he didn't offer me a job. He asked me about my plans and I told him I had every intention of sitting out a year from baseball. He then made a point of encouraging me to stay in the game, telling me I was too young to get out. He kept saying that baseball needed people like me in the game, and he said that I should at least consider talking to Bob Watson, who had been hired as the Yankees' GM, about the job as pitching coach. George can be very persuasive, and I have to admit, I was charmed by him.

Basically George's phone call allowed me to justify the idea of going back to the Yankees, and almost as soon as I got off the phone I started getting excited about the idea. I thought about Jason, how much he'd loved the Yankees and how much he would want me to go back to work for them. I talked to my other sons, Mel Jr. and Todd, and though they had been old enough when I was released by the

Yankees to hold their own grudge toward George, they too thought the time was right. And Jean loved the idea of returning to New York.

So I began talking to Bob Watson, whom I knew because he'd just left the Astros as GM to take over the same job with the Yankees. He told me they were going to hire Joe Torre as manager, and though I didn't know Joe personally, I had a high regard for him, having watched him manage the Atlanta Braves and St. Louis Cardinals during my time as the Mets' pitching coach. After a couple of discussions, Bob offered me the job as pitching coach and I accepted.

The next step was talking contract with Joe Molloy, George's son-in-law who, at the time, looked to be in line to take over for the Boss someday. Later Molloy's marriage to George's daughter ended in divorce, and he is no longer involved with the Yankees. But at the time, Molloy, a former phys ed teacher, was handling contract negotiations. By the time I left the Mets I had been making $140,000 a year, a long way from the $40,000 where I started in 1984. The Astros didn't pay as well, $75,000 for the first year, $90,000 for the second, and now, after some discussion, I agreed to a $100,000 salary for my first year with the Yankees. But for me that was just a base salary, if you will. I hadn't forgotten the $40,000 that George had promised—but never paid—me during that phone call in 1975 when he convinced me to rehab my shoulder with his kinesiologist friend, Charlie Beech, at Michigan State. Over the years I'd given up on the idea of ever getting that money, but now, given the opportunity, I wasn't about to let it pass.

I told Joe the story and explained that I had to have an additional $40,000 to seal the deal. I told him it was my way of bringing closure to my bitterness toward George. Joe didn't seem surprised by the story. He even chuckled a bit, and I got the feeling that he'd heard similar stories about his father-in-law. By the time I had this discussion with Joe, the Yankees had acknowledged reports that I was returning as pitching coach, and the New York newspapers played up the story. That gave me a little extra leverage, as I mentioned to Joe, because he knew that George wouldn't want my story about the $40,000 to hit the papers as the reason I backed out of the deal. If Joe had said he couldn't do it, I was determined to walk away. I felt that strongly about holding George to his word. It never got to that point, however, as Joe agreed that I was owed the money. I'm not sure if he ever even brought it to George, because George didn't say anything to me about it, but in any case, the money wasn't part of my contract. I had it put in writing, but the money was paid separately. I told Joe the additional money could be deferred, if the club preferred, and that's what he did.

For two years the $40,000 was deferred, and at that point, George called me up to his office to tell me he wasn't in the business of banking, that he wanted to conclude this transaction. I think Joe explained it to him at some point, but George never did say anything to me about our original conversation, so I don't know for sure. I just know that I ended up with $80,000 plus interest. At first George said he wasn't going to pay any interest on the money, but I figured I'd push him as far as I could, and I told him I had only agreed to defer the money with interest. Maybe he felt guilty about never paying me in the first place, but in any case, he agreed to pay the interest and it turned out to be a nice little piece of change, some twenty years in the making.

With that old score settled, I was delighted to be a Yankee again. I wasn't naïve, though. I knew George's history of hiring and firing very well, and I knew that the pitching coach had been a prime target over the years whenever the Yankees were underachieving. So I took the job with the attitude that it might only be a one-year stay. I was going to enjoy it and do things my way, so that if I did get fired, I wouldn't have any regrets. I soon found out that, as the new manager, Joe Torre felt the same way. Joe, who I knew only from a distance, didn't have a great record as a manager in three previous stints with the New York Mets, Atlanta Braves, and St. Louis Cardinals, but I quickly learned that he was a smart, savvy man who was very secure in his ability to manage, to the point where he wasn't going to be intimidated by the Yankee owner's famous temper.

I'm sure I would have enjoyed my first spring training back with the Yankees, 1996, no matter who was managing, because it really was emotional for me to wear the pinstripes again. But working with Joe made it feel all the more special. It was so easy working with him. From the start Joe was very straightforward. His message to me was simple: You've got a job to do and I trust you. I know what you can do, so just do your thing and I'll support you 100 percent. Joe treated all of the coaches that way, and it created a feeling of kinship that helped us bond quickly as a staff.

I remember my wife asking early in spring training how it was going, working with a new manager and coaches, and by then I already felt amazingly comfortable. Joe instantly created an atmosphere of goodwill by the level of trust he had for all of the coaches. That's what makes Joe such a great manager. He's the same way with his players. He just has a feel for people. He talks a lot about trust, and it's that trust that makes people want to go the extra mile for Joe.

As that first season unfolded, I found out just how important Joe thought it was to maintain that atmosphere of goodwill, not only among the coaches, but the support staff as well. Any time we had a night free on a road trip, Joe would organize a group dinner that included coaches, trainers, the conditioning coach, the traveling secretary, and so forth. It was a way of getting everybody together, maybe to talk a little baseball at times, but mostly just to relax and learn to enjoy one another's company. I had been on clubs that might do something like this once or twice a season, but in this case it was more like once a road trip.

Joe loves to do things first class, and he has a network of five-star restaurants around the country. He is quite a wine connoisseur, as well, and if we were going to a city where the wine didn't quite meet his approval, Joe would bring wine on the plane with us, and then to the restaurant. We had some great times, and I do believe those dinners paid dividends over the years. They were the kind of thing we needed for maintaining a feeling of togetherness over the course of a long season, especially during tough times. Joe never used them as a place to talk business formally. He never made speeches. He'd just make a toast at the start, to a good season, a good game, or whatever. After he survived prostate cancer in 1999, and then I had my own ordeal with cancer the next year, the toast was always to good health for everybody. As the wine was consumed, the baseball stories became more and more entertaining. There was a lot of laughter at those dinners, and usually over dessert everybody would play liar's poker with dollar bills, or a dice game that trainer Steve Donahue brought.

Joe likes to sample the restaurants in New York as well. He doesn't mind eating late, so he'll go into the city and have dinner with his wife, Ali, after we've played a night game. He invited me many times but I rarely went with him because I don't like to eat that late. Joe has become such a celebrity during his tenure as Yankee manager that he can walk into any restaurant in the city and get the best table, and he enjoys that lifestyle. He's always playing the role of host. Sometimes I don't know how he has time for everybody that he entertains, but it just seems to come natural to him. In his next life I think he's coming back as a maitre d'.

In some ways, Joe seemed to become as much host and narrator as manager during that first season. He'd grown up in Brooklyn, after all, and he had a personable touch with the media, so as we rolled along winning games, he seemed to be entertaining the entire city of New York. He really became the storyline to that season in many ways, as the national media also picked up on his careerlong quest to reach the World Series. The story transcended baseball in some ways, as Joe was surrounded by family heartache—the sudden death of his brother Rocco to a heart attack in June, then the need for a heart transplant for his other brother, Frank.

It wasn't only Joe, however; that entire season was filled with melodrama. Doc Gooden came back from two years of drug suspension to revive his career and pitch a no-hitter the night before his father underwent heart bypass surgery; Darryl Strawberry, out of baseball after his own drug problems, played his way off the independent league St. Paul Saints, and back to the Bronx; David Cone came back from surgery for a shoulder aneurysm to pitch the most crucial game of the World Series for us, after we'd lost the first two to the Braves. And then there were all the comebacks in October. Of the eleven postseason wins we needed to win a championship, we trailed in seven of them, four as late as the seventh inning.

For all of that, however, the emergence of maybe the greatest relief pitcher in baseball history proved to be the most significant development and, for me, at least, one of the lasting images of that first championship season. I'd love to be able to say that I knew Mariano Rivera was going to be a Hall of Famer from the first time I saw him, in spring training of 1996, but that would be a stretch. I was impressed, to be sure, because he was a great athlete with a smooth, easy delivery that made his 95–96 mph fastball seem even faster to hitters, and from the first time I saw him he was throwing his legendary cutter. I've never seen another pitcher throw that pitch at the same speed as their fastball. As a right-hander, you make the ball cut, or move sharply right to left, with finger pressure, almost like a modified slider, and it usually takes speed off the pitch. But with Mo, as we called him, it was just a natural thing, maybe because he has such a loose wrist. The ball cut hard and late toward left-handed hitters, away from right-handers, at 95 miles per hour, and the combination of the movement and the speed made it very difficult to hit, even when hitters knew it was coming. That late movement broke so many bats of left-handed hitters that we often joked that Mo should be the only pitcher with a contract with Louisville Slugger because he was ensuring them so much business.

Still, we weren't quite sure what we had in Mariano that first spring. He had opened some eyes in the '95 playoffs, coming out of the bullpen in the decisive Game 5 against the Seattle Mariners in the ninth inning, striking out Mike Blowers to escape a bases-loaded jam and temporarily extend the Yankees' season. But he was still an unknown commodity in '96, and I remember discussing him in meetings that spring, as the club tried to decide how to best use him: Was he a starter or a reliever?

We decided to start the season with him in the bullpen, not as the setup man for John Wetteland that he soon became, but as our long man. It seems hard to believe, looking back, but two weeks into the season, we brought him into a game in the fourth inning of a 7–1 blowout loss to the Minnesota Twins when Doc Gooden was knocked out early. Mo threw three hitless innings that day—I know, because I still have all my pitching charts—and he was so good that Joe and I sort of looked at each other knowingly, as if to say, we might have something special here. Over the course of a week we used him three different times for three innings apiece, and he didn't give up so much as a hit. Two walks were all that kept him from throwing the equivalent of a perfect game.

This was at a time when offense was exploding throughout the majors. We thought it was due mostly to a juiced ball, as it would be years before the truth about steroid use in that era would come to light. Regardless, Mo's dominance was all the more startling, considering that many teams were posting slow-pitch softball-league scores. Once again we had discussions with the front office about putting Mo in the starting rotation, as Doc was really struggling and another of our starters, Scott Kamieniecki, was having elbow problems. But Joe and I liked the idea of having such a weapon in our bullpen. We had started the season with the idea of using Steve Howe and Jeff Nelson as setup men for Wetteland, but after Mo's three consecutive three-inning stints, we gradually began sliding him into the setup role. He was just phenomenal early in the season, when the league was getting its first look at him. He extended that hitless streak to fifteen innings before he finally gave up a single to White Sox outfielder Tony Phillips, and his scoreless streak continued for another two weeks before ending at twenty-six innings.

By the end of the year, you could make a case that Mariano was our MVP. Wetteland was the closer, racking up the saves, but many times Mo made the job easy for him, stopping rallies or polishing off the tough hitters in the seventh and eighth innings in a way that just demoralized teams. Mo was such a force that teams felt like they were playing a six-inning game against us—they knew if they were behind after six, they weren't beating us with that combination of Rivera and Wetteland. He threw 107 innings that season, posting a record of 8-3 with 2.09 ERA with 130 strikeouts, and because he wasn't a very big guy, I worried at times that he was going to wear down, but I came to learn that Mo was blessed with a wiry strength, as well as great athleticism and toughness. We were careful that first year, trying to make sure to rest him enough, since he was usually throwing at least two innings per appearance. But he seemed to thrive on regular work and bounce back without a problem. Mo turned out to be more durable than I could have imagined, making the transition to the role of closer easily when Wetteland left as a free agent after the '96 season.

Eventually I thought hitters would catch up with his cutter and he'd have to use other pitches. But over those first few years he learned how to best use the pitch, and how to control the movement on it. He had to work harder at throwing the ball straight, without the cut on it, but eventually he was able to throw a two-seam fastball that actually moved the other way, down and in on right-handers. It was important because it kept right-handed hitters from diving out over the plate, anticipating his cutter moving away from them, the way Sandy Alomar Jr. did in the '97 playoffs when he beat Mo with a home run to right field. But mostly Mariano just mastered the movement and the location on that cutter, and because it broke so late, with such velocity, it didn't matter how many times hitters had faced him or whether they knew it was coming.

In addition, Mariano had a quiet confidence that was the perfect temperament for the high-pressure job of closer. Though he took his bad outings to heart, he was very good at shaking them off, showing up the next day with a smile, wanting the ball, believing nobody could beat him. If he had to sit for two or three days after a bad outing while waiting for another save opportunity, that's what really bothered him because he wanted to get back on the mound and restore order, you might say. Mo didn't have a big ego at all, even though he became such a star over the years, which made him a delight to coach.

Mariano and Andy Pettitte are the two Yankee pitchers with whom I developed the closest bond over the years. Most pitching coaches tend to develop closer relationships with their starters because you do more individual work with them. But I became close to Mariano over the years, partly because he cared very much about the state of the ball club and wanted to share his thoughts with someone. Pitchers tend to get wrapped up in their own state of affairs, but Mo was very much in tune with how other players were doing and concerned when things weren't going right. If we were going to have a captain on the pitching staff, it would be Mariano because he always had the team in mind.

I think when he walks away from the game, he'll go down as the greatest relief pitcher in history. Obviously, without him we wouldn't have won those four world championships. Quiet as he is, Mo is as fierce a competitor as I've coached, and he always seemed to welcome the pressure of the postseason, when he was often at his best. In that '96 postseason he allowed only one run over fourteen and one-third innings in the three series against the Texas Rangers, Baltimore Orioles, and Atlanta Braves.

It was truly a remarkable October. We spent much of it feeling as if we were hanging from a cliff, needing to be rescued. After losing Game 1 of the best-of-five series against the Rangers, we needed comebacks in the eighth inning of Game 2 and the ninth inning of Game 3 to pull out wins, and then fell behind 4–0 in Game 4 before rallying again for the clinching victory. Against the Orioles we needed the infamous intervention of a twelve-year-old fan named Jeffrey Maier in Game 1, who turned Derek Jeter's fly ball into a game-tying home run in the eighth inning by reaching out over the right-field wall. In Game 3 we were trailing 2–1 in the eighth inning against Mike Mussina before rallying for four runs to win 5–2. The most memorable comeback of that postseason came in Game 4 of the World Series, when we rallied from a 6–0 deficit, tying the game on a three-run home run by Jim Leyritz in the eighth inning and winning it 8–6 with two runs in the tenth inning. That rally allowed us to tie the Series 2–2, but to me the pivotal moment in that Series happened in Game 3 in Atlanta, after we lost the first two games in New York.

At the time, the whole world thought the Series was over. The Braves were the defending champs, they'd just waxed us in the first two games. And though it's easy to forget, after we won four championships and went to six World Series in eight years, we were the upstarts in '96, playing in the World Series for the first time since 1981, and in the postseason for only the second time since then. The Braves were huge favorites, defending world champs who had appeared in four of the previous five World Series.

We had decided to save David Cone for Game 3, partly for just this circumstance, the pressure of needing to win on the road in a dire situation. Coney was as gutty a competitor as anyone I've ever coached. I've often said that if I was in combat and I had to pick one guy to be with in a foxhole, it would be David Cone. He'd find a way to get you through it; that's just the way he was. I'd coached him with the Mets, and in his younger days his competitiveness could occasionally work against him, when he'd get a little overheated on the mound sometimes. There was also the one time in Atlanta when he got so mad about a call at first base that he just lost his mind for a minute, so wrapped up in arguing with the umpire that he didn't notice two guys continuing to run the bases and scoring on the play. It was an embarrassing moment, but that kind of intensity helped Cone far more than it hurt him over the years.

The day he sold me forever on his mental toughness was the final game of the 1991 season with the Mets. We were in Philadelphia, long since eliminated from playoff contention. Buddy Harrelson had been fired as manager with a week left in the season and Mike Cubbage was serving as interim manager. Coney was scheduled to pitch the Sunday afternoon finale, but when I got to the ballpark that morning, Cubbage told me we'd better start thinking about another pitcher because the Philadelphia police were investigating Cone for a rape charge brought by a woman the previous night. Nothing ever came of it, as charges were dropped in subsequent days, but at the time the police were taking it seriously, and they had questioned David at our hotel in the middle of the night.

As Cubbage and I were talking about who we should start, Coney walked into the clubhouse. I made my way over to him and told him I'd been made aware of his situation.

"Obviously you didn't get much sleep," I said, "and with all of this going on, we're going to start someone else."

"What are you talking about?" he said, his eyes getting real wide. "You're not starting anybody else. I'm pitching."

"We didn't think you'd feel up to pitching," I said.

"I'm fine," he said. "I'm ready to pitch."

So we went into the manager's office, and Cone told Cubbage that there was no way he was letting anything interfere with his start.

Meanwhile, the Philadelphia police had informed GM Frank Cashen, who was on the trip, that they were gathering evidence and even threatened to arrest Cone during the game if they felt the situation warranted it. Cone was aware of this, and yet he went out and pitched maybe the most dominant game of his career. His stuff was electric. His slider was unhittable. He wound up striking out nineteen hitters, matching Tom Seaver's single-game record for the franchise.

It was a close game, though, and by the late innings he had a high pitch count. At some point I went to the mound and told him that he had to let me know if he was getting tired.

"I know it's the last day of the season," I said, "but I still need to protect your arm."

Coney looked straight into my eyes and said, "I'm not going to get tired today."

And he finished as strong as he started, winning the game.

That was David Cone. He was such a competitor that he never wanted to give up the ball. Even if his arm was falling off, he tried to talk you into giving him one more hitter, one more inning, assuring you that everything was okay. As a pitching coach that's a big part of the job, getting to know your pitchers well enough to know how to read their body language, maybe their facial expressions or even the look in their eyes, and not necessarily listen to what they're telling you, because most guys always want to stay in the game.

And that's the situation in which we found ourselves in the sixth inning of Game 3. We were leading 2–0 but the Braves had loaded the bases with one out against Cone, with left-handed slugger Fred McGriff coming to the plate. As was his habit, David had already thrown a lot of pitches, as he worked carefully through the Braves' lineup, and Joe had left-hander Graeme Lloyd warming up. Joe asked me what I thought, and I was such a David Cone guy that I told him I thought he'd find a way to get out of the inning. Joe nodded but said he wanted to look Cone in the eye and get his own feel for the moment. So he went to the mound and demanded, "Tell me the truth, David, this is very important. Are you okay?"

Joe told me that Coney looked him straight in the eye and never wavered.

"I lost the feel for my slider a little bit, but I'm okay. I'll get this guy."

Joe continued to stare hard at Coney.

"Don't bullshit me, David," he said. "Are you sure?"

"I'm sure," Cone said.

Joe came back and said he liked the look in his eye. He hadn't wanted to take him out. Cone was such a leader for us that year, and after he'd come back from surgery to repair a shoulder aneurysm, he'd earned even more respect of his teammates. We were better when he was on the mound, as long as he wasn't gassed. So Joe left him in and, after getting ahead with a called-strike slider, Coney challenged McGriff inside with a fastball and got it in just far enough to produce a pop-out to Derek Jeter.

He wasn't out of trouble yet, however. He went to 3-2 on another lefty slugger, Ryan Klesko, and then threw a fastball that he thought was strike three on the inside corner, but home plate umpire Tim Welke called it a ball, and the walk forced in a run. So our lead was 2–1, and now Joe and I gritted our teeth one more time, as Coney got Javy Lopez to pop out to end the threat. We got three more runs in the eighth and the bullpen did the rest as we won 5–2 to change the momentum in the Series to begin our comeback.

Even after we'd lost the first two Joe had remained upbeat, telling the team that it would only take one win to change the momentum and give us a new outlook on the Series. And he was right. We won all three games in Atlanta, overcoming Kenny Rogers's poor start in Game 4, as Jim Leyritz hit his famous home run off of Mark Wohlers, then riding one of the best-pitched games I've ever seen in the postseason to victory in Game 5, as Andy Pettitte outdueled John Smoltz 1–0.

Finally, we came home and finished off one of the great turn-arounds in World Series history, beating Greg Maddux 3–2 as Jimmy

Key gave us a solid start, and Mariano and Wetteland took care of the late innings one last time. We had to hold our breath at the end, as the Braves scored a run against Wetteland in the ninth and put the tying run at second with two outs, before Mark Lemke popped out in foul territory to third baseman Charlie Hayes for the final out.

While the players piled on one another in celebration at the mound, Joe and the coaches exchanged hugs in the dugout. The TV cameras immediately zoomed in for close-ups on Joe, who had tears in his eyes. His quest to win a World Series had captivated fans around the country, the drama intensified by his brother's well-publicized wait for a heart transplant. When a heart became available and Frank Torre received the transplant the day before Game 6 against the Braves, there didn't seem to be any doubt we were destined to win. I mean, that's Disney-movie stuff. Yet in my mind it was my fairy tale, too. After all those years when I wouldn't so much as utter George Steinbrenner's name, I'd made my peace with the Boss and come back to the team that meant so much to me. Then we put together this miracle of a postseason to win the championship that I never won as a player with the Yankees. It seemed almost too good to be true.

Of course, I didn't know how long it would last, given George's volatile nature. With the emergence of young players like Mariano, Pettitte, Derek Jeter, and Bernie Williams, to go with veterans like Cone, Paul O'Neill, Tino Martinez, and Joe Girardi, I knew we had a chance to be a good club for a while. But at the time I probably wouldn't have told you that I saw a dynasty in the making. Too much could go wrong, as I'd found out after 1986 when I thought the Mets would win at least a couple of more championships. But this time, remarkably, most everything went right.

9

Perfect

It was only fitting, I suppose. The most perfect season I've ever been a part of included the first perfect game I'd ever witnessed. It was in May of 1998, the year we won 114 games and then went 11-2 in the postseason to complete one of the most dominant championship seasons in baseball history. Two years earlier Dwight Gooden had become my first pitcher to throw a no-hitter, for the Yankees against the Seattle Mariners, and I was thrilled for him after all of his drug-related problems. In 1999 David Cone would throw a perfect game as well, and on that day, too, I was ecstatic, mainly because I thought it was a just reward for one of the fiercest competitors I've ever coached. This time it was David Wells, and while I was happy for him, I can't say his feat meant as much to me as the other two. David just wasn't an easy guy to coach, put it that way. In fact, he's the only guy I've ever called out publicly because I was so frustrated with his work habits.

We hadn't reached that point yet by 1998, his second season with the Yankees. But we had butted heads in a way that made his perfect game a bit ironic, considering he threw it on a Sunday afternoon against the Minnesota Twins. It's no secret that David likes his nightlife, and he had struggled in some of his afternoon starts during the '97 season. I did some research and found that his record over the previous three years was significantly better at night than during the day, especially during the hot months of the season, so when I reset the rotation at the All-Star break in '97, I put him at the back of it because, the way the schedule fell, that would allow him to pitch more at night. He'd been pitching well going into the break, so he became upset when he saw where I had him penciled in coming back.

"Whose decision is that?" he demanded.

"It's mine, David," I said. "Joe approved it, but it's my decision."

"That's bullshit," he said. "I'm throwing great. Why aren't I pitching sooner?"

"You really want to know?" I said. "It's because I've looked at your record, and you haven't pitched well in day games during the hot months. This way, your first four starts after the break are scheduled so that you'll pitch at night. I think it's better for you and better for the team because I don't think you always adequately prepare yourself for afternoon games."

Well, he didn't like hearing that.

"That's bullshit," he said again, and stormed off. David barely talked to me when we came back from the All-Star break. He did his between-starts work in the bullpen without any conversation, but he continued to pitch well in his first few starts in the second half of the season.

Finally, because a rainout a few days earlier had pushed everyone in the rotation back a day, David's fourth start was on a Wednesday afternoon at home against the Oakland A's. At the time he had the highest career daytime ERA of all active pitchers, 4.92, but he went out and threw a gem, striking out sixteen in a 7–0 victory. Afterward I went over to congratulate him in the clubhouse.

"That was awesome, David," I said. "Your stuff was great, your command was great. Awesome."

He just gave me a hard look and said, "Tell me something. Was that a night game or a day game?"

At the time the whole day-game, night-game thing had slipped my mind. I just laughed and said, "Hey, if that's what it takes, I'm glad you remember that."

I told Joe about it and we had a chuckle. That's the way David was. He took any kind of criticism very personally and used it as motivation because he was determined to prove people wrong. By '98 our relationship was pretty much back to normal. But with David we never seemed to be able to go long before hitting a bump in the road of some kind. Only two starts before his perfect game, in fact, he had a major meltdown against the Texas Rangers and angered Joe Torre in the process. His teammates had given him an early 9–0 lead, but it was a hot night in Texas, and David didn't like the heat. He was a big guy who didn't work hard to get in shape, and sometimes when things weren't going his way he would sort of give in to the circumstances rather than dig in and fight.

This was one of those nights. The Rangers were hitting him hard, David's shoulders were sagging, and suddenly it was 9–5 with a couple of runners on base when Joe decided enough was enough. David wasn't happy when he saw Joe coming to the mound. He thought he should have been given more of a chance to get out of the inning, at least get five innings in and get the win. He sort of turned away as Joe neared the mound, then flipped the ball to Joe as he stormed off the mound. It was just disrespectful enough that a manager could have taken it personally and escalated the situation, but Joe was pretty good about not letting those things bother him. Usually anything in the heat of the battle, unless it got out of hand, he chalked up to frustration and let it go. But I'm sure he didn't appreciate it, and the proof was a couple of remarks he made to the press afterward. Joe almost never criticizes his players publicly because he believes in creating a trust with them, so when he takes even a subtle jab, you know he's boiling. On this night, when reporters asked him about Wells being unable to hold such a big lead, he told them he thought Wells needed to work harder on his conditioning.

"Maybe he's not in shape," he said.

He knew Wells wouldn't like that. David was very sensitive to any criticism about his weight, even though it was obvious he was almost always carrying extra pounds. He was fortunate that he could get by pitching fat, if you want to put it bluntly, because he was such a natural athlete. For a guy his size he was very agile, even light on his feet. And most important, he was blessed with a strong, durable arm. Over the years he has had injury problems with his back and his knees, but almost never his arm. David was one of those guys who could pick up a ball in the dead of winter and go out and give you five or six innings. Still, we felt his weight was an issue, in terms of his stamina, especially in July and August. I always felt he shortchanged himself by not being in shape for those tough months. But you also knew you could count on him in big games, especially in the postseason. That's where his personality seemed to pay dividends, because he lived for the spotlight, and he loved being counted on by the team to produce when it mattered most. It was nights like the one in Texas where you wished he would have brought that big-game type of attitude to the mound more often.

David didn't say anything after the game that night, but the next day he asked for a meeting with Joe and me, so we closed the door in the manager's office and listened as he complained that he deserved a better shot to stay in that game. The bottom line was that he wanted his five innings so he could get the win, and he implied that another pitcher would have been given more rope. Joe cut him off quickly on that notion and told him that he needed to take another look at the way he was pitching when he was taken out of the game. Speaking for both of us, Joe told him that our only objective was to win the game, that we weren't going to jeopardize it just to give a pitcher a chance to earn an individual win. In these situations, Joe had a way of putting a player in his place without insulting him, which was part of what makes him such a great manager in these modern times when multimillion-dollar egos are such an inescapable fact of life in the big leagues. David wanted to hear that we still believed in him, and Joe made him feel appreciated while essentially lecturing him on the need to give us his best effort at all times.

The meeting seemed to appease David, but I knew he probably still harbored some hard feelings toward us. He was convinced that Joe didn't like him, and he probably questioned how I felt about him. It wasn't that I didn't like David so much as I didn't agree with some of the things he did, mostly in terms of game preparation, work ethic, that kind of thing. I knew him long before I coached him because he pitched with my son, Todd, when they were both in the Toronto organization as young pitchers. I knew he had been a headache for the Blue Jays, to the point where they ended up releasing him in 1993. We had talked a few times over the years when we saw each other in spring training, and once when he was still with the Blue Jays, I remember him saying he'd like to pitch for me. At the time I told him I'd love to coach him, so long as he was willing to take off the earring that he was wearing.

I was still with the Mets at that time, and they didn't have a policy about earrings or facial hair as the Yankees do, but I felt strongly about the importance of appearance. I'm just old-fashioned, I guess, but I feel major leaguers have a responsibility as role models. I know how much kids in this country worship ballplayers, and I don't think it's a lot to ask them to present a clean-cut image for those kids to emulate.

That's one thing I guess I have in common with George Steinbrenner. I admire him for enforcing his rules of appearance, no beards or goatees, and reasonable hair length. I had to enforce my own rules with Todd and Mel Jr. as they were growing up as teenagers in the late 1970s, reminding them on occasion they needed haircuts. Of course, I have to admit, I let my own hair grow a little bit when it became fashionable in those days, and I even had sideburns for a while, but compared with other guys at the time, I was still on the conservative side. I guess I got it from my dad. He instilled certain values in me and I took them to heart. Not that I judge people by their appearance—I recognize that young people, especially, often see long hair or earrings as a way of showing their independence, or, in David's case, maybe a certain rebellious image. I just don't think it belongs in baseball, and though I didn't give David my speech, I think he understood. Surprisingly, he was agreeable when I mentioned the earring.

"For you I'd take it off," he said.

So I knew what I was getting when he became a Yankee, and I felt I could talk to David more than maybe some other people who had tried. Actually, I felt like I did get through to him at times, and we did have some interesting talks. But the bottom line was that he was an enormous talent who didn't always work hard enough to maximize that talent, and when someone called him on it, he reacted by claiming that he was being picked on unfairly. But sometimes that was okay, because situations like the one in Texas usually brought out the best in him. He took it as a challenge to go out and prove us wrong. Over the years I found that I could challenge him in different ways that might make him mad but usually produce results.

In this case, I wasn't surprised when David went out and pitched a strong eight innings in his next start, against the Kansas City Royals, retiring the last ten batters he faced and seventeen of the last eighteen. Five days later he pitched his perfect game against the Twins. It's funny, but what I remember most is how good he was in the bullpen warming up before the game that day. The ball was coming out of his hand with more life than usual. He was popping the fastball, snapping off sharp-breaking curves, and hitting his spots with just about everything he threw. Now, that doesn't always translate to success once the game starts, but he was so good in the bullpen that I remember thinking he could really be dominant that day.

Of course, that memory took on added significance years later when David made the claim in his autobiography that he was badly hung over that day from a long night of drinking. Supposedly he was still feeling a little woozy in the bullpen before the game, but I really have to question that because of the type of warm-up he had. I certainly saw no signs of a guy who wasn't feeling his best. I have to believe he stretched that story for the sake of the book, but with David, I guess anything was possible. If he did have a rough night, that wouldn't have been unusual for him. All I know for sure is that he was so good in the pen, the last thing I told him was to make the extra effort to concentrate on what he wanted to do with each pitch, and not just take it for granted that everything would take care of itself because his stuff is so good. That's the tendency that all pitchers have sometimes, when everything is working for them.

In any case, I left the bullpen that day expecting Wells to throw an excellent game. You never think about something like a perfect game, and especially with David because his whole approach is to come right at hitters, challenge them with strikes. He was never one to pick at the corners, trying to make the perfect pitch. He believed in working quickly and throwing strikes, knowing he had the control, the movement, and the change of speeds to keep hitters from squaring up his pitches. One of the things I spent a lot of time talking to him about was doing more to finish hitters off when he had them in advantageous counts, and against the Twins that day he did that, making great finishing pitches when he had guys on the ropes.

He also gave hitters a different look the last time he went through the lineup that day, which I believe was critical. It was something else I'd emphasized with him. David worked mostly inside to right-handed hitters with his fastball and his cutter, and when you start to tire a little in the later innings you're more apt to run into some-body's bat for a home run that way because your pitch doesn't have the same life. So I'd been after him to use the outside part of the plate later in the game more, with his two-seam fastball and his changeup. And I have to give him credit because he worked at that and became less predictable. I saw it even more when he pitched against us in subsequent years, after we traded him for Roger Clem-ens the following spring. But I remember that day against the Twins he got some easy outs in the late innings by going away when hitters were looking inside.

As he got close to the ninth you could feel the tension in our dug-out. As a pitching coach I tended to think much the way I did as a pitcher—more about how a guy was executing his pitches than the results. If you're making your pitches, you always figure the results will take care of themselves, but you never get ahead of yourself, which is why it's so often true when you hear a pitcher say he wasn't thinking of a no-hitter until the late innings. On Wells's day, by the seventh inning it was impossible not to think about it. The crowd, fully aware, was roaring with every out. At the time the Yankees weren't quite the must-see that they became by 2005, when they drew more than four million fans, and the Twins weren't a big draw then. But there were 49,625 fans on hand, largely because the club was giving away Beanie Babies, which were all the rage as collector's items. So it was loud and getting crazier with every out.

I stayed away from David in the dugout because I didn't want to mess with his karma, and there wasn't really anything I needed to tell him. I was getting excited myself. It's a great thrill for any pitch-ing coach to be part of a no-hitter or perfect game, especially for me since I'd never thrown a no-hitter. The closest I ever came was tak-ing a no-hitter into the eighth inning against the Oakland A's in 1971. I was pitching against Vida Blue, who was practically unhit-table that year, winning twenty-four games and the Cy Young

Award. In fact, what I remember most about that day was having my family with me because it was late August and they were going back home to Yakima after the game to start school. Before I left the hotel that morning, Todd, who was only about seven years old, asked me who was pitching against me that day. When I told him it was Vida Blue he said, "Oh, Dad, you don't have a chance today."

I laughed and told him thanks for the confidence boost, then I went out and held the A's hitless over seven innings. My sinker was really biting that day, and we were leading 1–0 when Rick Monday led off the bottom of the eighth by dropping a perfect bunt down the third-base line, beating it out easily for a hit to break up my no-hitter. Obviously that's not the way you want to lose out on a no-hitter, but I couldn't fault Monday because in a one-run game it was a good play in an attempt to win the game. If it had been 5–0 I would have felt differently. I was disappointed, but I'd never really thought I would throw a no-hitter because I was such a contact pitcher, relying on my sinker to get ground balls, not strikeouts. With such a slim lead, I was more worried about hanging on for the win, anyway, and I did end up pitching a 1–0 shutout.

In David's case, we had a 4–0 lead so he was truly gunning for the perfect game at the end, and it was fun to see him get it. He was very appreciative, having rings made for all of the players and coaches that commemorated the perfect game. David went on to have a great season, finishing with a record of 18-4 as he pitched well and managed to avoid further conflicts with Joe and me. David and I would have our parting of the ways, so to speak, in 2003 during his second go-round with the Yankees, when I criticized him in the press for not doing his work between starts, and basically he stopped talking to me, right up until his back went out on him before Game 5 of the World Series. I'll revisit that ugliness ahead; fortunately, in '98 there were only good memories as we piled up the wins all the way to a championship.

It was a year like no other. Of course, it started as some sort of theater of the absurd, with talk of Joe's job being in trouble when we opened the season on the West Coast by losing four of our first five games. Keep in mind that in his first two seasons Joe had produced the franchise's first world championship in eighteen years, then lost in the first round of the playoffs in 1997. Now, five games into the '98 season the New York newspapers were full of speculation that Joe might lose his job if the losing didn't end quickly. Usually those types of stories didn't materialize out of thin air. It meant that somebody in the Yankee organization was whispering such things to reporters, probably for what George Steinbrenner considered motivational purposes. It was the price a manager had to pay for the privilege of managing the Yankees and having a chance to win the World Series every year. To his credit, Joe handled it with his usual unflappable style. His calm demeanor wasn't some act he put on for the press, either. Joe was the same guy behind closed doors; he was able to shrug off such antics as George being George, and as long as it didn't directly affect his relationship with the players, which it eventually did on a couple of occasions, Joe was never flustered by the Boss.

Not that we thought it was beyond George to be impulsive enough to make good on the whispered threats. After all, he did fire Yogi Berra just sixteen games into the 1985 season, with a 6-10 record, after telling the world during spring training that Yogi would manage the entire season. Three seasons before that he had fired Bob Lemon fourteen games into the 1982 season, with a 6-8 record, so the possibility of him firing Joe wasn't as ludicrous as it sounded. For what it was worth, Davey Johnson's name was being floated in the newspapers as Joe's possible successor.

Fortunately, we quickly started winning, and never stopped. In fact, we won so many games with improbable, late-inning rallies in '98 that I recall looking at Joe and Zim on the bench more than once that season and saying in amazement, "Who are these guys?" That group was really hungry, as the players carried the memory of losing in the '97 playoffs with them into the '98 season. We wound up winning 114 games that season, the most in American League history at the time (the Seattle Mariners won 116 in 2002), breaking the record of 112 held by the 1954 Cleveland Indians, as well as the franchise record of 111 held by the legendary 1927 Yankees.

All of that led to a first-round playoff matchup with the Texas Rangers that I'd been dreading for weeks. I wasn't so worried about the Rangers; I just didn't want to have to sit in the opposing dugout with my son Todd on the mound in such an important game. Todd had been in the majors since 1988 but I'd managed to avoid facing him. He was in the American League with Toronto and Oakland through 1995, while I was in the National League with the Mets and Astros. He went to the St. Louis Cardinals in 1996, the year I took the job with the Yankees, but finally he was traded to Texas at the July 31 trading deadline in '98, and only a few weeks later he pitched against the Yankees in New York.

Over the years we'd talked often about the likelihood that it would happen eventually, but all of that talking didn't make it easier on either of us emotionally. Before that game in August, Todd admitted to reporters that he considered it bigger than the playoff and World Series games he'd started in the past because he wanted to make me proud. Todd gave up five runs in the first two innings, but he hung in there for six innings while the Rangers pounded Hideki Irabu, and Todd wound up earning the win in a 16–5 victory. I squirmed some on the bench that day, especially when Todd was struggling early, but because we were cruising to the playoffs by then, I was able to feel good about him pulling it together to get the win.

Obviously there was much more at stake when we met the Rangers in the first round of the playoffs. Todd pitched Game 1 for the Rangers, against David Wells, who had been our most consistent starter over the course of the season. That was one of the toughest days I've ever had at the ballpark. On the day of the game, I was kind of uptight, knowing I was going to be torn between my team and my son. It wasn't a good time to run into George Steinbrenner, but that's just what happened in the clubhouse an hour or so before the game. He was coming out of Joe's office as I was coming out of the coaches' office across the hall, and suddenly we were practically face-to-face.

"We gotta win this game tonight," George said, which was his way of saying hello. "We really gotta beat on this pitcher of theirs."

"How about if we beat him 2–1 or something like that?" I said, figuring that George would laugh and let it go at that. But he didn't.

"No, we really gotta beat on this guy," George said again, with no hint that he might be kidding. And because I was on edge already, I sort of snapped at him.

"George, that's my son out there," I said. "Imagine if it was one of your sons or grandsons on the mound. Can't we just beat him by one run and be happy?"

George gave me a quizzical look that I wasn't sure how to read, and he never did smile as if to let me in on the joke. But finally he said, "All right, I guess so," and walked away.

It bothered me at the time that George didn't have the courtesy to say he understood I was in a tough position, something like that. Eventually I decided he was just trying to kid me, and simply wasn't very good at it, probably because he didn't do it very often. But it didn't help me relax.

As we got closer to game time, it was impossible to go about my business as if it were a normal day. Before the game I walked out with Wells, as usual, for his warm-up in the bullpen and there was Todd walking toward the other bullpen. All kinds of thoughts were running through my mind. Obviously I had a job to do, and I had to pull for our club, but I have to admit, a lot of my thoughts were in the other bullpen.

In the dugout before the game a couple of the guys tried to loosen me up a little bit. Derek Jeter came over and said, "Hey, what does this guy throw? You gotta tell me what this guy throws."

Unlike George, Jeter knew how to get a laugh without hitting a nerve.

Once the game started, it was just real difficult to sit there, wanting Todd to pitch well yet wanting us to win the game. I've never been so intense for nine innings. Normally I focus on how our pitcher is throwing, then get a little breather when we come to bat. But on this day I didn't want to miss a pitch on either side. As it turned out, the game went about as well as I could have hoped. Todd pitched nicely, going the distance, but we won the game 2–0 as Wells dominated the Rangers. The only better scenario would have been for us to score after Todd was out of the game so that he wouldn't have been tagged with the loss, but as it was, he couldn't have pitched much better. I was proud of him. The hardest part was not being able to cheer for him.

Meanwhile, my wife had decided she wouldn't have that problem. She may have been in Yankee Stadium, sitting in the section with families of other players and coaches, but Jean wasn't going to pretend to be neutral. It wasn't like Todd was pitching against me, so as far as she was concerned, her loyalty was with her son. I understood that, but it turned out that George didn't. He watched the game mostly on TV from his office at the stadium, as he usually does, and the Fox-TV people kept showing reaction shots of Jean in the stands. One time they caught her standing up and clapping after Jeter was thrown out on a play at the plate, and I heard through the grapevine that George was very upset by that. Families were allowed on the team plane during the playoffs, and Jean made all the trips in that postseason, as did George, but after that game, he seemed to make a point of not talking to or even looking at Jean when he was around her on the plane. It wasn't until I went public with my cancer two years later that he talked to her again.

All in all, it was quite an emotional way to start the playoffs, and everything else seemed easy by comparison, at least to me. We swept the Rangers in three games to advance, but then we had our moment of truth in that postseason against the Cleveland Indians when they beat us in Games 1 and 3 to take a 2–1 lead, with Game 4 in Cleveland. As the defending AL champs who had knocked us out of the playoffs in 1997, the Indians were a powerhouse team, and, on top of that, there was enormous pressure on us to win it all that October and validate our 114-win season.

So suddenly we were facing what felt like a must-win game because falling behind 3–1 in the series might have been too much to overcome. And all that pressure fell on the shoulders of Orlando Hernandez, or El Duque, as everyone calls him. That was El Duque's first year with the Yankees, after defecting from Cuba, and it didn't take long to see we'd been smart to get him. He was a guy who really knew how to pitch, how to read the swings of hitters, which gave him a better idea of what they were looking for and how he could get them out.

When I first saw his big leg kick, I thought I would need to try to change it, but once I saw it a few more times, I realized that even as awkward as it looked, his mechanics were outstanding. He had tremendous control of his body, and the leg kick was something that could disrupt a hitter's timing, so I never messed with it. El Duque had an assortment of pitches and arm angles, but more than anything, he just had a feel for pitching that you can't teach. He was as good as anybody I've coached at knowing how to read individual hitters, whether a guy might be sitting on a particular pitch, or a location, and that dictated the way he pitched to him. He had a knack for keeping hitters off balance, and he had command of all of his pitches. El Duque had an impressive first season, going 12-4 with a 3.31 ERA, but we didn't know he'd turn out to be a great postseason pitcher.

In fact, by the time he made that start against the Indians, El

Duque hadn't pitched in two weeks, and I didn't know what to expect from him. Because we swept the Rangers in three games, El Duque hadn't pitched in that series, and he had assumed he would start the next series against Cleveland. However, with a few days off before the next series, we reset our rotation, slotting Wells, Pettitte, and Cone for the first three games, and El Duque for number four. He was guaranteed to pitch because this was a seven-game series, but he was very upset at being skipped, to the point where Joe and I had to bring him into the office and try and explain the situation to him. It wasn't that we didn't trust El Duque, but at that point the other three guys had proven track records in the playoffs, so we felt they gave us the best chance to win. El Duque didn't seem to care how we explained it to him; he wasn't happy. He was a very proud guy whose status as an ace in Cuba had afforded him preferential treatment. Basically he was accustomed to calling the shots, on and off the mound, which made him a little difficult to handle at times.

He wanted to do things his way, especially as far as his between-starts work. Sometimes it would be kind of a guessing game for me, whether he wanted to throw the second day or the third day after his start. He went a lot by feel. We talked about that quite a bit, and most of the time I would give way, catering to what he wanted to do. But he got his work done, and he worked very hard, which is what was most important. Because he spoke very little English at first, I communicated with him mostly through an interpreter the club hired for him. During games I was fortunate that Jorge Posada, our catcher, spoke Spanish, so he could translate for me on the mound. The only problem was that El Duque and Posada clashed at times, and that caused some difficulty.

Both of them could be a little hardheaded, and both were very temperamental, so you never knew when they were going to go at it. At times they got along great, but it seemed there was always at least one inning where they would come into the dugout arguing heatedly with each other. El Duque liked to call his own game, so he often shook off Posada on signs, but besides that, El Duque at times liked to decide on his own whether he was throwing his four-seam or two-seam fastball. And there were other times he'd nod at Posada's sign for a fastball, only to decide to throw his changeup instead. This kind of thing drove Posada crazy, and understandably so. If you're looking for a four-seam fastball to take off in the strike zone, and it sinks the other way at the last second, it can be murder on the catcher.

It took a lot of talking to El Duque to make him realize that Posada needed to know what he was throwing. In the meantime, all those disagreements actually led to a fight between them in the club-house one time after a game. I was in the coaches' room at the time and I never did find out what started it, but guys who saw it said they went after each other viciously. Fortunately, there were enough guys around to pull them apart, and neither one was hurt, but Joe had to bring them into his office for a meeting the next day. Joe seemed to talk some sense into them because from that point they got along better. As a former catcher himself, Joe made Posada real-ize that he had to give in to the pitcher regarding pitch selection without taking it personally, and eventually Jorge did a much better job of that with all of our pitchers. From my end, I tried to make El Duque understand he needed to be a little more thoughtful of his catcher.

As a whole, pitchers are respectful of catchers because they rec-ognize how much impact that guy behind the plate can have on their performance. Before every game, in fact, as a pitching coach I would sit down with the starter and the catcher to go over the scouting re-port on individual hitters, how we wanted to attack each one. From there the decision-making process on pitch selection depends some-what on the dynamic between the pitcher and the catcher. A young pitcher typically will be less likely to shake off a catcher's sign, especially a veteran catcher, where an established pitcher often won't hesitate to shake off signs and make sure he's throwing the pitch he believes is best in every situation.

That can get a little tricky at times because I've found catchers to be proud people who consider it their job to call pitches based on their knowledge of both their pitcher and the opposing hitters. Some guys take it a little more personally than others if you shake them off. Posada has come a long way in that area, understanding that a pitcher has to feel good about every pitch he throws, and that a shake-off isn't necessarily a reflection on the catcher's thinking. I was fortunate as a young pitcher because Elston Howard went out of his way to make me feel comfortable. The first time he ever caught me, Ellie made a point of telling me to let him know how he could help me in any way, and he said, "Don't be afraid to shake me off." That meant a lot to a nervous rookie, but I didn't shake him off much, mainly because I had a pretty basic repertoire, sinker and slider, and I threw my sinker most of the time.

Over the years, when I did shake off a sign, particularly in a crucial situation, I always made a point of going to the catcher between innings and telling him what I was thinking, as both a courtesy and a way of allowing him to get to know me better. That's the job of the catcher, to get to know each of his pitchers well enough that he can think along with them in every situation. That's where Thurman Munson excelled. He was the best catcher, in terms of his overall game, I ever had, and he knew how to work his pitchers. He was a cocky guy by nature, and he wasn't afraid to go to the mound and kick you in the butt to try and fire you up at times, but he also knew when to calm you down or when you might need a little encouragement.

There's a knack to handling pitchers, since their personalities are all different, and guys like Joe Girardi and John Flaherty were great at it because they were such defensive-minded catchers whose only concern was to get the most out of their pitcher on any given day.

Mickey Mantle congratulates me after my first victory with the Yankees, August 12, 1964. That day Mickey hit the longest home run I've ever seen.

Killing time in the Yankee clubhouse with some exclusive company: Mickey Mantle, Elston Howard, and Thurman Munson.

Spring training in Fort Lauderdale, 1972. The boys—Mel Jr., Todd, and Jason—were always ready for a game of catch. My wife, Jean, had her hands full when I was at the ballpark.

Our beloved son Jason, taking a swing on Family Day in 1971. He died of leukemia at age eleven.

Thurman Munson congratulates me after a complete-game victory. Thurman was the best all-around catcher I pitched to during my eleven years with the Yankees.

Pitchers love to brag about their hits, and this was the ultimate for me—sliding home for an inside-the-park grand slam at Yankee Stadium against the Boston Red Sox in 1965. I was so tired that I didn't slide so much as collapse coming home.

Posing with fellow pitchers (*from left*) Al Downing, Fritz Peterson, and Whitey Ford in spring training 1966. Whitey taught me more about pitching than anyone.

Following through on a pitch at Yankee Stadium in 1973. I won sixteen games that year and felt I was still in my prime, only to have my career ended by a rotator cuff injury in 1974.

Talking pitching grips with Dwight Gooden. Doc was like a son to me, which is why it pained me so much to see his career ruined by his problems with drugs. (*Photograph courtesy of the New York Mets*)

Making a point to a young David Cone before a game with the Cubs in Chicago. Coney was one of the fiercest competitors I ever coached, as both a Met and a Yankee. (*Photograph courtesy of the New York Mets*)

With my son, Todd, in spring training when he was pitching for the Toronto Blue Jays. He had a successful career that included two championships with the Blue Jays and one with the Arizona Diamondbacks. (*Photograph courtesy of the New York Mets*)

Posing with my eldest son Mel Jr. Four shoulder surgeries cut short a promising career after just one season with the Kansas City Royals. (*Photograph courtesy of the New York Mets*)

With Joe Girardi looking on, I made a trip to the mound to settle Andy Pettitte down. Andy was one of my all-time favorites to coach.

Sharing a light moment with Roger Clemens. I had my doubts when the Rocket became a Yankee, but coaching him turned out to be a great experience.

Watching Mariano Rivera throw during spring training. I'm looking forward to the day I go to Cooperstown for Mo's induction into the Hall of Fame.

Joe Torre and I became as close as brothers during our ten years together.

Posada has gotten better with that over the years, but it has been a process. Because he was more offensive-minded, there were times, especially when he was younger, when Jorge let a bad at bat or maybe a prolonged slump affect the way he called a game and dealt with pitchers. If he struck out in a big spot, he wasn't always thinking clearly behind the plate the next inning, and I would watch closely as to what pitches he was calling. But Jorge has gotten much better in his game-calling and his energy with the pitchers. I thought Tony Pena, a former All-Star catcher who joined the Yankees as a coach in 2006, had a significant impact in raising Jorge's overall level of defense and throwing, to the point where he was doing his best catching ever.

I can't say I've ever seen a pitcher and catcher go at it quite the way Posada and El Duque did, but through all their fighting they eventually formed a very strong bond. Personally, I didn't have those kinds of arguments with El Duque, but developing a relationship with him wasn't easy, partly because of the language barrier. He didn't seem to be a real trusting guy, which I could understand, after what he'd been through escaping from Cuba. At some point he had a birthday party for his wife at a hotel in New York, and I showed up with my wife. That seemed to mean a lot to him, and from that point he seemed to trust me more. He made an effort to learn more English as well, so we were able to communicate better over the years. I would have liked to have talked to him about leaving Cuba and some of the things he went through to escape, but he didn't seem to want to share that with many people. El Duque could be very sensitive about certain things. He had some issues with the front office that affected his pitching. Some of the injuries he developed seemed to be his way of sending messages to the front office regarding contract negotiations and that type of thing.

In short, El Duque could be high-maintenance at times, but he was more than worth the trouble come playoff time, as evidenced by his career postseason record with the Yankees of 9-3, with a 2.55

ERA. Of course, we couldn't know that when he took the mound in Cleveland in '98, but he opened everyone's eyes that night. He was very sure of himself from the start, pitching with the kind of confidence in October that guys either have or they don't have. He pitched seven shutout innings as we won 4–0, and that win turned the series around.

From there we won the next two games to finish off the Indians, and then another four straight to sweep the San Diego Padres in the World Series and finish in a style befitting a team that won a total of 125 games against only 50 losses. El Duque pitched another gem in Game 3 against the Padres, going seven innings, allowing one run. As for David Wells, he made headlines before the Series started by going on Howard Stern's radio show and predicting that we would beat the Padres in five games. When he found out the Padres were angry about it, Wells insisted he was only kidding. He also blamed the press for writing about it, but I had to wonder if the controversy messed with his head because he wasn't himself in Game 1 and the Padres hit him hard for five runs. For a pitcher with a well-deserved big-game reputation, it was certainly out of character. Then again, this is what you got with David: sometimes perfect, sometimes perfectly exasperating.

In the end, it didn't matter. We came back from a 5–2 deficit that night, the way we had all season, as Tino Martinez hit a grand slam and we won 9–6 to start the countdown to our second championship in three years. This one wasn't as emotional as finally winning that first title in Yankee pinstripes had been two years earlier. But it was no less memorable. In many ways it was the perfect season.

10

Zim vs. the Boss

Even after we'd won two championships in three seasons, I could see the honeymoon with George Steinbrenner wasn't going to last forever. It became all too clear to me in the spring of 1999, when Joe Torre was diagnosed with prostate cancer and forced to miss the early part of the season while recovering from surgery. By then Joe had become the toast of the town in New York, embraced by the media and fans alike for his personable, well-spoken style of managing, not to mention the two championships.

More and more Joe's calming influence and insistence on a team-first approach were cited as important reasons for the Yankees' success, and rightly so. The more time I spent around Joe, the more I appreciated his ability to create a bond among players by making them feel responsible to one another for their daily effort and commitment. Yet Joe's influence became an issue inside Yankee headquarters because as much as George loved being in the winner's circle again, he also wanted credit publicly for being the driving force behind the return to glory. And at least in his eyes, he wasn't getting it because the whole world was in love with Joe.

In addition, Joe had become a master at handling the Boss, which no doubt irritated him as well. No matter how well things were going, George liked to create conflict at times, thinking it was a good way to motivate his people and maintain control over his employees, but he found out early on that Joe was as unflappable behind the scenes as he was stoic in the dugout, expressionless whenever TV trained the camera on him.

Joe had a way of taking subtle jabs at George during our meetings, dismissing suggestions he made in a way that let him know he didn't understand the nuances of baseball. Anytime we had a problem during the season, George wanted to come up with some kind of special strategy. After all of his years in the game, he still approached baseball more like the assistant football coach he had been at Purdue for a couple of years in the 1950s. He wanted to draw up trick plays at times to fool the other team, and I guess he drove his past managers nuts with this stuff. But Joe had a way of deflecting suggestions with humor that disarmed George.

During the 1996 season George was in a panic when pitching injuries put us in a difficult position. We had to play the Cleveland Indians, then the defending American League champions and owners of the most powerful offense in the majors, in a doubleheader in June with two untested rookie pitchers, Brian Boehringer and Ramiro Mendoza. The games were in Cleveland, but George, as he often did, called an emergency meeting in New York to devise a strategy. He gathered his executives in a conference room and called Joe on his cell phone. We were off that day, and Joe was playing golf with me and a couple of the other coaches.

"Where are you?" George demanded.

"I'm playing golf," Joe said.

"Well," said George, "while you're out in the goddamn woods

having fun, we're trying to figure this damn thing out for tomorrow."

"How the hell did you know my ball is in the woods?" Joe shot back, and from what I was told, he cracked up everyone in the conference room. Even George had to laugh.

It was classic Joe, his way of telling George to relax, that we'd be fine. And wouldn't you know it, we swept that doubleheader the next day with those two rookies on the mound. We didn't hear from George again for a while after that.

But by 1999 there was a feeling around the club that George was growing restless. He liked ordering people around, and he couldn't do that with Joe. Then, suddenly, Joe was gone during spring training after being diagnosed with cancer, and, in Don Zimmer, who took over, George had somebody he knew he could provoke, if nothing else. He also knew that messing with Zimmer was one way he could actually anger Joe, who was protective of his coaches.

Zim's first showdown with George involved Hideki Irabu, the Japanese pitcher who, in two years with us, hadn't lived up to his reputation coming over as the Japanese Nolan Ryan. Irabu had pretty good stuff but he never made the adjustment to pitching against a better caliber of hitters in the major leagues, and it always seemed to shock him whenever someone would hit one of his split-finger fastballs out of the park. Part of Irabu's problem was that he didn't work very hard at staying in shape, and by 1999 he was beginning to wear out his welcome with us. In spring training he had failed to cover first base a couple of times on ground balls to the right side, and we started to lean on him pretty hard. All pitchers do drills in spring training covering first base, but we brought Irabu out on the back field for some extra sessions, making him repeat those drills by himself.

So then in our last spring training game in Florida, Irabu was late again covering first. Actually, this time it was as much the fault of the first baseman, Clay Bellinger, because it was a ball hit so far into the hole that he should have let the second baseman take it. Still, it was Irabu's job to be there, and he was late, allowing the runner to beat the play for a hit. It ended up costing us a run, and, as I found out later, George was very upset about it. Irabu hadn't pitched very well during spring training, and his weight had been an issue with the club, to the point where George had implored the trainers to stay on top of it. Now, as he often did when he was upset, George immediately made himself available to reporters and went into a tirade, calling Irabu a fat toad, among other things.

After the game reporters asked Irabu, through his interpreter, George Rose, for his reaction to George's comments, and I guess he took offense because Rose came into the coaches' locker room and told me that Irabu wanted to speak to me in the manager's office. Zim was in there packing his stuff for our flight to Los Angeles, where we had two exhibition games with the Dodgers before opening the season in Oakland. We had penciled in Irabu to start the third game of the season, but now, through his interpreter, Irabu was telling us that he couldn't pitch that day. At the time we hadn't heard of George's comments, so we didn't know what the problem was.

"What do you mean?" Zim said, looking at Irabu. "You're my guy. You threw well today. I'm counting on you."

It was obvious that Irabu had told George Rose this wasn't a matter for debate, because the interpreter didn't hesitate.

"No," he said. "Hideki feels he is not ready to pitch."

Now, Zim wasn't the most patient guy in situations like this, but he was keeping his cool.

"Okay," he said, again looking at Irabu. "If that's the way you feel, we'll pitch you out of the bullpen until you're ready to start."

Again George Rose responded without even looking at Irabu.

"No," he said. "Hideki doesn't think he can do that, either."

Now Zim and I looked at each other, trying to figure out what was going on. Just about then George Steinbrenner walked in, and

Zim explained the situation. George seemed to know immediately that Irabu had heard about his criticism, and he began to apologize, explaining that sometimes he says things in the heat of the moment, that he didn't mean to offend him. Irabu wasn't responding to George, and his interpreter said the pitcher wasn't changing his stance that he needed more time to get ready for the season. Suddenly we had a full-blown crisis on our hands that wound up delaying our departure on the team buses to the airport for about an hour. When it was clear we weren't making any progress with Irabu, George finally said, okay, Irabu could stay in Tampa for a few days and work on his own while the team went ahead to the West Coast. Irabu more or less agreed that he would join the team at some point, but nothing was definite as he left the office that day.

Zim and I talked about it on the plane to the coast, and we decided that Ramiro Mendoza would start in Irabu's spot in the third game. We couldn't sit around waiting to see what happened with Irabu, but I had a feeling that George would get involved with the decision. I told Zim, don't be surprised if we get a call from somebody in Tampa in a couple of days, saying that Irabu is fine and ready to make his scheduled start. Zim announced his decision the next day, Friday, to start Mendoza on the following Wednesday. But then, after Irabu had a bullpen session in Tampa with Billy Connors on Saturday, George began campaigning for him, telling reporters all was well and that he hoped Irabu would make his start on Wednesday. His fit of temper aside, George was in Irabu's corner because he was the one who had pushed so hard to acquire the Japanese pitcher, telling everyone at the time that he would be a star.

Meanwhile, Zim was ticked when he heard that George had publicly questioned his decision to start Mendoza. And Zim being Zim, he responded by telling reporters that George needed to back off and let him manage. Zim, who had been friendly with George for more than twenty years, was upset by this soap opera, but I'm convinced that George loved it. To him, making headlines seemed to be as important as winning, and he could never draw Joe Torre into this sort of controversy, the way he did for years with Billy Martin and Lou Piniella.

Anyway, Billy Connors called Zim the next day to tell him that Irabu was ready. Zim said he'd already told Mendoza he was starting, and that he wasn't going to rearrange things again for Irabu. Zim felt he'd look bad in the eyes of the other players if he bowed to such pressure, and he was probably right. He tried to call George to explain his reasoning, but the Boss didn't call him back. So then Billy called me.

"Everything's fine with Irabu," Billy said, "and George really wants him to pitch on Wednesday."

"Sorry, Billy," I said, "but Zim has named Mendoza as the starter Wednesday and I'm 100 percent behind him."

"George isn't going to be very happy with this," Billy said.

"Well, I can't help that," I said. "I'm supporting Zim because I was in that room last week when Irabu said he couldn't pitch, and I don't think it's the right thing to do to let him pitch after we've already told Mendoza and the team that he's starting."

George apparently decided not to push Zim any further on the matter. Irabu, meanwhile, showed up while we were in Los Angeles and he was very contrite. He apologized to the team and told us he was ready to pitch whenever we needed him. Mendoza wound up making the start against the Oakland A's, pitching eight shutout innings, and, with us holding a 4–0 lead, Zim and I decided we'd use Irabu to pitch the ninth. He got the last three outs, and afterward Zim joked that everything had worked out perfectly.

"George said he wanted Irabu to pitch on Wednesday," he told reporters, "and he did."

It was a good line, but George didn't usually have a sense of humor when he was the punch line for a joke. In truth, I think the Irabu controversy was the start of the problems between George and Zim that finally led Zim to resign bitterly after the 2003 season and vow never to speak to the Boss again. Zim wound up managing the team for six weeks that season, before Joe returned from surgery, and he was hurt that George never said a word, publicly or privately, in appreciation of the job he did. I don't think their relationship was ever the same after that, and I got the feeling that George wasn't happy with me either for supporting Zim on the Irabu situation.

Without Joe around, George was making his presence felt more than I'd seen to that point, as we got off to a sluggish start. Two weeks into the season we were swept in a three-game series at home by the Detroit Tigers, dropping our record to 7-5, when George called a meeting with Zim and all of the coaches. We all went up to his office and George launched into a speech about how he wanted to talk out a few things, discuss some of the areas where we'd been having problems. But before we got into anything, George said, "Now if anyone in here thinks they're doing the absolute best job they can do, they can get up and leave right now."

It was really just George's way of saying everybody needed to work harder, and I'm sure he didn't expect anyone to take him up on his offer. But the words were barely out of his mouth when Zim popped up out of his chair and marched right out of the room without so much as a sideways glance at George. I think George was so taken aback that he didn't say a word, and suddenly Zim was gone.

Well, now I was mad as hell. I'd gone into the meeting in a rotten mood as it was because I'd found out before the game that Billy Connors had made another of his phone calls from Tampa to one of my pitchers to offer some unsolicited advice. As the organizational pitching coordinator and, more important, a confidant to George, Billy had carte blanche to tinker with our pitchers, and I would have been okay with that as long as he went through me to do it. Instead he went behind my back at times to talk to my pitchers, and by now, in my fourth season as pitching coach, I knew we were heading for a showdown that eventually we had, a few years later. But at the time, I was just exasperated, to the point where I was ready to throw my hands in the air and say, "Fine. I'll leave. Let Billy be the pitching coach."

Above all, it made me resent being in this meeting with George that much more, and now Zim had bolted on us. So I stood up and said, "George, if you really mean that, I think I should leave too because I don't know what else I could be doing."

I took a step or two toward the door but George, in that high-pitched voice that he gets when he's agitated, stopped me in my tracks.

"Wait a minute, wait a minute," he barked. "Stottlemyre, sit down, sit down, let's talk about this, let's just talk."

Reluctantly I sat down. None of the coaches were happy about being there. We felt like we were all doing our very best to hold the team together in the face of injuries and Joe's absence. And really, nothing came of the meeting other than George getting a chance to offer some opinions about what we needed to do with this player or that pitcher. More than anything George just wanted to vent a little bit. Most of us offered a few obligatory responses to placate him, and after he'd weighed in on several issues, he seemed satisfied that he'd solved all of our problems.

"Now that's what I wanted out of this meeting," George said. "That's exactly what I wanted. We made some real progress here."

And with that we were dismissed. I left the meeting not knowing whether to be mad at Zim for leaving or fearful that he might not be coming back at all, since his bitterness toward George seemed to be growing by the day. He'd been threatening to leave, in part because he was dealing with severe knee pain at the time, after having arthroscopic surgery in the winter. I didn't take him seriously until we were in Texas at the end of April. By then we were winning again, but Zim was growing more and more agitated about his silent treatment from George. Finally, after losing 8–6 to the Rangers on Wednesday, April 28, Zim called a meeting and told the team he would be leaving to go home after the final game of the series in

Texas the next night. Joe, who had been in St. Louis to see one of the doctors treating his cancer, was going to join the team in Kansas City, the next leg of the trip, and I guess Zim was thinking that Joe would take over. But from what I knew Joe was just showing up for a couple of days to support the team and wasn't ready yet to take over managing.

Normally after night games on the road, I just went back to the hotel, watched a little TV, and went to bed, but on this night I could see that Zim needed somebody to talk to, so I asked him if he wanted to get a beer. We sat down at the hotel bar and he said he was serious about leaving.

"I think you're making a mistake, Zim," I said. "I guess you've gotta do what you've gotta do, but I have to ask you: Does Joe know you're leaving?"

He just shook his head and said no. I'm laughing just thinking about it, because Zim is such a stubborn so-and-so, but it wasn't funny at the time. He'd been getting calls from time to time from Brian Cashman, our GM, sometimes with less-than-supportive messages from George, and he was at the end of his rope. I sure as heck didn't want any part of taking over the team in case Zim really did leave, so I tried to make him feel a bit guilty about the idea.

"You know, Joe's probably not ready to take over," I said. "Don't you think you owe it to him to hang in there? At the very least, don't you think you should talk to Joe before you do anything?"

Zim agreed he should talk to Joe, so I called him right there from the bar. Joe told Zim that physically he just wasn't ready to start managing yet, and that he was only coming to Kansas City to lend some support. Talking to Joe did make Zim feel guilty enough to rethink his decision to leave, and he agreed to stay until Joe came back. So I guess maybe I kept him from leaving because who knows what would have happened if he didn't talk to Joe that night?

Zim wound up managing for another couple of weeks. By the time Joe returned we were in Boston playing the Red Sox, with a

21-15 record. Considering that we'd been missing Roger Clemens and Jeff Nelson, who were both on the disabled list, I thought Zim did a great job. The two of us got along well during that time, largely because we both had the same outlook. Neither one of us was looking for any personal glory—we were only interested in keeping the team running smoothly until Joe came back. Both of us made an effort to do things the way we thought Joe would have done them. Zim left the pitching decisions almost entirely up to me, so I had a little more responsibility than normal. Occasionally Zim would suggest doing something different, and if he had a good reason for it, I went along with him.

I got to know Zim better during that period. We spent more time talking than we had in previous years and became closer as friends as a result. Zim's got a lot of pride, and he cared very much about the team and doing the best job he could for Joe. All he wanted was a thank-you at some point from George, but he never got one. It hurt him because for years he'd considered himself a good friend to George, which makes me chuckle because sometimes it's hard to be George's friend.

Over the next few seasons there were a few more insults from the Boss before Zim finally walked away after the 2003 season, vowing never to speak to George again. I believe he'll keep his vow, although I do think that George could mend the fences by reaching out to Zim and saying the right things. I don't see it happening because George is not that kind of guy, but, then again, he did call me and talk me into forgiving and forgetting my own grudge with him.

In any case, nobody was happier than Zim to see Joe return as manager. Actually, everybody was overjoyed, first because Joe was healthy, and second because, while the players played hard for Zim, Joe had a presence around the team that no one could duplicate. We'd all been shocked when he was diagnosed with prostate cancer, and he'd been shaken pretty hard by the news. Now, more than two months later, I was anxious to see if he was the same old Joe.

He was a little different at first. He seemed to be feeling his way back, guarding against doing too much because he became tired more easily than he had in the past. At first the everyday things he went through on the job made him very tired, so he was very aware of the need to pace himself to keep from becoming exhausted. He and I talked a lot about our conditions. By then I had been diagnosed with multiple myeloma, though it hadn't reached the stage where I needed treatment, and it wasn't until the next year that I let anyone other than Joe and Zim know about it. But by this time I knew my cancer was going to have to be addressed eventually, so Joe and I served as something of a sounding board for the other, as far as our health situations. We would compare notes any time one or the other of us went to see our doctor for a checkup and gave each other high fives when the news was good.

As far as managing, I think Joe became, if anything, more secure than ever in his decision making after his cancer scare. He was never one to worry about being second-guessed anyway, but I just got the feeling that when he came back the baseball decisions were easier than ever for him because he'd dealt with real life-and-death decisions during the previous three months. He was always good at handling the little brush fires on the ball club that popped up from time to time because he always believed in addressing such matters immediately, but now anything like that seemed even easier for him. As his strength began to come back over the next several weeks, I could see that he was enjoying the job as much as ever, maybe more so.

As much as we talked, one subject that never came up for discussion was how much longer Joe would want to manage. At the time I never thought either one of us would stay on the job as long as we did. Actually, I always thought I'd outlast Joe. I thought he'd get tired of dealing with some of the distractions from George, and I thought that maybe having a young daughter at home might be a factor as well. But Joe relishes the job and he seems to be great at leaving it at the ballpark so that he can enjoy his time at home with his family. I only saw him affected by George during one particular season, in 2003, when the interference from above seemed to get to him. Joe had one more year on his contract at the time, and I know he thought that would be it for him, after the 2004 season. He just felt at the time that George didn't want him anymore, but then in spring training of 2004 George's attitude toward Joe changed, and that led to another contract extension.

I don't think even he could have foreseen that kind of longevity when he returned in '99, but it was only a matter of weeks before Joe seemed to be the same as before his prostate cancer. And though we were in first place throughout the summer, it wasn't an easy season, mainly because the expectations were so high after what we'd done in '98. It wasn't realistic to think we could be as dominant again, but we couldn't escape the comparisons, so every little losing streak brought all kinds of scrutiny and analysis from the media and fans. There was no denying that we weren't playing at the same level, and much of the dropoff centered around Roger Clemens and Andy Pettitte.

Clemens was a newcomer, after we'd traded David Wells to the Toronto Blue Jays for him in spring training. And as much as Roger wanted to play for the Yankees and win a championship, it wasn't a comfortable transition for him. He had been very intimidating while pitching against us for the Red Sox and Blue Jays, and there were some hard feelings toward him after he hit a few of our guys with pitches. I sensed that he was a little uneasy coming into our clubhouse because of that, but Derek Jeter helped lighten the mood when he put on full catcher's gear the first time he stepped in for live batting practice against Roger in spring training. Jeter was one of the guys Clemens had plunked, and joking about it indicated a willingness to accept Roger as a teammate. Other teams may not have been so quick to forgive and forget, but those guys were so team oriented that they always put winning ahead of anything else. That attitude was a reflection of Joe Torre, who believed it was his job to fully sup-

port and accept anyone wearing pinstripes, in the interest of winning.

Roger turned out to be more of a pleasure to coach than I ever
imagined. Just from my impressions over the years being in the other
dugout, I was expecting a star pitcher with a big ego who was set in
his ways and wasn't going to listen much, but Roger was just the opposite. Eventually I enjoyed working with Roger as much as any
pitcher I've ever been around. He was very open to trying different
things, wanted to talk about his mistakes during an outing, and became a great leader and influence on the rest of the pitching staff.
Still, I got the feeling that he was feeling his way in his first few
months as a Yankee. He was bothered by a groin pull, which didn't
help, but Roger just seemed to be very conscious of not wanting to
mess up the chemistry of a team that had enjoyed a historic season in
1998. As a result, he seemed to be pitching more not to lose than
anything else. For example, let's say he'd just finished six innings in
a 2–2 game, and thrown about a hundred pitches. That first year he
was ready to come out at that point, where in the same situation in
subsequent years, he would say, "No, no, I'm not coming out. I'm
going to give you one more." The more comfortable he became with
us, the more his competitive nature came to the forefront. But he
wasn't dominant that first year with us.

As for Pettitte, he sprained an ankle late in spring training and
didn't find his form the first half of the season, and as we approached
the July 31 trading deadline, Andy became the focus of trade rumors. I didn't understand why but I always felt like there was someone in the front office who wasn't sold on Andy, right up until he left
as a free agent after the 2003 season. Personally, I always had faith
in him because I worked with him every day. I knew what kind of
person he was and how much heart he had. But more than once during organizational meetings I found myself defending Andy in those
early years. Somebody would say, "Well, you know, his body is soft,
he doesn't work hard . . ." and I would say, "Wait a minute. Time

out. He does work hard. His body may be a little bit soft, but that's Andy."

Usually those kind of comments would come from George's people in Tampa, most of whom I didn't know at all because I had such limited dealings with them. But one time I was shocked when Gene Michael, who was our superscout at the time, made a similar statement at one of our meetings. He said that he didn't think Pettitte could be counted on as a consistent winner over the long haul for those same reasons. I defended Andy during the meeting and then afterward I asked Stick, which is what everyone around the Yankees calls Gene, if I could talk to him in private. I've known Stick since I played with him in the 1960s, and I've always thought he was one of the sharpest baseball people in the game, so I wanted to get a better idea of why he felt that way about Andy.

When we talked I was emphatic in telling him that he was dead wrong about Andy's work ethic. Stick is an excellent talent evaluator who wasn't one to let someone else influence his opinions on players, but at the time he made it seem as if he'd merely been voicing the company line on Pettitte.

"I'm glad to hear you say that," he told me when I made my case for Andy, "because I hear this stuff all the time, and I'm going to take the other side now."

I'm not sure if Stick was just saying that to appease me, but the static in the organization regarding Andy never did seem to go away, and I was never sure why. I know there was concern about his elbow, which bothered him from time to time with us, but the front office just seemed to make more of it with him than they would with somebody else. Every year his elbow would be a little cranky for periods of time, yet Andy would be able to pitch and put up good numbers with it.

And I don't know how anyone could doubt his heart and toughness after what he'd done in the '96 World Series, outpitching John Smoltz in that 1–0 victory in Game 5. Joe has always said that per-

formance convinced him about Andy forever, and then the next season was even more proof to me that Andy was a gamer. He won
eighteen games in '97 even though his elbow was barking the whole
second half of the season. He had to be careful how much he threw
between starts, and he was often getting treatment on his elbow, but
he was always ready on game day. He wanted the ball and he was as
intense as ever on the mound, even on days when his elbow was really bothering him. I could never question anything about him after
that year.

I'll be the first to admit I'm biased about Andy. He and I became
very close over the years, probably closer than any pitcher I'd ever
coached. His father had some medical problems that he needed to
talk about with somebody, and as a result we developed a relationship that went beyond baseball, sharing thoughts on family and personal matters. Then when I went through my cancer ordeal in 2000,
Andy was the one player I talked to the most about my ups and
downs. Even when I was in the hospital I'd call the trainer's room at
Yankee Stadium and Andy would come to the phone. Or he'd be in
Joe's office when Joe would call me, and get on the phone to talk to
me. He was the guy that other players would go to for information
about how I was doing, that type of thing.

Not that he and I hit it off from the start. He could be stubborn
about wanting to do things his way on the mound, and we had some
disagreements as we got to know each other, especially in '96, our
first year together. For a while it was a toss-up over who was more
stubborn, him or me. In my view, Andy fell in love with his cutter a
little too much, throwing it hard down and in to right-handed hitters. It was his most effective pitch, but I thought he was throwing it
so much that it was taking a toll on his arm, and his velocity was
dropping because of it. I told him about pitchers who had damaged
their careers by relying too much on splitters and cutters. Both
pitches put extra strain on the forearm. With the cutter you're putting more pressure on the ball with your index finger, throwing al-

most like you would with a football, spiraling it to one side of the plate. Mariano Rivera is one of the few guys whose natural release produces a cutter, which is why he is about the only guy who can throw a cutter at 94 miles per hour.

So I spent a lot of time talking to Andy about the need to throw a fastball that would stay on the outer half to right-handers, give them something else to keep them from looking inside all the time, while also helping maintain his velocity. It took awhile but eventually I convinced him, and he worked hard to be able to pitch outside as well as inside to right-handers, with a four-seam fastball and a sinker. In addition, Andy was so intense during games that he could be difficult to talk to at times, but I understood that, and eventually we developed a trusting relationship where I could pick my spots with him during games, and he became very good about listening.

In '99 he was just in a rut during the first half of the season, unable to get anything going and feel good about his pitching after the ankle injury early in the year. I knew he'd turn it around, but by July the trade rumblings were getting louder and louder, to the point where I was afraid it was going to happen. Finally, I felt I had to try to intervene, so I went to talk to Brian Cashman.

"Brian," I said to him, "I don't know if you've ever thought of it this way, but look at Andy Pettitte as being on another team, not the Yankees. Look at what he's done, his record during the season and in the postseason, and let's say you had the opportunity to make a deal for him and have him pitch here in Yankee Stadium, where you love having left-handers. You'd give up almost anything to get a guy like him. Yet we already have him and there's all this talk about trading him. I can't understand it."

Brian didn't give me much feedback.

"I can't argue your point," he said, but he didn't give me any assurances that he wasn't going to trade him. I understood that Brian had to be careful about what he said. I've gotta believe that George wanted him to trade Pettitte at the time, and I'm not sure exactly where Brian stood, but at least I'd made my point.

Joe argued on Pettitte's behalf as well with Cashman, and once even talked directly to George about it. All of our lobbying seemed to have an effect. After the trading deadline passed and Andy was still a Yankee, George made it sound as if Pettitte had received a reprieve from the governor.

"He should be very relieved," George told reporters after the deadline. "Certain people put a lot of faith in him. Now we'll see what kind of man he is. This is a very defining moment for him."

That was classic George, trying to motivate people by challenging their manhood—while also putting us on notice for arguing on his behalf. In Andy's case, such a strategy was ridiculous, considering he'd been a vital part of our two championships in his first four years in the big leagues. George just never seemed to warm up to Andy. He loved to call guys like Paul O'Neill and Roger Clemens "warriors," but to me, Andy Pettitte was as much a warrior as anybody who played on those championship teams. He won 149 games for the Yankees in his nine seasons, and another 13 in the postseason, and if he had stayed a Yankee he would have become one of the winningest pitchers in club history.

In his final year with the club, 2003, Andy had a 21-8 season and then delivered big-time in the postseason, winning Game 2 in each of our three series, every time with pressure on him after we'd lost Game 1. His elbow bothered him some during that season, and the doctors told us that he'd probably need surgery at some point down the road. But I was still shocked that the front office didn't take a harder run at signing him. It worked out well for him, getting a big contract to play in Houston, since he'd grown up in that area and still lived there. But I know how much he loved pitching for the Yankees, and I know he would have stayed if the club had made him more of a priority that winter. By then I think the elbow was a big factor in the club's thinking, and it did go out on him the next year with the Astros, requiring surgery. But he came back to win seventeen games in 2005, and he still has plenty of good years left—maybe with the Yankees, as it turns out. Cashman was smart enough to sign him last winter after his contract ran out with the Astros, and having Pettitte back in 2007 should pay dividends, especially in October.

In any case, I'm just glad George backed off on the idea of trading Pettitte in '99. At the trading deadline he was 7-8 with a 5.65 ERA, yet he finished the season 14-11 with a 4.70 ERA, then pitched two outstanding games in the American League playoffs to help us breeze past the Texas Rangers and Boston Red Sox en route to another World Series. Andy didn't pitch as well in the Series, getting knocked out in the fourth inning in Game 3 against the Atlanta Braves, but by then there was no stopping us from another championship. We'd won the first two games in Atlanta and we weren't about to let the Braves do to us what we did to them in '96, coming back to win the Series after losing the first two at home. Sure enough, we rallied in Game 3 from a 5–1 deficit to take Andy off the hook and then won 6–5 in ten innings on Chad Curtis's home run.

That set the stage for Roger Clemens to finish off the sweep, which he did with a strong game, allowing one run in seven and two-thirds innings as we won 4–1 for our third championship in four years. Joe always cried when we won it all, allowing all those emotions he kept stored in the dugout all season to come pouring out, but this time there were tears all around after a particularly trying year on the personal side. A year that had begun with Joe's cancer diagnosis ended with the tragic news that Paul O'Neill's father had died in the early morning hours on the day of Game 4. Paul wanted to play to honor his father, and after we won everyone sort of gathered around to give him a group hug. There was a lot of sorrow late that season, as Luis Sojo's father had died only a week earlier, and Scott Brosius lost his father as well, in September. In addition, Yankee legends Joe DiMaggio and Catfish Hunter died in 1999, Catfish much too young, at fifty-three, because of ALS, better known as Lou Gehrig's disease. So in many ways this championship was a time of reflection for many of us. Joe and I drank a toast that night to our health, each of us knowing that my time for treatment was coming soon. We just didn't know how soon.

11

Cancer

In the quiet of a doctor's office, the oncologist was talking to me about high protein levels in my blood, good cells and bad cells, and I really didn't know where it was all leading until he casually dropped the "C" word on me.

"Some of the cells may be cancerous," he said, and though he continued on without so much as a pause, I'm not sure I remember anything else he said that day.

You hear the word *cancer* and it shakes you to your bones because of the uncertainty, the fear of death associated with the word. For me it was especially chilling because it instantly conjured the painful memory of losing my son Jason to leukemia, a blood cancer that is related in some ways to myeloma, the cancer I was diagnosed with that day in the spring of 1999. Worse yet was hearing there was no cure. Treatment, yes, but there is still no known cure for multiple myeloma. The first doctor who diagnosed me, in fact, told me I shouldn't expect to live more than another six years, and that was if chemotherapy and a cell transplant went smoothly.

For my wife, Jean, it was hard not to think the worst, that she was going to lose me in much the same way we'd lost Jason. After I was diagnosed, she began reading everything she could find on the Internet about multiple myeloma, and it was virtually all gloom and doom. What made it harder in some ways was that while I was diagnosed in '99, the cancer wasn't active enough in my body at the time to necessitate aggressive treatment, so for a year we were kind of waiting for the other shoe to drop, so to speak.

The first sign of trouble had been my annual physical with the Yankees before spring training of '99. I was told there were abnormalities in my blood, which led to my having a bone marrow aspiration. That was no fun, believe me. They bend you over and stick a needle in the bone in your back; it's difficult for the needle to penetrate the bone, but eventually it draws marrow from the bone, and the marrow confirmed that I had cancerous cells in my blood. The doctor who diagnosed me wanted to begin treatment immediately, but after confiding in Joe Torre, I decided to get another medical opinion.

By this time Joe had been diagnosed with prostate cancer, and his doctor set up an appointment for me with Dr. Steven Nimer at Memorial Sloan-Kettering Hospital in New York. Dr. Nimer confirmed the diagnosis but said the cancer was in what he called a smoldering stage that didn't need to be treated aggressively right away. He said it needed to be watched, so I began going once a month to have my blood tested and get an IV treatment that helps keep your bones hard and less susceptible to fractures. The disease can weaken your bones and cause fractures, and it can make you anemic, so that you feel tired, but I didn't have any of those symptoms.

So for a year, the IV treatments were all I needed as I went about the business of coaching during that 1999 season, feeling fine all the way to a second straight world championship. It wasn't until the next season, on our first road trip in 2000, when things changed. We were in Seattle, so I went to my local doctor to have my blood checked, and bad-cell counts had started to rise significantly, which meant I needed aggressive treatment. Dr. Nimer outlined a plan that called for four to six months of chemotherapy, followed by a stem-cell transplant. He was very positive, very confident the treatment would allow me to live well beyond the six years the first doctor had discussed. And he assured me the stem-cell transplant, assuming all went well, would only force me away from my job temporarily, for the few months it would take my immune system to recover. So Dr. Nimer was already talking about returning to the Yankees in 2001, but to be honest, I was just hoping to get through the 2000 season and had no intention at the time of coming back in 2001. I had enough to think about because, despite the doctor's reassurance, it was scary that suddenly the cancer was attacking my body. Chemotherapy is another word that you more or less associate with death, so I knew I was in for a rough ride.

I also knew the time had come to tell people that I had cancer. I would have preferred not to, because I planned on continuing to work during my treatment, but I knew I'd be recognized going in and out of Sloan-Kettering Hospital for my chemo treatments, and people would start asking questions, so I figured I might as well get it out in the open. I talked to Joe about it and he knew that it would be too emotional for me to tell the players, so he volunteered to do that. So while I had a little press conference in Seattle to tell the media that I had cancer, Joe gathered the players in the visitors' clubhouse and told them about my situation. I had asked him to tell the guys not to treat me any differently, that I wasn't staying on the job to try to be a hero but because I fully expected to be healthy enough to handle my duties. I asked the press much the same thing, telling reporters to feel free to ask me about our pitchers, as usual, but to refrain from asking me about my cancer.

The news of my condition drew more attention than I expected. I guess that being in New York for so many years as a player and a coach, with the Mets as well as the Yankees, made me familiar to a lot of baseball fans, and I was grateful for all the well-wishing cards and letters I received. But to the media the story was bigger than my misfortune because the team seemed to be haunted by such occurrences. Newspaper stories reminded fans that cancer had struck Joe Torre and Darryl Strawberry in recent years, while Yankee legends Joe DiMaggio and Catfish Hunter had died from illness in 1999, as had three fathers of Yankee players.

Players were uncomfortable with all the sickness. Reliever Jeff Nelson went so far as to ask reporters: "Is Yankee Stadium cursed?"

More likely it was all coincidental—but a bit eerie nevertheless. I didn't give it much thought at the time because I was consumed with my own condition. And, if anything, I benefited from what I considered a little divine intervention that allowed me to attend the home opener. My first chemotherapy treatment was scheduled for the afternoon of our home opener, Tuesday, April 11, so I was going to have to miss the game. But the forecast of cold temperatures and snow was so ominous that the Yankees postponed the game a day ahead of time, and rescheduled it for Wednesday, allowing me to be there as we defeated the Texas Rangers 8–6.

It was quite a day, too. I handled my first chemo treatment pretty well and felt good at the stadium. My condition had received so much attention that I figured the fans would respond, but I was overwhelmed by the ovation I received upon being introduced. I'd heard plenty of those types of roars there in recent years as we won championships, but pitching coaches aren't supposed to get the loudest ovation on opening day. I had the feeling the fans were trying to lift my spirits for the ordeal ahead of me with the sheer decibel level of support, and it was humbling to think people cared that much. Actually, for the rest of that season fans were always calling out to me during batting practice, or when I'd walk out with the pitcher to the bullpen, wishing me good health and saying they were pulling for me. It meant a lot to hear that kind of support, especially on the days when I wasn't feeling so good.

Once the game started against the Rangers that day, I wasn't thinking about my cancer or my chemo, but rather concentrating hard on trying to help David Cone find his rhythm on a day when he was out of synch and fortunate just to make it to the sixth inning. And though I was a little more tired than usual that night, I realized that staying on the job was going to be the best possible therapy for me because it was going to keep me from sitting around and either worrying about my fate or feeling sorry for myself.

It wasn't always easy going to work, but I never would have guessed that I'd be able to do my job with minimal interruption from the chemotherapy. After the initial treatment at the hospital, at which the doctor had inserted tubes into my chest, I was able to take the chemo while on the job. I wore a little bag that was attached around my waist containing a bottle with the chemo in it. I'd wear this for three days, as it worked off my heartbeat, pumping it into my system by a thin tube that someone would connect to the tubes in my chest, then disconnect it after the treatment. The tubes just had to be cleaned daily for those three days when I was getting the chemo. It wasn't the simplest thing in the world, because the tubes had to be disconnected, cleaned, flushed, drained, and reconnected in specific steps, and it took some time. The nurses at the hospital taught Jean how to do it, and she changed them for me when I was home. She made road trips during the first half of the season, while our long-time trainer, Gene Monahan, volunteered to learn from Jean and take it from there.

Geno was a lifesaver for me during this time. He made sure that I roomed next to him or across the hall in our hotels, and he'd come to my room every morning to take care of me. It could be a little in-timidating, with all the medications, needles, plugs, and cords, and the masks we wore as a precaution against infection. Geno was a little nervous about it at first. He even called the hospital a couple of times to make sure he was cleaning, flushing, and reconnecting in the right order, but after a few times he had it down. I've known Geno since 1963, which is when he started with the Yankees as an assistant trainer. I call him the Dean because he has been with the organization longer than anyone else. He preferred that I didn't remind everyone just how long he has been on the job, which, of course, was all the more reason for me to do it. Geno's really a great guy, and even though I didn't particularly like having those tubes in my chest, I enjoyed those mornings with him, the two of us solving the world's problems while he worked on me.

He really watched out for me, too. He was always keeping an eye on me, making sure I was behind the big screen beyond second base during batting practice, so that I was protected from getting hit. After a while it was like Geno was my doctor, and I had to check with him before I did anything on the field. Before games I'd tell him I was going out to the outfield to put the pitchers through some running work, and he'd tell me, "No, it's too hot." I'd say, "Ah, come on, Geno, let me go. I'll be fine."

Usually I could talk him into it, but not without an argument. He knew I wasn't trying to prove anything, but rather that I just loved doing my work as a coach. On the days I felt strong, I'd tell him I was going to throw batting practice.

"But you've got all these tubes and wires," he'd say.

"Ah, just tape the stuff down," I'd say, "and it'll be fine."

"Well," he'd say, "I better call the doctor and see if it's okay."

"No, no, you don't have to do that," I'd say. "It's okay, believe me. Just tape it down."

So I'd go out and throw batting practice for fifteen minutes, then come in sweating heavily, and Geno would have to change my bandages. Sometimes I felt bad because he had enough to do. Our trainers, Geno and Steve Donahue, put in ungodly hours, taking care of player injuries and treatment, and he didn't need to be worrying about me. But we'd been friends for so long that he'd always tell me he enjoyed spending the time together, and we did share a lot of stories from over the years.

Anyway, I took those chemotherapy treatments that way for four months, and most people had no idea I was even doing it. I was lucky because I handled all the side effects without much problem. I didn't get nauseous and didn't lose my hair, so there were no outward signs of what I was going through. I did have a strong reaction one time, when they gave me a medicine called Cytoxin as part of my chemotherapy. For some reason, it brought my white-cell counts down really low, and I began running a fever on a Saturday night when I was at home in our apartment in New Jersey. Jean had to drive me to the hospital, where they gave me an IV to raise my counts back to normal. That was scary because it made me realize how susceptible my immune system was to any type of sickness.

For the most part, though, I came through four months of treatment in good shape. All along I knew I was going to have to go into the hospital in September and spend about three weeks there for the stem-cell transplant. I would have loved to have put it off until after the season, since we were heading for another big October, but it wasn't something you could postpone like a dentist appointment. Dr. Nimer had laid out the timetable, and I'd discussed it with Joe. The people in the front office, including George Steinbrenner, were aware as well.

George was great during this time. He had allowed Jean to travel with us on our chartered jet before Geno took over caring for me, and he made a point of telling me more than once not to hesitate to ask if I needed something, anything, especially when I went into the hospital. As I mentioned earlier, he pulled some strings, apparently calling Mayor Rudy Giuliani, so that I could get the Madison Square Garden network, which carried the Yankee games at the time, on the TV in my room. That made me quite popular among the nurses, many of whom were Yankee fans; they'd sneak into my room to watch an inning here or there in between tending to other patients. Being able to see the games made my stay much more bearable, as I managed to feel connected to the team at least in some way.

I was grateful to Joe for that. He made every effort to make me feel as if I was still in the loop. Billy Connors had joined the club on a daily basis to serve as pitching coach, but Joe continued to confer with me by phone every day, relying on my opinion for various pitching decisions. Still, the more time I spent away from the team, the harder it was to feel a part of things. For that matter, I was pretty much disconnected from everyone except my family during my time in the hospital. Because the chemotherapy was killing my cells and preparing me for the stem-cell transplant, my immune system was becoming weaker by the day, making me more and more susceptible to any kind of germs. I was on the eleventh floor, which was for transplant patients, and I was confined to my room, allowed to have only family visit. Anyone in the room had to wear masks as a further precaution.

Jean was always there for me, and my sons, Mel Jr. and Todd, both flew in to New York to spend time with me in the hospital. Junior was the pitching coach at UNLV at the time, and they were in their fall season, but he came and stayed for a month in New York to support both me and Jean. He was married with a couple of young kids by then, and I told him to go take care of his own family, but he assured me they were fine and insisted on being there. Todd was pitching for the Arizona Diamondbacks that year, but he left them and came to the hospital when I had my transplant, stayed around the clock for a couple of days, then flew to San Francisco and made his next start.

Todd was having a tough season, missing weeks at a time because of arm injuries, but he and I had enjoyed a nice moment earlier that season. He happened to be pitching in Philadelphia on a day when the Yankees were off, so Jean and I drove down the New Jersey Turnpike to see the game. It was the only time I'd seen him pitch live in a regular-season game when I wasn't in the other dugout, and his first time up at the plate he hit the only home run of his career—just got out in front of a fastball and nailed one. He loved going deep with me sitting right there, I can tell you that. Todd didn't pitch great that night, but he probably shouldn't have been out there at all, because at the time his shoulder was a mess: He had tears in his labrum, his rotator cuff, and his bicep tendon, but somehow he was able to continue pitching.

After the game I waited for him in the tunnel, the way my kids used to wait for me after I pitched. When he came out, I said to him, "How are you doing it? Your shoulder is hanging together by a thread—how the hell are you doing it?"

Todd just sort of shrugged, and later he told me that he couldn't say what he was thinking at the time—that if I could continue coaching while I was fighting cancer, he could sure as heck keep taking the ball with a bad shoulder. Not that I believed him. Todd was so ultra-competitive, and some of that goes back to his anger over losing his brother, that he pitched many a time when he probably should have been on the disabled list, but I do believe my positive attitude about my cancer helped him get through a difficult season. I could tell how much he appreciated me coming down to see him pitch, and I drove home that night feeling as if someone had just zapped the cancer right out of my body. I mean, every father can relate to how uplifting it is knowing you have inspired your son or daughter, whether it's by fighting cancer or just showing up at a game to see them play. I've been lucky to maintain that type of relationship with both of my sons, and that's why it meant so much to have them there at the hospital.

In fact, my family members were usually the only visitors I was allowed, but one day I did talk the nurses into allowing Jay Horwitz, the longtime Mets' PR director, to visit me in my room. Jay is a great friend but he is kind of a nervous guy, and I think he was pretty spooked by the visit, having to wear the mask and everything. I really appreciated him making the effort to come see me, though, as it was becoming depressing to be so isolated at a time of the year when I'd normally be gearing up for another postseason with the Yankees.

During this time, especially, I found myself thinking a lot about Jason, and what a tough little guy he'd been throughout his battle with leukemia. It gave me strength just remembering how he'd handled some of the same painful treatments that I was undergoing. I knew Jean had to be thinking about Jason as well, but it wasn't something we really talked about. Jean told me later that the medical people were trying to prepare her mentally for the transplant as I went through my chemotherapy. Dr. Nimer suggested that she see a therapist to deal with her fears of a repeat of what she went through with Jason, losing him after his body rejected Todd's bone marrow from the transplant. She told them no, she'd be fine, and she was until we got close to the transplant.

Jean kept this from me at the time, but one day she just kind of broke down, telling our nurse that she couldn't go through this again. It all seemed eerily similar to Jason's leukemia. I was even taking some of the same medicines they'd given Jason. Dr. Nimer called Jean that day and again suggested she go see a psychiatrist at the hospital, but she didn't want to do it. He was doing his best to keep Jean thinking positive, constantly reinforcing the thought that my case was different, that there was less chance of rejection with a stem-cell transplant than a bone marrow transplant. I'm glad I didn't know how hard Jean was taking it, or it probably would have added stress that I didn't need.

Meanwhile, my chemotherapy treatments became stronger as the time for the transplant neared. Basically the chemo was killing all my white cells where the cancer had formed. A few of those treatments knocked me for a loop, made me sick and tired as could be. I began to feel very weak, and all I really wanted to do was sleep. Just before the transplant it became really hard to stay awake and watch the Yankee games. Finally, on September 14, I had the transplant, and that turned out to be easy to handle. It wasn't much more than a transfusion, really. The transplant just made me feel warm and flushed—I was expecting something worse. They had taken my bad cells, cleaned them up and put them in a plastic bag, then injected fluid into the bag to freeze them, a process that kills any sign of myeloma. Those cells were then transplanted back into my body. It sounds strange, I know, but that's how they replace bad cells.

After the transplant it was just a waiting game to see if my body would accept the new white cells. If not, I probably wouldn't have made it because there weren't really any other options. At the hospital they began taking blood samples every day, and for two days there was no sign of a white-cell blood count. The doctors and nurses assured me this was normal, that it normally took a few days for the new cells to show up, but those were a couple of the longest days of my life. All I could do was wait, and for really the first time I began having my doubts, worrying that the transplant wasn't going to take. But then on the third day my blood showed that I had a white-cell count of .1. Though it was a tiny percentage, Dr. Nimer was thrilled because the appearance of any white-cell presence meant the transplant worked. That put my mind at ease, as my white-cell count began climbing little by little over the next few days. At that point I was allowed to get out of bed and leave my room for the first time in more than a week, but only to walk a little bit at night when the halls were pretty empty, and there was less exposure to germs.

I couldn't believe how weak I felt. Once around the hall and I was exhausted. But every day I could feel my strength beginning to come back, and I was starting to believe what Dr. Nimer had been telling me from the time he began treating me—that everything was going to be all right. He had been very positive from the outset, which was comforting to me. He was honest with me; he never pretended that I wasn't at risk, but he was very upbeat about the way I was handling the chemo, saying it improved my chances the transplant would work. My nurses were great, too. They dealt only with transplant patients, and they were continually making me feel like there was a good chance my transplant would work.

Looking back, I see it was really an unbelievable process, leading up to and then undergoing the transplant. Sometimes I think I was kind of stupid for continuing to work during that time because there were a lot of days when I didn't feel like going to the ballpark and just had no energy to do my job. But being around Joe and the players always raised my energy level enough to get me through the night, and focusing on the game kept me from thinking about everything else. That was part of my motivation. I felt a loyalty to the Yankees, but I also knew that if I was working, it would help keep me from sitting around feeling sorry for myself and getting depressed.

In any case, as happy as I was after the transplant, it took a long time to feel close to normal. I was released from the hospital on September 21, a week after my transplant, and three weeks after I'd been admitted on September 1. I went home but I was pretty much confined to our apartment in New Jersey, as my immune system remained weak. And I didn't have the strength to do anything anyway. I took walks outside but initially I couldn't make it around the block. I'd just run out of gas. But slowly my strength began to come back and I was able to take longer walks. By then the Yankees had wrapped up a third straight divisional title and were preparing for the playoffs, but Dr. Nimer said it was much too risky to go to Yankee Stadium and see the team. As the playoffs began, however, at least I was able to watch the games again without conking out.

It was odd, feeling so detached from the team at such a critical time in the season. I hadn't been able to continue my talks on the phone with Joe before and after my transplant, so I really felt like I'd lost touch with the club. When we reached the World Series against the Mets, I begged Dr. Nimer to let me go to the Stadium for the first two games. As I noted earlier, I watched those games from Joe's office, where I wound up eating cheeseburgers with George Steinbrenner as the Yankees won both games to start us on our way to defeating the Mets in five. I stayed at home for the three games at Shea Stadium, so I wasn't there when we won our third straight championship. As happy as I was for the guys, it was hard, watching from my couch in New Jersey while everybody celebrated in the locker room. Same thing for the parade a couple of days later. Not that I lost sight of the big picture: I felt fortunate to be alive and well, with a prognosis for a full recovery. Still, I had a feeling of sadness because at the time, weak as I was, I really didn't think I'd be going back to coaching in 2001.

After the World Series I really just wanted to go home to Washington. But I still couldn't be around people. Because my white-cell count was still low, the danger was that if I caught a cold I'd be highly susceptible to getting pneumonia, which in my state could be dangerous. It was November before I was allowed to go to a restaurant for dinner, and even then Jean and I would go during off-peak hours and get a table in the back, as isolated as possible. Finally, Dr. Nimer said it was okay to fly, and we went home on November 15. He wanted me to wear a mask, but I didn't want to call that kind of attention to my condition.

One of my regrets during that time was missing my younger brother's funeral. Keith, the brother with whom I'd played all those games of pitch-and-catch as kids—me pretending to be the Yankees, him the Dodgers—had been diagnosed with a brain tumor two years earlier. We hadn't spent a lot of time together for years because he lived in Alaska, but after he got sick we took some fishing trips together, and in 1999 he came out to New York during the season to visit. I took him to the stadium, and he got a big kick out of watching batting practice, taking some pictures with some of our players. We both knew he didn't have a lot of time because the doctors had performed surgery and said they were unable to remove all of the cancer. Keith passed away right around the first of November, and at the time my doctor said it was much too dangerous to be around people, especially in a closed environment on a plane. So unfortunately I wasn't able to be there for Keith's family at the funeral in Olympia, Washington.

It was late December before I was cleared to resume a normal life, though Dr. Nimer asked me to continue to avoid crowds if I could. By then I was starting to feel like I did want to return for the 2001 season. As I began to regain my strength, I didn't want the cancer to be the reason that I left baseball. My wife and sons felt the same way; they were encouraging me to return because they thought it would be good for me in the long run. In addition, though the doctors told me my form of cancer was very rare, the response I received from people told me maybe it's not as rare as they think. Everywhere I'd go it seemed I'd run into somebody who knew of a friend or relative who had myeloma. And I received so much mail at the stadium, most of it from fans wishing me well, but a good portion of it from people telling me they were suffering from the same cancer, and urging me to continue coaching because I was an inspiration to them.

As much as my doctor told me about the disease, I became more educated about it from the mail I received. I learned a lot about symptoms, about what happens if it's not detected as early as mine. I came to learn that some of these people were really suffering, and they were looking to me for hope. Some of them told me they were watching the Yankee games on TV, just waiting to get a look at me, either in the dugout or maybe going to the mound to talk to a pitcher. They made it sound as if they were watching my every move, because just seeing me in good condition gave them reason to stay positive about their own condition.

It wasn't long before I felt an obligation to respond. I wrote some letters but then I found that it meant even more to people if they heard from me by phone. It started when someone on the ball club would tell me he had a friend who had the same cancer. Roger Clemens was one of the first, and he asked if I'd call his friend and "give him some of your attitude," I guess because I was very positive, always convinced that I was going to beat the cancer. So then, whenever someone included a phone number in a letter, I tried to call them and talk for a few minutes, just compare notes about how each of us was doing, and maybe lift somebody's spirits. It was kind of funny, people were usually shocked to hear from me. But I got a lot of satisfaction knowing I was helping somebody, because I could usually hear it in their voice that it meant a lot to them.

I only made calls on days when I was feeling good myself and felt I could impart some good vibes. On those days I'd usually make a few calls in the morning from home before going to the stadium in the afternoon. Other days I didn't feel I could call anyone because I was feeling a little down myself. I know that a lot of Yankee people have said they couldn't believe how upbeat I was throughout my cancer, but believe me, I had my days where it got to me a little bit. For a while it was kind of a day-to-day situation as to my state of mind. Some days I was fine, and I didn't think of my disease the whole day. Other days, it was hard to think about anything else. Those were the days when I knew I made the right decision as far as continuing to work, because I needed something to take my mind off the cancer and where it could lead. Just being at the ballpark, doing my work, interacting with the players as well as Joe and the other coaches, I kept my mind occupied and I was around the people who could always make me laugh, no matter how I felt.

One real source of motivation for me was meeting a man at a banquet for multiple myeloma who had been diagnosed with the disease eleven years earlier. He looked and felt great, and that gave me hope at a time when I was still trying to build up my immune system and overall energy level. Like a lot of people who contacted me, this guy told me I was an inspiration to him. I heard that so often that I started to feel I'd be letting down a lot of people if I didn't go back for another season. The Yankees gave me all the time I needed, and finally in January I told them I would be coming back. Spring training was tougher on me than normal, and I had to take precautions to guard against getting sick, avoiding players who had colds, things like that. I held up okay physically but I still didn't have my normal energy level, and I did come down with colds a few times during the season.

It wasn't until midseason that I began to feel like my old self, and since then I've been blessed with good health. Over the years I've been back to the hospital to have my physical, get blood work done, and all that stuff, and the doctors say they can't believe how well I've done. My blood counts now are probably better than 90 percent of people who have never had any form of cancer. That's partially because of the transplant and partially because of the medicine I've taken since then to keep my blood clean. I still have signs of myeloma in my blood, and I'll never be entirely free of the disease, unless medical research finds a cure for it. But it's under control and I continue to feel good, more than eight years since I was first diagnosed.

In a way, it seems like a lifetime ago since that spring day in the doctor's office, when the mention of an incurable cancer painted the bleakest of pictures. I try not to ponder the question of whether I was a victim of fate or all those ill-advised radiation treatments I received on my shoulder when I was playing for the Yankees. Considering the outpouring of support I received from so many people, most of whom I didn't even know, and the satisfaction I felt in serving as an inspiration, I don't feel like a victim at all.

12

The End of the Run

After surviving cancer, I started thinking seriously about an exit strategy, if you will, from a life of baseball that would allow me to spend more time hunting, fishing, visiting my sons, and throwing batting practice to my grandchildren rather than to major leaguers. I wanted to coach at least one more season, partly because I'd missed the thrill of a third straight championship in 2000 while I was recovering from my stem-cell transplant, and partly because I was determined to show people that your life doesn't have to change because of cancer.

I never intended to stay another five seasons, but I wanted to go out with another championship, and the way we were going, I figured I could name my year. Who knew that October would suddenly bring us heartbreak, as if the baseball gods had decided we had to pay for our years of domination. In truth, it was bound to happen. When Major League Baseball added an extra round of playoffs in

1995, it multiplied the odds against winning a championship, yet the Yankees had won it all in four of the first six seasons the new system was in place.

So when we lost the 2001 World Series to the Arizona Diamond-backs, obviously it was shocking because you never expect to lose with Mariano Rivera on the mound, but that convinced me to stay another year, win that last championship, and get out. Then the Anaheim Angels ambushed us in 2002, beating up on our pitching staff so severely that I felt a personal responsibility to come back. A year later, after our epic League Championship Series victory over the Boston Red Sox in 2003, we let down and allowed the Florida Marlins to beat us in the World Series. Finally, unbelievably, we be-came the first team in baseball history to blow a 3–0 lead in the postseason, losing those four straight games to the Red Sox in 2004 that put to rest the Curse of the Bambino. Every one of those years I'd gone to spring training feeling sure that we'd win and I'd sail off into the sunset in my fishing boat.

At some point, of course, I started wondering if I was going to get to go out on my own terms at all. With each of those postseason losses, I could feel the wrath of George Steinbrenner starting to move in my direction. Never mind that four championships in six years should have assured any manager and his coaching staff a decade of immunity in the playoffs. It's not as if we stopped being a very good team; it's just that the difficulty of the October crapshoot, which is about the only way you can describe a three-tiered system of playoff series, finally caught up with us. But no matter how much we won, George needed to assign blame when we lost. So in 2001, when the Diamondbacks ended our dynasty by beating us with their ninth-inning rally against Mariano in Game 7, George fired hitting coach Gary Denbo and bullpen coach Tony Cloninger. It didn't seem fair, especially considering the way the Series was decided, on a broken-bat single that barely reached the outfield grass. Indeed, that was surely the most gut-wrenching of our October defeats.

It had been an unusually emotional World Series in many ways, mainly because it was played in the aftermath of the September 11 terrorist attacks on New York City. I didn't lose anyone close to me in the tragedy, but I think everyone felt a sense of loss and heartache. I can remember so many times, standing during the playing of "God Bless America" in the seventh inning in the ensuing days, having tears come to my eyes, and then suddenly having to refocus on baseball. I'd look around and see other guys wiping tears away as they went back to the dugout, so I knew I wasn't the only one. It was heartwarming to see the reaction of fans in other cities, displaying signs of support for New York, when normally we were considered the enemy. And I can't tell you how many fans in the stands tried to bargain with us for the hats that we were wearing in the days following 9/11, bearing the insignia of the New York Police Department, the Fire Department, or the Port Authority Operations.

Throughout October we kept hearing that we were doing the city a service by making another run at a championship, giving people a reason to forget the horrors of the attacks for a few hours a night. Yankee Stadium is always loud and rocking during the playoffs, but you could definitely sense a spirit of community among the fans during that time, as if the setting provided the opportunity for New Yorkers to show the world they were going strong and united, going on with life as usual. The highlight, in that regard, had to be the night that President George Bush came to the stadium to throw out the ceremonial first pitch for Game 3 against the Diamondbacks, our first home game of that World Series. I know it made an impression on the players and coaches that he made himself so visible at a time when there was still considerable fear about more attacks.

The funny thing was, the president took his task of throwing the pitch very seriously, warming up his arm by throwing for a couple of minutes in the batting cage underneath the stadium. I think he was nervous about it, especially after Derek Jeter kidded him when they shook hands that he better not bounce his throw to the plate because the fans would boo him. We've seen it happen a lot. People get out there on the mound and don't realize just how hard you have to throw the ball to reach the plate. And Yankee fans do like to boo any sign of weakness. So when I was introduced to President Bush, I raised my arm above my head and said, "Get your arm on top and aim high, because everybody usually bounces it." He laughed and said thanks, then went out there and threw a strike, as the stadium erupted with a roar. He came off the field and exited through our dugout, and you could tell he still had some adrenaline pumping. All in all, it was quite a moment in one of the most thrilling World Series in baseball history.

Actually, I've never seen anything like what we pulled off against the Diamondbacks, hitting game-tying home runs in the bottom of the ninth on consecutive nights, by Tino Martinez in Game 4 and Scott Brosius in Game 5. We won both games in extra innings, and the miracle wins sent us back to Arizona with a 3–2 Series lead, confident that we'd find a way to beat either Randy Johnson in Game 6 or Curt Schilling in Game 7 and win our fourth straight championship.

I had a lot of confidence that Andy Pettitte would end it for us in Game 6. He'd been lights-out in Game 2, dominating the Diamondbacks all night but losing 4–0 because he gave up a three-run home run to Matt Williams in the seventh inning. Before Game 6, however, the D-Backs studied tapes of Game 2 and picked up something, noticing that Andy was tipping his pitches, bringing his glove to his belt during his delivery when throwing his cutter, while bringing it to a position maybe six inches higher on his other pitches. He did it in both the windup and the stretch, setting his glove in slightly different positions. It doesn't sound like much, but if you're looking for it from the batter's box, you can tell the difference, in time to know when Andy was throwing his cutter. As a result, from the start the Arizona hitters were right on just about every pitch, blitzing Andy by scoring six runs on seven hits and knocking him out before he recorded an out in the third inning. It happened so fast that we were all stunned, and it wasn't until I looked at the tape the next day, after word had filtered back to us, that I saw what Andy had been doing. I felt bad because it was something he had done from time to time over the years, just as a habit, and it's something we watched for. But he had been so effective in Game 2 that I hadn't noticed anything, and the damage was done so quickly in Game 6 that I was focusing mostly on trying to settle Andy down and keep his head in the game.

Sometimes tipping pitches isn't such a big deal if a pitcher is on top of his game, hitting spots, using all of his pitches, but in Andy's case he relies on right-handed hitters chasing his cutter out of the strike zone, as it breaks down and in on them at the last second. They had taken a lot of bad swings in Game 2 doing just that, chasing his cutter, but in Game 6 they were laying off the real good ones, and hammering the ones he left in the strike zone. To see the tapes of Game 2 and Game 6 you'd have thought it was two different pitchers, but Andy actually had good stuff in Game 6 as well— he was simply forced to throw more hittable pitches and the Arizona hitters were just sitting on them. It made for a short night for Andy, a long night for our club as our bullpen took a pounding and we lost 15–2.

One night later, however, I didn't think it would matter because we gave the ball to Mariano Rivera in the eighth inning of Game 7 with a one-run lead. There wasn't a better feeling for us than having Mo on the mound with a lead, and when he blew away the Diamondbacks in the eighth inning, striking out the side despite giving up a single to Steve Finley, it looked like business as usual for the greatest postseason closer of all time. Then, unbelievably, it unraveled in the ninth. Everybody remembers the Gonzalez broken-bat game winner, but the hit that killed us was a double down the right-field line by Tony Womack that tied the game 2–2 and put runners on second and third with one out. At the time our scouting report on him was to bust him inside, which, of course, played to Mariano's strength with his cutter to left-handed hitters. But after getting the opportunity to see more of Womack when he played with us for part of the 2005 season, I concluded that we probably had the wrong book on him for the 2001 World Series. With his short, quick stroke, he's tougher to tie up with the inside pitch than most guys, and because he doesn't have any power, you can pitch him away and play him shallow that way in the outfield.

So maybe we can second-guess ourselves a little bit about that, but we certainly didn't expect Womack to pull a pitch from Mo down the line the way he did. Mo didn't get the pitch inside as far as he wanted, and with that short, choppy stroke, Womack made him pay. After Mo then hit Craig Counsell with a pitch, trying to get in on him, Gonzalez won it with his blooper. It was a shame because if the infield was back, Jeter catches that ball with no trouble. Ironically, however, that's part of the reason we brought the infield in; more often than not, hitters aren't able to center the ball on their bat against Mo's cutter, and we were worried that if we kept the infield back, we might not be able to turn the double play on a slowly hit ground ball. So we felt we had no choice but to bring the infield in and go for the force out at the plate.

As it turned out, the thinking was right. Mo made a great pitch, got in on Gonzalez's hands and produced a weak hit, but it just happened to be a broken-bat bleeder that landed in the perfect spot for the D-Backs, giving them a 3–2 victory and the championship. It was shocking to watch, because we'd gotten to the point where we always expected to win in October, especially with Mo on the mound. Afterward there were a lot of hugs in the locker room because we knew changes were coming, with Paul O'Neill and Scott Brosius retiring, and free agent Tino Martinez aware that George was going to pursue Jason Giambi as the new first baseman. As badly as we felt about losing, especially the way it happened, I didn't sense that real bitter taste of defeat in the locker room. We realized we were fortunate to push the Series all the way to the end, with those ninth-inning home runs in New York, and just as we'd snatched victories from them, they'd done it to us in Game 7. It was a great Series, with the home team winning every game. Even in losing there was a real feeling of pride about our team that night.

The next year was quite the opposite. I don't know if I'll ever be able to explain what happened in 2002 against the Angels, losing three of four games in the best-of-five divisional series. We won 103 games during the season and I thought we were primed to win another championship, but the Angels just completely manhandled our pitchers. They were a hot team full of scrappy, contact hitters who always seem to play us tough, but it was hard to believe the way they buzzsawed through a starting rotation of Andy Pettitte, Roger Clemens, Mike Mussina, and David Wells. In four games our starters gave up twenty runs in seventeen and one-third innings, a 10.39 ERA. The Angels set a record by hitting .376, the highest ever by a team in a postseason series. Looking back, I think we had good information on their hitters, we had good game plans to attack their weakness, but we just didn't execute our pitches in that series, and the Angels were hot enough to make us pay for it.

By the end of the series, after we lost 9–6 in Game 3 and 9–5 in Game 4, I felt kind of numb. Anytime one of my pitchers gets hammered I feel their pain. Seeing our staff get massacred left me feeling as if I'd gone a few rounds in the ring with Mike Tyson, and I decided right then and there I couldn't leave the game feeling like this. For one thing, I'd feel like I was deserting my guys if I walked away after this kind of beating. As I told reporters who cornered me after the series, "When my guys get abused, I feel abused."

So now we'd gone two seasons without a championship, which wasn't exactly a crime, but we knew that getting bounced in the first round of the playoffs would make George furious. The surprise was that he didn't fire anyone that winter, though he did fire off a warning shot that set the stage for a bitterly contentious relationship in

2003 between George and Joe, as well as our coaching staff. In a lengthy Q & A interview that appeared in the *Daily News* that winter, George took some not-so-veiled shots at all of us, intimating that Joe was a lousy manager in previous jobs with the Mets, Braves, and Cardinals and should be grateful to the Yankees for salvaging his career, while implying that our coaching staff had slacked off in 2002.

Here were his comments in the *Daily News* that seemed to hang over us for months:

"I want his whole staff to understand they've got to be better this year," George said, speaking of Joe. "I will not see him drop back into the way he was before. Right now he's a sure-fire Hall of Famer. Before he came to the Yankees he didn't even have a job. Three different times as a manager he didn't deliver, and was fired. Look how far he's come. He's come that way because of an organization, and he's got to remember that.

"I'm glad Joe is an icon. He's a hell of a guy, a tremendous manager and a tremendous figure for New York. I just want his coaches to understand that just being a friend of Joe Torre's is not enough. They've got to produce for him. Joe Torre and his staff have heard the bugle."

Now remember, we had won 103 games that season, the most in the majors. So it was hard not to feel insulted by the tone of George's comments. Especially Joe. He had always been considered a quality manager, winning a division title with the Braves but otherwise finding himself in situations where the Mets were a disaster in the late 1970s and the Cardinals weren't spending any money in the early 1990s. George made him sound like a bum. And he made the coaches sound like some kind of lazy freeloaders.

Joe never said anything to me directly about George's comments, but this was one time I could tell he was really stung. He always had a lighthearted way of fending off George publicly, but not on this occasion. When asked by reporters about George's barbs at the

Hideki Matsui press conference a few weeks after the *Daily News* story, Joe said flatly, "I don't even want to respond to that."

So basically that's how 2003 started for us, feeling as if we were in George's crosshairs. As coaches we were more vulnerable than Joe, as the *New York Post* depicted with a cartoonish illustration on its back page, showing George as a hunter taking aim at our six-man coaching staff, each of us drawn as sitting ducks. That made for quite a conversation piece in our coaches' dressing room, as you can imagine. I was going to have someone take it upstairs and ask George to sign it, but I never did have the nerve. We kept that back page in our dressing room all year, occasionally reminding one another that it was only a matter of time before George fired at one of the sitting ducks.

Though we tried to joke about it, we were bothered by the lack of respect. We knew that sometimes George took shots at us as a way of irritating Joe, but there were also signs of something more personal. George and Don Zimmer, once close friends, hadn't had much of a relationship since the '99 season. As I've mentioned, Zim never forgave George for refusing to acknowledge him, publicly or privately, for the job he did that year, taking over as manager when Joe was out with prostate cancer. Now, for some reason, George seemed to be looking to pick a fight with Zim, doing things like refusing to get him a rental car for spring training, as the Yankees did for all of the coaches. There was also a time during the season when George made a comment to a member of the front office, telling him not to talk to "those assholes downstairs," which was relayed to us and convinced us that George wanted some of us gone.

Still, it was Joe's position that as long as none of this affected his relationship with his players, he refused to take issue with George publicly. But early that season Joe drew the line when George interfered in our business and made the two of us look like liars in the eyes of Jose Contreras, our prize pitching acquisition that season.

George had won a bidding war with the Red Sox for Contreras, a

Cuban defector, that winter, signing him to a four-year, $32 million contract. However, Contreras wasn't nearly as major league ready as you'd expect for that kind of money. He had great natural talent, as he went on to prove with the Chicago White Sox during their 2005 championship season, after we'd given up on him and traded him at midseason in 2004. And in retrospect, the organization probably didn't handle him as well as it could have, perhaps confusing him by having him work with two different pitching coaches, me in New York and Tampa pitching coordinator Billy Connors whenever he could work himself into the picture.

Contreras had dominated hitters for the Cuban national team, but pitching to major-league hitters required some adjustment. I got the feeling that he'd relied heavily on his off-speed forkball as his out pitch in Cuba, to the point where he could throw it thigh high over the plate and either get called strikes or weak swings from hitters who were geared up for his fastball. Big-league hitters were too good for that, however. His forkball was effective when he got them to chase it below the knees, but if he left it in the strike zone, often they'd smack it all over the ballpark.

One of Jose's big problems was that whenever he'd get in a jam, he'd lean heavily on that forkball. I tried to get him to trust his fastball more, but it was a process. As it was, our scouting reports said he'd thrown 96–97 miles per hour, but when he first pitched for us he only threw a two-seam, or sinking fastball, at 92–93 miles per hour. I asked him why he wasn't throwing his four-seamer, which has more takeoff up in the strike zone, and he looked at me as if he didn't understand. After much back and forth through his translator, Jose explained that he didn't throw a four-seamer, which made me wonder about our scouting reports. But in any case, I worked with him on a four-seamer, and eventually he incorporated it into his repertoire.

Throw in the fact that he was a sensitive guy who obviously missed the family he'd left behind in Cuba, and it seemed clear he needed time to work some things out. He was having so little success his first few weeks of the season that Joe and I felt he'd benefit from going to Triple-A to work on his pitches in a less stressful environment. We told GM Brian Cashman we wanted to send him down for a few starts and then bring him back. There was some back and forth between the New York and Tampa factions of the Yankee front office, as always, with pitching coordinator Billy Connors apparently lobbying to bring Contreras to Tampa for some individual work. Finally, George sent word through Cashman that it was Joe's call, so we went ahead with plans to send him to Columbus. Joe and I sat down together with Jose one day while we were in Detroit and spent nearly an hour explaining our thinking, while assuring him we still believed in him and had every intention of bringing him back after a few starts in Triple-A. Our traveling secretary made arrangements for him to fly to Columbus the next day, and that was that.

Except Contreras never made it to Columbus. Apparently Connors finally convinced George to let him have a crack at solving Contreras's problems, and George had Jose rerouted to Tampa. We knew nothing about it until Cashman called Joe the next day to tell him of the change in plans. By then Contreras was gone, so we had no chance to explain what happened. At that point, he had to be thinking we'd lied to him, and that's what made us both furious. It's one of the few times I ever saw Joe truly enraged. He takes great pride in being honest with players, creating a bond of trust that is the foundation of his managing style, and now George essentially had made it seem as if he'd lied to Contreras. I felt just as strongly, because I need my pitchers to trust that I have their best interests in mind when I'm working with them on a daily basis.

So the first thing Joe and I did was get Leo Astacio, Jose's interpreter, on the phone and tell him to explain the situation to Contreras and apologize for us. He did that and eventually we talked to Jose ourselves about it, but from that point I always wondered if he trusted everything I told him. And that bothered me. Joe felt so

strongly that, for once, he aired his unhappiness publicly, telling reporters how upset he was with George for going behind his back. I
think Joe also felt the move was a slap at me, as though George was
saying that maybe Connors could fix what I couldn't with Contreras, and Joe wasn't going to sit for that quietly.

Personally, I had no problem with George wanting Connors to
look under the hood, so to speak. The problem was the way he did
it, without consideration for my relationship with my pitchers. Even
after Joe sounded off about it, no one ever really explained why it
happened the way it did. Certainly no one in the organization ever
apologized, which bothered me because it was as if they didn't care
that it may have damaged my reputation.

Anyway, this was the first time I began to question whether I was
still wanted as pitching coach by George. I have to admit, I didn't
have the greatest respect for Connors. For years he'd been around as
organizational pitching coordinator, occasionally irritating me by
going behind my back to talk to one of my pitchers during the season
with some advice for this or that. I'd spoken to him about it, but it
wasn't a huge issue. In the next couple of years it would become
more serious, to the point where I finally went to Billy and told him,
point-blank, to stop talking to my pitchers without my knowledge.
His answer had always been that George wanted him to do it that
way, but I told him that wasn't going to fly anymore.

"Then you tell George that's not the right way to do it," I said.
"Because I know he listens to you. So I don't want to hear that again.
And if I hear about you going behind my back again, we're going to
have a problem."

That seemed to get through to Billy, but obviously we didn't have
a trusting relationship. In the case of Contreras, we should have been
communicating our thoughts on how to best help him, and I'll have
to take some blame for that. I didn't make the effort to talk to Billy
during that time, probably because I was afraid of what I might say
to him. The funny thing was, Billy and I got along fine during spring

training, when we were more or less working together. The problems always seemed to arise during the season, when Billy was in Tampa. He and George had begun palling around, going to hockey games together, going to dinner, spending a lot of time together. I knew he had George's ear, and there were times I felt he was undermining me. Not that he wanted the job of pitching coach, because, for one thing, he had weight and heart problems and probably knew that he couldn't have handled it physically. And for another, then he would have been the one getting second-guessed.

It's one of the problems inherent to the way George runs the organization, with separate control centers in New York and Tampa. Billy wanted to know everything that was going on with the pitchers, be able to make evaluations, and it's just impossible to do that from a thousand miles away when you're only reading statistics and watching games on TV. For all the success the Yankees have had over the years, it's just hard to believe the way decisions are made sometimes. I always felt during my ten years that there just wasn't enough trust put in the people in New York to be allowed to do their jobs. Why George has chosen to run the organization that way, with so much long-distance interference, I'll never understand.

In the case of Contreras, I definitely think the organizational split contributed to his problems. I honestly don't know if he ever would have had the success in New York that he had in Chicago in 2005, because he just seemed overwhelmed by the pressure he felt as a Yankee, but we could have helped him feel more comfortable. Not that Billy made any dramatic changes when he had Contreras in Tampa for a week, before finally sending him to Columbus for a few starts. I know they worked a lot on his breaking ball, but I didn't notice any changes in his mechanics.

And nothing changed much for Contreras when he came back from the minors. He remained inconsistent all season, and again in 2004, even after his wife and two daughters were allowed to leave Cuba and come live with him in June of that year. Finally, the front office decided Contreras would never win consistently in New York, and we traded him to the White Sox at the July 31 trading deadline for Esteban Loaiza, a right-hander who provided little help the rest of the way.

The Contreras controversy was only one reason for tension around the ball club in 2003, as we went through a rough stretch in May and June, losing twenty-four of forty games to fall into second place behind the Red Sox. That gave George an opportunity to take another shot at Joe, telling reporters that "we spent a lot of money and got the people Joe wanted. It's his team to turn around."

That, in turn, made Zim furious, and he decided to speak up on Joe's behalf.

"I get fed up with talk about the manager," he said to reporters. "We're struggling for two weeks and all of a sudden it's Joe Torre's team. For seven years it was Tampa's team. It's not right. We all know who the Boss is. But what does that mean? You're supposed to clam up like a mouse when he's rapping everybody?"

Zim's rant made back-page headlines, including one that read, "The Mouse That Roared."

We hung that back page up in our coaches' room right next to George taking aim at the sitting ducks.

Fortunately, all this internal strife didn't keep the team from hitting its stride over the summer and once again playing well enough down the stretch to overtake the Red Sox and win a sixth straight division championship.

Then, somehow, we survived a grueling League Championship Series with the Red Sox, winning in seven games in the most emotionally charged atmosphere I've ever experienced. The Yankees–Red Sox rivalry is always intense, especially in the postseason, but that was the year we had the brawl in Boston, with seventy-two-year-old Zim thinking he was thirty-two, making his unfortunate decision to charge Pedro Martinez. Zim was lucky he didn't get seriously hurt when Pedro threw him to the ground, but the incident racheted up the intensity in the rest of that series to the highest level. When it all came down to a Game 7 at Yankee Stadium, the pressure to win was suffocating. I thought we showed remarkable resolve in rallying for three runs against Pedro in the eighth inning to tie the game, 5–5, giving Aaron Boone his opportunity to leave a Yankee legacy with his game-winning home run against Tim Wakefield in the eleventh inning.

I have to admit, when Grady Little made the decision that eventually cost him his job as manager of the Red Sox, leaving Pedro in as we were rallying in the eighth inning, I was stunned. When he went to the mound, I thought sure he was taking Pedro out of the game. Pedro was showing signs of getting tired, missing location with pitches, and getting under some of his pitches rather than over the top, making them flatten out and become more hittable. It was Pedro's history that when he becomes tired, he becomes far more hittable than usual, so I thought they'd go to the bullpen. When Grady left Pedro in, I remember the feeling in our dugout was that he'd done us a favor.

On the other hand, we weren't happy about seeing Wakefield come into the game in the eleventh inning. He had been lights-out in two starts in that series against us, better than I had ever seen him pitch. His knuckleball was almost unhittable, yet he had great command of it. Of course, the problem with the knuckleball in such a situation is that it's still a pitch that is hard to control. And, in this case, it only took one that didn't knuckle to cost the Sox their shot at the World Series.

When Boone, a Yankee for only a few months, launched his game winner into the seats in left to win the game 6–5, it ended the most emotionally draining series I've ever taken part in. Honestly, I can't imagine another series ever matching the start-to-finish intensity that one had. If ever a team needed a few days to decompress and reenergize, it was us, but Game 7 ended on Thursday night and the World Series against the Florida Marlins started on Saturday night.

A number of guys talked about how they'd stayed up into the wee hours of Friday morning, too exhilarated to sleep, and you could see the exhaustion in their faces during our light workout that Friday. I was worried that mentally we'd have a tough time being ready for the Marlins, a surprise team with few big names, which made it easy to take them lightly. I remember even the crowd at Yankee Stadium seemed to have a Red Sox hangover for Game 1, unable to work up the usual postseason noise level for the Marlins.

We were definitely flat in losing 3–2 to the Marlins in Game 1, but after Andy Pettitte got us even with a brilliant effort in Game 2, I thought we'd be okay. Give the Marlins credit, they were hungry and they played well, but I just don't think we were able to find that energy level we had for the Red Sox. We didn't hit much against Florida's good, young pitching, but in the end, the Series turned on a couple of pivotal moments involving two of our pitchers who were never among my favorites: Jeff Weaver and David Wells.

Weaver had been an enigma to me since coming over from the Detroit Tigers in a three-way trade with the Oakland A's in which we gave up Ted Lilly in 2002. Jeff had a great arm and looked unhittable at times, but he was prone to making key mistakes, partly because he was stubbornly in love with his cutter, a pitch on which he too often gave up home runs.

Jeff didn't have the greatest reputation for attitude and work ethic when we got him, and I don't think he helped himself when he began palling around with Wells as a Yankee. When I saw it happening I tried to offer him some friendly advice:

"Jeff," I told him one day, "David might be a lot of fun and everything, but he's not the guy for you to run around with."

I didn't want to make too big a deal of it, but I don't think it mattered anyway. I think Jeff basically had his earplugs in during that conversation because he continued to hang out with Wells. He wasn't a problem to work with or anything, except that I couldn't get him to ease off his cutter.

Home runs were what really hurt him, and he gave up a good portion of them on his cutter. It's meant to be a pitch that looks like a strike, but breaks off the outside corner to a right-handed hitter. Only he tried to throw it for strikes, thinking it would fool hitters. But it had a tendency to hang in the strike zone, and hitters would hammer it. Basically that's what happened in the twelfth inning of Game 4, when light-hitting shortstop Alex Gonzalez ended the game with a line-drive home run to left.

I knew that Weaver was the last pitcher that Yankees fans wanted to see in a World Series game. He had been booed heavily during the season, partly because he pitched poorly, partly because he made some inflammatory comments about the fans after being booed one night. We had moved him from the starting rotation to the bullpen for the postseason, but we hadn't used him in either of the first two rounds of the playoffs. By the eleventh inning of Game 3 against the Marlins, however, it was either Weaver, Mariano Rivera, who we didn't want to use with the game tied, or left-handers Felix Heredia or Chris Hammond, neither of whom had been pitching well at the time.

So Joe and I talked about it and we felt that Weaver was our strongest available arm at that point. I know we caught a lot of flak for it but there wasn't anybody else that we had more trust in than Weaver. And there had been many a start that season where Jeff had pitched with dominance for three or four innings, only to blow up with a bad inning, so we were hoping he could give us a few good ones until we could break through and win the game. The thing is, he looked great in the eleventh, getting three easy outs, but then he served up the fat one to Gonzalez, and instead of taking a 3–1 Series lead, we were tied 2–2, giving the Marlins new hope.

That made Game 5 crucial to us, and with Wells on the mound, I liked our chances. His reputation for being a big-game pitcher was well earned over the years, and he had pitched superbly throughout that postseason, in wins against the Twins and Red Sox, and a Game 1 loss to the Marlins. He and I weren't on the best of terms by this point, to say the least, but I like to think our little conflict had something to do with him raising his game over the final weeks of the season.

By August of that season, David wasn't pitching well. His back was bothering him off and on, and he had stopped doing his between-starts bullpen sessions, which I felt were important for him to stay sharp. He rarely did much work on his own at this time of the year, because of the heat, but in this season he just quit doing any kind of conditioning. I watched him pretty closely, and some days he would come out with the rest of the pitchers, but rather than join them for running, he'd play catch for about five minutes, then go back inside. And I know he wasn't going to the weight room, because I checked on that.

A couple of times I went to him and told him he needed to start working harder, and throwing between starts again, but he didn't want to hear it. Finally, after David was shelled by the Chicago White Sox on August 27, giving up ten runs and eleven hits in five and a third innings, I was fed up with his lazy work habits, but I had no intention of going public with my frustration. Instead I went looking for him when the game ended, ready for a battle. But David bolted the clubhouse the second the game ended, so the press came looking for me to explain Wells's poor performance, and I decided I wasn't going to cover for him. I didn't blast him so much as I explained that I thought he needed to get back to a better work routine between starts as a way of improving his performance. I admitted I wasn't happy with him skipping his bullpen sessions, and the reporters knew that, for me, this was harsh criticism, considering I almost never said a discouraging word in public about any of my pitchers.

It made headlines, naturally, and David was very upset in the clubhouse the next day. I felt I owed it to him to explain the circumstances that led to my comments, but he cut me off immediately.

"I don't want to hear it," he said. "It's all bullshit, and I don't want to hear it."

I told Joe we might have a problem, and he called us both into his office, where David let off some steam, telling Joe he felt I'd betrayed him by going to the newspapers. He said something about both of us having it in for him.

"This has nothing to do with Joe," I said to him at that point. "This is me. We don't have some plot against you. But I've tried to get you to do your throwing for weeks now, and you won't do it. I think you need to work harder to stay sharp and get back to pitching well."

David didn't exactly leave the office with a smile on his face. In fact, I didn't think we made much progress that day, or the next day when he walked past me in the clubhouse without a hello. But that was his throw day and, without a word from me, he showed up in the bullpen and did his between-starts throwing for the first time in weeks. I think it was partly for that reason, and partly because David now had motivation to prove something to Joe and me, that he soon raised his level of pitching and maintained it all the way into October. He barely spoke to me the rest of the year, but I can't say I lost any sleep over his hard feelings.

As long as he was pitching well, I thought he was the right guy to pitch Game 5 against the Marlins for us. So there we were, in the bullpen that night, and he was just about finished with his pregame warm-up, only about five minutes from game time, when he told me he didn't know if he'd be able to pitch. Good thing I don't chew tobacco, or I might have swallowed my chaw on the spot.

"What?" I said.

"I just can't get my back loose," he said.

He'd been bending over between pitches during his warm-up, stretching his back, but that wasn't unusual for him, and I hadn't thought much of it. There had been a bunch of times when he said his back was bothering him as he warmed up, only then as he got loose he felt better and went out and pitched without a problem. This time he said it was worse, and suddenly I was in a panic.

"David, you gotta let me know what we're doing here," I said. "If you can't go, we'll have to get Contreras ready."

"All right, let me try it," he said finally. "I think I can go."

When he went out and pitched a 1-2-3 first inning, I thought he was over the hump. But at the end of the inning, he walked into the dugout, threw his glove on the bench, said "I can't go," and kept walking, all the way to the clubhouse. I followed him and tried to talk him into giving it another shot.

"I can't do it," he said. "My back's killing me. It's on fire."

"Are you sure?" I asked. "Because I've gotta know right now."

"I'm sure," he said.

So I ran back to the dugout, called to the bullpen, and had Contreras get up and start throwing. He had pitched well in relief during the postseason, but not on this night. He gave up three runs in his first inning of work, and over his three innings on the mound he gave up four runs that led to a 6–4 loss to the Marlins.

I don't doubt that Wells's back was killing him, but what angered Joe and me was that we found out later it had been bothering him the day before the game, and he never gave us or even the trainers a heads-up to have a Plan B ready in case he couldn't go. We weren't amused either that David had made jokes about his lack of conditioning at a press conference the day before the game, telling the national media that you didn't have to be a workout freak like Roger Clemens to excel at an advanced baseball age.

"Goes to show you don't need to bust your butt every day to be successful," Wells said in that press conference. "I've been blessed with a rubber arm. I'll leave the working out and conditioning to other guys. They can write books and do videos on how to last twenty years in the big leagues by conditioning. I'll write the one 'How Not to Work Out.' "

I read those quotes in the newspaper the morning of Game 5, and I didn't find them as funny as I'm sure David thought they were. Maybe he jinxed himself because those words sure came back to haunt him. The loss gave the Marlins a 3–2 lead in the Series, and when Josh Beckett overmatched us in Game 6, throwing a five-hitter to beat us 2–0 in New York, we'd lost to a team we knew we should have beaten. We all felt bad about it, but the Marlins dominated us with their young power pitching, and that's the nature of the baseball playoffs. Hot pitching and a break here or there can change the script.

Still, it was quite a ride that October. I'm sure our players will be talking about that Game 7 against the Red Sox long after they've retired. And they should. It was a memorable accomplishment, no matter what happened against the Marlins. What bothered me was that, because George Steinbrenner deemed it so, we were made to feel as if the season was a failure because we hadn't won a championship. To me, I don't care how much more money we were spending on players than other teams, your season can't be considered a failure when you win a series as tough as the one with the Red Sox to take the American League pennant and reach the World Series for the sixth time in eight years.

But that was the atmosphere George created, particularly that season, and his negativity took a toll on Joe and the coaches. Zimmer announced that he was through working for George, and I was upset because of that. I told reporters on the way out of the stadium the day after the Series that I felt "personally abused" by George, and I meant it. I went home feeling that I would have to think long and hard about whether I wanted to come back.

13

Raising the Ante

W hen Brian Cashman called my cell phone on November 13, 2003, looking for an answer regarding my future with the Yankees, I was in the MGM Grand casino in Las Vegas, which seemed appropriate because I was about to play some high-stakes poker with George Steinbrenner. Did he really want me around anymore or not? By the end of the turbulent 2003 season it didn't feel that way, but I figured there was only one way to find out for sure: go all in.

I had left Yankee Stadium the day after we lost to the Florida Marlins feeling that perhaps the time had come to walk away, but I wanted a couple of weeks away from baseball to let my emotions settle before I made any decision. After returning to Seattle, I went on a five-day hunting trip to Utah with my two sons that helped clear my head and let go of some of my resentment toward George for his shabby treatment of Don Zimmer and the negative vibes he cast toward all of the coaches in 2003.

Then I returned home to find my wife, Jean, about as mad as I've ever seen her. The *New York Times* had run a story that day quoting a Yankee source saying that I had decided to retire, and Jean had already answered a handful of phone calls from reporters asking if it was true. The two of us hadn't even discussed the subject yet, and Jean was furious because she interpreted the story as being planted by the Yankees for the purpose of convincing me to retire.

"If you had intentions of retiring," she said to me, "you can forget it. You're not retiring like this. You're not going to let them run you out like this."

It was Jean, of course, who had been ready for me to retire the last few years, believing it would be healthier for me to slow down a little. And we had talked before the season ended about maybe this being the right time. So now I had to chuckle at her change of heart.

"Are you sure?" I asked.

"I'm sure," she said. "You're going back for at least one more year. They can't do this to you."

I couldn't be certain, then or now, if someone really was trying to make my decision for me. But for a variety of reasons, I always suspected that Randy Levine, the team president, was the source for the story. And since he tends to voice George's thoughts, I had to wonder if the Boss preferred that I didn't come back. I couldn't think of any other reason why the story would be leaked, because I hadn't spoken to anyone in the Yankee organization since leaving New York after the World Series. After the story ran, I made a few calls trying to get some sort of explanation, voicing my displeasure to different people in the organization, but I never did get a satisfactory answer. I was tempted to call George myself, but if he didn't want me back, I didn't think he'd tell me, so I decided there was a better way.

I knew money would be the litmus test. It usually is with George. If he was willing to give me a big raise, then I'd be satisfied that he still wanted me. If not, well, I'm not sure what I would have done. Although Jean was determined that I go back, I'm not sure my pride would have allowed me to continue if I knew I wasn't wanted. In any case, I told Jean my plan, told her how much I was going to ask for, and she told me I was crazy, that there was no way I'd get it.

I'd rather not say what my salary was at the time, but I'd been getting steady, if unspectacular, raises since starting at $140,000 a year in '96. I did a little research and found out that Dave Duncan, Tony LaRussa's longtime pitching coach with the Oakland A's and the St. Louis Cardinals, and Dave Wallace, the Boston Red Sox pitching coach, were both making substantially more than me. Since neither of them had anywhere close to five world championships on their resume, I felt I had a good case.

So I decided I'd tell the Yankees I wanted an $80,000 raise, which isn't much compared to the millions George pays his players, but it's pretty much unheard of for a coach to get a raise like that. For the most part, coaches make a decent real-world salary, but peanuts in baseball-world money. George had given each of the coaches a $25,000 bonus when we won the World Series in 1996 and 1998— though he was reluctant at first when we won again in '98 and did so only after some prodding on our part. It was a nice gesture, but he didn't do it when we won in 1999 and 2000; I guess he decided it was getting too expensive.

In any case, Brian Cashman had told me he was going to be calling sometime in mid-November, needing an answer about my plans, so I figured I'd wait for his call to make my demand. In the meantime, Jean and I went to Las Vegas to celebrate our birthdays, which coincidentally, are both on November 13. So there we were at the MGM, having a good time, playing the slot machines, when Brian called.

As I walked outside to take the call, Jean asked if I was still going for the $80,000, and when I said yes, she said, "You've got no chance."

That was all I needed to hear. I thought, *Oh, yeah, watch this.* And with that, I decided to go for an extra $20,000 just to leave no doubt. So it was $100,000 or bust. I presented the figure to Brian, using Duncan and Wallace for comparison sake, as a take-it-or-leave-it proposition, telling him I needed to know that George truly wanted me back.

He said he'd take it to George and get back to me as soon as he could. I walked back into the casino, giggling as I told Jean that I'd raised the price, and she just threw up her arms in exasperation and said I really was out of my mind.

Personally, I didn't really know what to expect, but I was surprised that Brian called back so quickly, less than an hour later. He said George had approved it. He didn't offer any details, so I don't know if George had a particular reaction upon hearing my demand, but I could only take it as the sign of approval that I was looking for. It made me feel great and basically allowed me to put all the bad feelings from 2003 behind me and start fresh.

When I went back into the casino again, believe it or not, Jean had just hit a jackpot on her slot machine for $1,900. I told her I'd hit the jackpot as well, and I thought she was going to faint. Over the years it seemed that George never failed to surprise us, in good ways and bad, and this was one of the good days. It sure was a memorable birthday, and, as a result, I began looking forward to going back to work and getting that one last championship.

I was delighted also because I had wanted to be able to last as long on the job as Joe Torre, and I was now fairly sure that Joe and I would go out together after the 2004 season. For the first time since he'd taken over the Yankees, Joe hadn't enjoyed managing in 2003 because he felt George had tried to undermine his relationship with his players by criticizing and interfering. Just as important, Joe felt that George no longer wanted him around, and he wasn't going to stay under those conditions. Going into spring training of 2004, then, Joe was thinking that he would finish out the last year of his contract and walk away. There had been no indication from George during the off-season that he was going to be any easier to live with in 2004, so Joe had no intention of asking for a contract extension.

But then, after a winter when it seemed that Alex Rodriguez would be dealt to the Boston Red Sox, Brian Cashman pulled off a surprise trade to get A-Rod from the Texas Rangers for Alfonso Soriano only a few days before spring training began, and suddenly the Boss was the happiest man on earth. He loved acquiring stars as much as he loved winning championships, and A-Rod was perhaps the biggest star in baseball. That the deal meant sticking it to the Red Sox only added to George's joy.

So he was in his glory when we arrived in Tampa for spring training. Where George had largely avoided Joe's office and our coaches' locker room in 2003, he seemed to be omnipresent in the spring of '04. Maybe Don Zimmer's departure had something to do with it as well. I still don't quite understand how and why George allowed his relationship with Zim to deteriorate so badly, but George sure seemed a lot more comfortable in our locker room than he had been when he and Zim were feuding. And to Joe's utter surprise, George bounded into his office one day and said, "So what are you going to do next year?"

The tone was so friendly that Joe immediately sensed the rules of engagement had changed for the better. He accepted George's offer to discuss a contract extension over dinner in Tampa, and after a week or so of pondering this unexpected development, Joe agreed to negotiate a new deal that wound up being worth $19.2 million over three years. Smart as it was to want to keep Joe in the dugout, the contract was another case of never knowing what to expect when you're dealing with George Steinbrenner. In some ways he was still as unpredictable, if not quite as impulsive, as he had been back in the days when he was firing and rehiring Billy Martin like clockwork. In this case I suspect he was also aware that Joe would be a hot com-modity if he became a free-agent manager, and he didn't even want to think about the possibility of Joe going to the Red Sox or the Mets.

In any case, I was happy for Joe, but at that point I knew that I wouldn't be able to hang in there with him as long as he would con-tinue managing. With Joe locked in at that kind of money, I knew George would take out any frustration on the coaches, and that win-ter he had convinced Don Mattingly to return to the Yankees as hit-ting coach, eight years after he had retired as a player. Having Donnie around was great for the ball club, and he fit in nicely on the coach-ing staff for all the same reasons that made him such a beloved player and captain. But I knew that Donnie's status as an icon would be one more reason that George would look in my direction if we weren't playing up to his expectations. And despite his good mood that spring, I had a feeling he would become more and more impa-tient if we didn't start winning championships again, especially now that he had added A-Rod to our cast of stars.

But for all of our big names, I wasn't sure what to expect in 2004. We had lost Roger Clemens, Andy Pettitte, and David Wells from our starting staff, so it was really a transition year from a pitching standpoint. My concern was that all three of the guys we lost were proven big-game pitchers who had all pitched well in the postseason, which is how guys are judged as Yankees. In their place we acquired two pitchers in trades, proven veteran Kevin Brown from the Dodg-ers and talented young right-hander Javier Vazquez from the Expos. A year earlier we had signed free agent Jon Lieber, knowing he still needed several months to rehab from shoulder surgery, and now he was ready to join Brown, Vazquez, and holdovers Mike Mussina and Jose Contreras.

On paper it wasn't a bad staff, but more than anything, it was an indication of just how little quality pitching our minor-league system had developed for years. With Pettitte gone, we had no homegrown

starters in our rotation, and none on the horizon. Sometimes I wondered what the problem was with either our scouts or our development people because we just never seemed to have the kind of young,
power arms the Marlins had just used to dominate us and win a
championship. Some of it was bad luck, going back to left-hander
Brien Taylor, the number one pick in the country in the 1991 draft,
who was going to be a star before he injured his shoulder in an off-
the-field incident at home in North Carolina one winter. Some of it
was our win-now philosophy: In 1998 we traded Eric Milton, our
number one draft pick in 1996, as part of a deal for Chuck Knoblauch, and Milton blossomed into a solid major-league pitcher. But
mostly we just weren't getting much out of our draft. From 1993 on,
first-round pitchers Matt Drews, David Walling, and Jon Skaggs
never made an impact, and when we did draft a gem, Mark Prior in
1998, we couldn't sign him out of high school.

Finally, however, it looks as if that drought may be over. Chien-
Ming Wang, who was signed out of Taiwan at age twenty in 2000,
had a breakthrough season for the Yankees in 2006, and Philip
Hughes may not be far behind him. The hard-throwing right-hander
was our number one pick in 2004, a high school kid from California, and I got to see him in 2006 when I came back as a spring training instructor; he looks like he could be the real thing.

In spring training of 2004 I was already wishing that we had
some young arms, if only for depth and injury protection. Our staff
had some age and a history of injuries, and for a change we didn't
have any real surplus of starters. So while I was impressed with my
first look at Brown and Vazquez that spring, I was worried that we
were thinner than normal in the starting rotation. Sure enough,
Lieber pulled a groin muscle fairly early in March and wound up
missing the early part of the season. We were forced to move Jorge
De Paula, a marginal prospect, into the rotation, but he hurt his arm
in his only start and wound up needing shoulder surgery. We called
up a young left-hander, Alex Graman, to make a start, and he got hit

hard by the Chicago White Sox, and clearly wasn't ready for the big leagues. Meanwhile, Jose Contreras was off to a very shaky start, hit hard in two starts against the Red Sox. It was only April but we were so short on pitching that we decided to start Vazquez on three days' rest in a series against the Red Sox.

Lieber came back in late April, but by June both Brown and Mussina were out of the rotation, Brown with a bad back, Mussina with a pulled groin. It seemed as if we were patching a rotation together for much of the season, using another rookie left-hander, Brad Halsey, for a few starts, and at one point, pulling Tanyon Sturtze out of the bullpen to make an emergency start. Our offense was keeping us atop the AL East for most of the season, but Joe and I were concerned throughout that we may not have the pitching we needed in October, if we got there at all. By August it looked as if it might cost us the division title, as the Red Sox were making a charge.

We had given up on Contreras, dealing him at the July 31 trading deadline to the Chicago White Sox for Esteban Loaiza, but Loaiza didn't help us much. If not for El Duque Hernandez making a heroic return as a Yankee, we probably wouldn't have been able to hold off the Red Sox. Injuries and ineffectiveness had convinced the front office to trade El Duque in 2002, and he missed the entire 2003 season with the Montreal Expos because of rotator cuff surgery. The Expos didn't re-sign him, so he was a free agent looking for a job in the spring of 2004, and though he wasn't ready to pitch at the time, Brian Cashman took a chance on him, signing him to an inexpensive contract with the hope that he might return to his old form later in the season. With injuries to Brown and Mussina continuing to be an issue, El Duque returned in mid-July and wound up anchoring our rotation in August and September, winning his first eight decisions before a tired arm sidelined him late in the season.

All season I felt like I was trying to navigate my way through a minefield with our lack of pitching depth, and just when our starting rotation finally was clicking at full strength, Kevin Brown blew it up. During a start against the Baltimore Orioles on September 3, he took out the frustration of a difficult season on a concrete wall in the Yankee clubhouse, slamming his left fist into the wall and breaking a couple of bones in his hand. At least he had the sense not to use his pitching hand, but the injury knocked him out of the rotation until the final week of the season.

I happened to see Brown hurt himself because I'd followed him up into the clubhouse that night, and while it was rather shocking to watch him react so foolishly, I can't say I was surprised that he snapped. He was a perfectionist who couldn't accept the fact that, at age thirty-nine, a chronic back problem no longer allowed him to be the dominant pitcher he'd been in his prime. Kevin seemed to be full of anger on those days when his back was aching, which it was for most of his two seasons with the Yankees.

I think Kevin was kind of a loner by nature anyway, but he just sort of retreated into his own world as a way of dealing with his de-clining skills. The thing was, I thought he was still plenty good enough to be a winning pitcher, especially if he became a bit more of a finesse pitcher, changing speeds with his sinker, but it was almost as if he was too proud to adjust and be anything but a power pitcher.

As a result, he was terribly hard on himself. He wanted to be that guy who had once knocked the bats out of hitters' hands with a 95 mph fastball that sank hard and late enough that he didn't need to worry too much about location. Kevin still had good movement on his pitches, but he wasn't happy throwing 90 miles per hour. More than once I'd whistle admiringly at his pitches during workouts in the bullpen and tell him he looked great, at which point he'd turn around and say, deadly serious, "Yeah? Then you should go out there and try to pitch with this stuff."

And I'd laugh and say, "You don't know how much I'd love to."

Kevin started the 2004 season by going 5-0, and even then he wasn't happy. I tried to make him see the big picture, that he was winning games for us, but he was obsessed with finding his old form. I had to be creative just to develop a relationship with him. The first time I ever went to the mound when he was pitching, he was in a jam, and he just looked at me and said, "I don't think you can help me unless you've got a rabbit's foot with you."

I reached into my back pocket and said, "You won't believe it, but I've got one right here. So now, how about trying to keep that sinker down and get out of this inning with a ground ball."

I can't say he laughed but I think I made my point. And he was like "Okay, okay, time to go."

I remember walking off the mound thinking, *Boy, this guy is going to be something.*

It's not that Kevin was a problem for me. He was more than willing to work, but at times his back just wouldn't allow it. He was a problem for the trainers, however, because a lot of times he wouldn't give them much information about how his back was feeling. It seemed as if he didn't trust our medical people and only wanted to deal with his own people. Often on off-days he'd fly home to have his back worked on by his chiropractor. Sometimes he'd come back from those sessions and his stuff would be a little more electric for a couple of days, but then his back would tighten up again, and he'd lose that little extra pop on his fastball.

All of this led to his explosion in early September. By then Kevin had been back for a few weeks from a month on the disabled list, the result of both a bad back and the effects of an intestinal parasite, of all things. He was pitching against the Orioles when he twisted his knee covering first base on a ground ball in the fifth inning and had to be treated by the trainers in the dugout. He went back out for the sixth and made the mistake of sticking his bare hand out for Miguel Tejada's hard ground ball up the middle. The ball deflected off his hand en route to center field for a single. Kevin stayed in to finish the inning, at which point he'd given up three runs on five hits, with seven strikeouts.

So he was pitching fairly well, but he was losing 3–1. That and the two new injuries, which were more annoying than serious, set Kevin off on a rampage. He went storming up the tunnel before I could ask him if he could go another inning, so I followed him. By the time I got into the clubhouse, he was in the little hallway by Joe's office, back where we keep the bats. He looked like he was about to grab a bat and start swinging, which I could relate to.

All pitchers lose it occasionally. Andy Pettitte was real bad for a couple of years. He'd go in and just explode in the clubhouse, to the point where I was afraid he was going to hurt himself. And as much as I prided myself on being even-tempered during my own career, there were days during one of those bad years in the late '60s when I felt like, well, Kevin Brown.

One time, in particular, after a tough inning in a game I was losing, I came up the tunnel and into the clubhouse, looking for something to throw or break. I saw a bat leaning up against a locker and grabbed it as I went back into the old laundry room, which is now the players' lounge. There was a big equipment trunk back there, and I took the bat and started beating on that trunk, smashing away at it as the bat cracked and splintered. After a few minutes of maniacal behavior, I stopped, took a deep breath, and felt considerably better about life. Just about then, as I turned to go back through the clubhouse, I heard Tom Tresh yelling, "Hey, has anyone seen my bat?"

I looked down and, sure enough, Tresh's name was on the bat I'd destroyed. Tommy was one of my best friends on the team, but I didn't think he'd appreciate me ruining his bat. So I waited until he went back to the dugout before I came out of the laundry room. After the game I told him about the bat, and we had a laugh over it.

As frustrated as pitchers can get at times, we're a mild-mannered species compared to hitters. It's the nature of the game: Even .300 hitters make outs roughly seven of every ten at bats, and some guys can't handle that kind of failure well at all. In my experience, when it comes to tempers, three guys are in a class of their own: Paul O'Neill, Lou Piniella, and Mickey Mantle.

I'd have to give O'Neill the nod as the all-timer. He could blow up at any time, and, unlike the other two guys, he played at a time when TV cameras were everywhere, following guys into the dugout, so fans saw him beat up on the water cooler in the corner of the dugout on more than one occasion. Of course, they never saw him take a bat to the toilet facilities just behind the dugout. You could feel the explosions coming with Paul, depending on how his night was going, and guys in the dugout would run for cover at times when they could see he was about to snap. Piniella was the same way, though Lou tended to be more vocal. He would let loose with a rather colorful stream of self-hating verbiage after a particularly bad at bat that had guys biting their gloves in the dugout to keep from laughing, which, of course, was the last thing you wanted Lou to see, for fear that he might turn his anger on you.

Nobody scared people quite like Mickey, however. He didn't explode as often as O'Neill or Piniella, but when he did, the ferocity of such episodes was startling. Mickey was one of the strongest guys I've ever seen, even though I don't think he ever lifted a weight in his life. His arms and hands were unbelievably powerful, which explained some of his tape-measure home runs, but that strength would show in other ways as well. More than once I saw him slam his bat into the bat rack and snap the handle right off the bat, and I can't say I ever saw anybody else do that. One time Mickey struck out three straight times in a game in Oakland, and the first two times I made the mistake of being at the far end of the dugout, where he'd go to stew. When he struck out a third time, I ducked into the toilet, which was adjacent to the dugout. I had to go anyway, and I thought I'd be safe there. But it turned out that Mickey was ready to blow this time, and after slamming his bat into the bat rack, he grabbed the handle of the bathroom door and yanked it open with such force that it slammed into the dugout wall, and scared the hell out of me. It was embarrassing because some of the fans in the seats near the dugout were at an angle where they could see into that little bathroom when it was open, and when they looked to see what caused the explosion of noise, well, there I was, just wishing someone would close the door.

I can't say that all these memories came flooding to mind as I chased after Kevin Brown, but I knew enough to tread lightly when I caught up with him.

"Are you okay physically?" I asked.

"What's it look like?" he growled, which I took as a no.

He then began walking back toward the center of the clubhouse, when he suddenly turned and, without warning, smashed his fist into the wall. I only saw it out of the corner of my eye, so I wasn't sure which hand he'd used.

"Christ, Kevin," I said, "tell me that wasn't your right hand."

He didn't answer, but I was relieved to at least see that he was holding his left hand, and not his right, in pain. He was in a zombie-like state now as he walked over and sat down on the couch in the middle of the clubhouse.

I asked him if he was all right, but he didn't answer.

"Kevin," I said, "I need to know if you can go back out and pitch or not. You've gotta tell me something."

Finally, he looked at his hand and said, "No, I'm not all right."

I hustled out to the dugout to call the bullpen, and the next time I saw Kevin, a couple of days later, he was wearing a cast to encase the two broken bones in his hand, and looking as if he'd been sentenced to a prison term. At the time, I couldn't have imagined that we'd wind up needing to turn to him in desperation some five weeks later for a Game 7 start against the Red Sox in the League Championship Series.

We'd managed to hold off the Red Sox, as always, for the division title, and then dismiss the Minnesota Twins in the division series, twice winning games with late-inning comebacks against their bullpen. When we then won the first three games against the Red Sox, I was sure we were going all the way. It wasn't simply that no team in baseball history had ever blown a 3–0 series lead; we had been pounding Red Sox pitching, having scored nineteen runs in Game 3 alone, while our pitching had looked solid. I felt even more confident when we played Game 4 to a position where we could bring Mariano Rivera into the game in the eighth inning with a one-run lead.

Joe was second-guessed for that move, people wondering why he didn't save Rivera for just the ninth. It wasn't that we had no faith in Tom Gordon pitching the eighth—although he had been a little shaky for us against the Twins the previous series. It was mostly just that Mo was well rested, and we'd won championships doing it this way, giving him the ball in the postseason for some crucial two-inning saves.

This time it backfired, though. After an easy eighth, Mo gave the Sox an opening with an uncharacteristic walk to Kevin Millar. That was the real surprise of the inning, because Millar's a free swinger who, in that situation, is looking for a pitch to try to go for the pump. He's not a guy who walks a lot, and Mo rarely gets himself in trouble with walks. But it happened.

When the Sox sent Dave Roberts to first to pinch-run, we were sure he was going to try and steal second. It was partly my job to keep him from doing it because I call the throw-overs to first and the pitchouts via signals to our catcher. I had Mo throw over a couple of times before making his first pitch, but I thought Roberts would wait for at least one pitch to get a look at Mo's movement toward the plate. I was hoping that Mo would throw a strike, get ahead, and then I was going to call for the pitchout. I guessed wrong, and I was kind of second-guessing myself afterward, but it's a tough call either way. If you pitch out and he doesn't go, you put yourself at a disadvantage because you don't want to pitch out twice in a row and put your pitcher in a hole.

Anyway, Roberts got a decent jump, and that was enough because Mariano was pretty slow to the plate with his delivery. He worked to get better at holding runners the next year, mostly by varying how long he holds the ball in his stretch before coming to the plate. The stolen base was pivotal, allowing Roberts to score on Bill Mueller's ground-ball single up the middle, tying the game 4–4, and the Red Sox went on to win in twelve innings on David Ortiz's home run.

The next night we wound up with another late-inning lead, 4–2 going to the eighth, only this time the situation was trickier. Because Mariano had worked two innings the night before, we didn't want to use him for more than one. As a result, Gordon, who'd come on in the seventh to get an inning-ending double play, started the eighth. I was a little concerned about Tom because I'd been told by our guys in the bullpen that he had been more nervous than usual in the bullpen during the playoffs, to the point where he had vomited before one of his appearances. They said it wasn't as bad as it sounded, because he'd done that in the past occasionally, but it made me a little nervous thinking about it.

When Tom gave up a leadoff home run to Ortiz, our lead was down to one run, and now we figured we'd better have Mo start getting loose, just in case. We were still hoping that Gordon could do the job, but then he walked Kevin Millar. Now Joe and I were looking at each other, wondering: Should we or shouldn't we? We decided to give Gordon another batter, and Trot Nixon promptly singled Millar to third.

Now we felt we had to go to Mo to keep the game from getting away from us. But he couldn't prevent the Sox from tying the score, as Jason Varitek hit a fly ball deep enough to deliver the run from third. Mo got out of the inning, which at least gave us a chance to win it with our bats, but the game went fourteen innings before the

Sox won on another Ortiz hit, this one a soft single to center, scoring Johnny Damon. As a result, it was easy to second-guess our decision, and, in retrospect, if we were going to bring Mo in to get us out of trouble, we probably should have gotten him in one batter earlier, with just a runner on first. But at that point we were still hoping that Gordon could get at least a couple of outs because we were worried about overtaxing Mo.

In any case, a second straight extra-inning loss shook our confidence a little, but we were heading home needing to win only one of the two games, and I had the sense that we believed we'd find a way. As many tough games as we'd played against the Red Sox in 2003 and 2004, we always seemed to win the one game we really needed. As much as the teams may downplay such things, everyone on both sides was well aware of the history of the rivalry, and after all the years when the Yankees won the big one, I'm sure at least some of the Red Sox players had to wonder if there was something to all that talk about the Curse of the Bambino.

On our end, meanwhile, we felt like we absolutely needed to win Game 6, mainly because we didn't really have a starter for Game 7. Brown had returned from his broken hand at the end of the regular season but hadn't found his form again. He had been ineffective in Game 3, pitching only two innings, and we knew that his back continued to be an issue, so we weren't thrilled about the idea of having him pitch Game 7. Our only other option, however, was Javier Vazquez, a talented right-hander who seemed to lose all of his confidence over the last couple of months during the regular season, to the point where we put him in the bullpen for the Red Sox series. Basically Joe and I didn't even want to think about a Game 7, so we never even sat down and talked before Game 6 about who we would start if we lost that night. Obviously we were hoping we wouldn't have to make that decision, and we felt good about our chances with Jon Lieber pitching Game 6. Lieber had been our best pitcher the final month of the season, and he gave us a solid outing in Game 6, but we lost 4–2 to Curt Schilling and his famous bloody sock.

After the game I sat down with Joe in his office and he said, "What do you think?" I told him that Brown had looked good in his bullpen workout two days earlier, and that I thought he should get first consideration. So we called him in and asked him to be honest with us about the condition of his back, and whether he thought he could give us a strong start the next night. He assured us his back was good enough that it shouldn't be an issue.

"Give me the ball," he said. "I'll get the job done."

There was no hesitation in his voice, no hedging about his condition. I'll never know if Kevin was putting up a false front, trying to convince himself, but he did a good job of selling us. Of course, we wanted to believe him because, if nothing else, we knew he was tough-minded enough that he wouldn't be affected by the magnitude of the situation. We couldn't say the same thing about Vazquez.

In his first season as a Yankee, Javy had been something of a mystery to me. He had a great first half and looked like the star the front office thought it was getting when it traded promising first baseman Nick Johnson to the Expos for him the previous November. I really thought we were going to make a deal with the Arizona Diamondbacks for Schilling, but after seeing what the Marlins' young power pitchers did to us in the World Series in 2003, Brian Cashman was determined to make our rotation younger. I was impressed when I got to see Vazquez up close in spring training; his stuff was dynamic. He was a quiet kid who hadn't been exposed to an environment like New York, so that was my only concern with him, but by midseason, when he made the All-Star team, he seemed very comfortable in New York.

Javy's only problem in the first half had been the home run ball, as he had a tendency to throw too many fastballs right down the middle. In the second half he started making more mistakes with his breaking ball, partly because he seemed afraid to throw his fastball at times. He had developed some type of nagging soreness in his arm, not enough to keep him from pitching, but enough that his velocity dropped a bit, taking some of the life out of his fastball. I was talking to a couple of scouts about Vazquez one day, and they told me they were seeing the same thing—he was still throwing 90–92, nearly as hard as always, but they said the late life was missing. It may have been that with his arm bothering him, he wasn't turning the ball loose with the same authority, and the fastball was straightening out on him. His stuff was still good enough to get hitters out, but as he lost confidence his results suffered and suddenly everything was snowballing on him late in the season. I tried to talk to him, make him feel good about himself, but he wasn't real responsive.

After Javy made a so-so start against the Twins in the first round of the playoffs, we put him in the bullpen against the Red Sox, and he'd pitched poorly in relief of Brown in Game 3. He just didn't look like a guy who would have a lot of belief starting Game 7, and he didn't seem surprised when I told him we were starting Brown. I don't know, maybe he would have responded to getting the start—I still wonder about that at times. Then again, he didn't do the job coming out of the bullpen that night.

I have to admit, I didn't have a good feeling as I watched Brown warm up in the bullpen that night. He didn't seem to be getting much push off the rubber, probably because of his back. But he was always hard to read, and I was hoping the adrenaline would make a difference when the game started. Obviously, it didn't happen, as David Ortiz hit a two-run home run in the first inning, and when Kevin got in trouble in the second inning, Joe and I decided to take a shot with Vazquez and hope he could keep us in the game. Maybe bringing Javy into a bases-loaded situation wasn't the best idea, but we were pretty desperate at the moment, looking for a life raft. Javy wasn't up to it, giving up a grand slam to Johnny Damon, the first batter he faced, as the Red Sox took a 6–0 lead, and right there I had a feeling it wasn't meant to be. The final was 10–3, and after falling behind early, the game seemed to last forever, a humbling night if ever there was one.

It still seems hard to believe that we could lose four straight games after the way we'd handled the Red Sox in the first three. Though our bats were partly to blame, going silent for most of the four losses, our concern about a lack of depth in starting pitchers came to fruition at the worst possible time. Though Joe was second-guessed more heavily by the media for some of his moves than at any time during our run with the Yankees, I thought Brian Cashman might take the most heat from George. From the time the Red Sox made a trade to get Schilling the previous winter, we were hearing that George was upset with Cashman for letting it happen. Even before Schilling's heroics in October, George considered Schilling a "warrior" in the mold of Clemens, who he loved so much. He had been on Cashman throughout the season, especially when Vazquez faded in the second half, telling him he should have made a deal for Schilling. After the playoffs, Brian admitted publicly that he had misread the Schilling situation, thinking he might be able to get him later that winter because Schilling had stated publicly that he would only go to either the Phillies or the Yankees. He didn't anticipate the Red Sox wooing him over Thanksgiving dinner at his home in Arizona, convincing Schilling to agree to be traded to Boston.

I went home after that Series thinking that George would lash out in some way over our collapse. Surely after perhaps the most humiliating loss in the history of the organization, George would fire somebody. But strangely enough, he didn't react much at all. In fact, I found out later that he made a point of telling Cashman, only a couple of hours after the Game 7 loss, that his job was safe. It was a telling sign of just how much George had come to rely on Brian, even while riding him hard via daily phone calls when things weren't going well during the season. He didn't even order Cashman and other executives in New York to Tampa for emergency meetings, as he had done in recent years when we'd failed to win it all. It made me wonder if the Boss was losing his bite now as he got older. But as it turned out, after deciding one more time that I couldn't retire with such a bitter taste in my mouth, I would come back for still another season and quickly find out that George was just waiting to pounce on someone. This time I wouldn't be able to shrug it off.

14

Enough Is Enough

As much thought as I'd given to retirement during the years after my cancer ordeal, I hadn't been able to walk away for one simple reason: Baseball was my life, and while I enjoy hunting and fishing, there was no feeling like being in the dugout, with the adrenaline flowing, your intensity level raised, joining forces with Joe Torre and the players to try to win a ball game on a nightly basis. In addition, I loved the quiet times just as much, the hours spent working with my pitchers between starts, when we were tinkering with a delivery, or maybe just talking about the mental part of pitching. It was rewarding enough to allow me to shrug off the steady flow of second-guessing and criticism, some of which never made the newspapers, that had been coming from George Steinbrenner and the Tampa faction of the Yankee organization since we had stopped winning championships.

But then something changed for me in 2005. We got off to a

rough start, going 11-19 through early May, partly because our re-vamped pitching staff was struggling, and instead of the usual rum-blings of discontent that I would hear second or third hand, George this time went public with a knockdown pitch.

"Our pitchers are not improving," he told a reporter for *USA Today.* "That's what a pitching coach is supposed to do—make your pitchers improve. I don't know whether we have to think of some changes there or not."

I had become accustomed to the whispering campaign, but this was different. To me it was a sign that maybe I had stayed too long, that George was ready to make a change. I was hearing things through the organizational grapevine that George was more irratio-nal than ever, even blaming me for pitching injuries. I found out later that Joe had to go to bat at least once for me with George, and I heard at one point the only thing keeping George from firing me was his fear of how it would look, considering my record, my history with the club, and the way I'd continued to coach for his team the year I had cancer.

Well, I had too much pride to be a sympathy case, so it was about that time I decided 2005 definitely would be my last season. For the first time, I was letting all the flak from George get to me, to the point where I couldn't leave it at the ballpark. I'd find myself sitting at home, getting worked up thinking about the criticism, and it was taking all the fun out of the job. Though I was healthy, I had begun taking medication a year earlier because my white-blood-cell counts had started to rise, and I realized this kind of stress wasn't good for me. So while I didn't say anything to anyone, not even Joe for a while, I vowed to myself that I would retire at the end of the season. It was a good decision because it allowed me to stop worrying about George so much and smell the roses, as Davey Johnson once liked to say to me, over what I knew would be my final months with the Yan-kees.

Looking back, I think by then George pretty much had decided that 2005 would be my last year, one way or another. When I told Brian Cashman the previous November that I wanted to return for the 2005 season, I mentioned that I thought this might be it for me, and I got the feeling that comment was relayed to George. I was in New York for Joe Torre's Safe at Home charity dinner at the time, and when George heard I was returning, he sent word that he wanted me to fly to Tampa for a meeting. So I went down and met with George, as well as Billy Connors, minor-league pitching coach Neil Allen, and our bullpen coach, Rich Monteleone. The meeting was basically to address the changes we were making in the bullpen. George was adding Neil, who had been our Triple-A pitching coach, as a second bullpen coach, and I think it was a way of grooming Neil to take over for me the following year. That seemed to be the plan at the time, and I'm sure Billy wanted it that way, because Neil had worked with him in Tampa, which Billy assumed would give him more control of the major-league staff when I was gone. George basically said as much during the meeting.

"You watch and learn and get everything down straight," George said to Neil from across a conference table, "because after next year it'll be your baby."

This rather blunt projection for 2006 caught me off guard because it wasn't as if I'd announced my retirement, but George didn't seem to give it a second thought that I was sitting there listening as he gave my job away. Then he turned to me and asked if I was going to be comfortable having both Neil and Rich Monteleone on the staff as bullpen coaches.

What could I say? I did have some reservations about it because I knew that Neil was one of Billy's guys, and I could envision problems. But I could see that I wasn't going to have a choice in the matter, so I said sure, I'd be fine with both of them.

Fortunately, Neil turned out to be an honorable guy. Basically he refused to be a spy for Connors. From the start of the season, Billy tried to use Neil as a go-between to communicate with my pitchers.

He was faxing messages daily to Neil, making observations on what he'd seen watching the game on TV the previous night, and he wanted him to relay the message by talking to the particular pitcher. But Neil didn't think it was right, going behind my back, and he told me what was going on. He also didn't give the pitchers the messages, though he didn't tell Billy that.

I don't know if Billy ever found out, and I'm sure he probably still wanted Neil to get the job of pitching coach when I finally did step down. But when Brian Cashman negotiated assurances from George that he would wield more power in the organization before agreeing to return as GM after the 2005 season, he allowed Joe Torre to decide on a new pitching coach, and Joe wanted Ron Guidry. Gator, as we call him, had been a star Yankee pitcher, of course, and both Joe and I had grown comfortable having him around as a spring training instructor for years. I thought it was the right choice, and I was happy to see Gator get the job. To some extent, I knew it would keep Billy on the outside, looking in.

In any case, after I heard about Billy's faxes to Neil early in the 2005 season, I was pretty sure that he was in George's ear, maybe even the real voice behind that quote in *USA Today*. After the story appeared, in fact, there was speculation in the New York newspapers to that effect, suggesting Billy was once again a strong influence on George. I guess that set Billy off because he demanded a meeting with Joe and the coaches in New York not long after that.

Or as I heard it from someone in the organization, "Billy wants to know who threw him under the bus."

So we had a meeting in New York. Joe and I were there, as was Brian Cashman, team president Randy Levine, and our two bullpen coaches. George was on a speaker phone from Tampa, and he opened the meeting.

"Our purpose here is to air our differences," he said. "We're all in this together and we need to be on the same page if we're going to win."

He then gave the floor to Billy, who said he wasn't getting "the cooperation from New York" that he wanted. He had asked to have the pitching charts sent to him on a daily basis, and I had refused. The charts are individual records of each game, how many pitches were thrown and what type, as well as notes about a pitcher's performance. I like to keep them so I can refer to them from time to time as a way of picking up on patterns, good or bad habits, that sort of thing. In the meeting George wanted to know why I wasn't sending the charts and I gave him those reasons, as well as one more: "By sending the charts," I said, "I think it opens up the opportunity for a lot of nitpicking."

George didn't like hearing that.

"Nitpicking?" he said in his high-pitched voice that tells you he's agitated. "What do you mean? There's no nitpicking going on."

"Well," I said, "maybe there's not now but there has been some in the past. And I want to avoid it at all costs. But if you think it's that important for Billy to see the charts, I guess I can send them."

At this point, George addressed Billy, asking him what he wanted to see in the charts. Connors told him that he was mainly interested in getting the velocity readings for each pitcher from the previous night.

"All right," George said. "Stottlemyre, can he get the velocities?"

Now it was becoming comical, George's voice on the speaker phone acting as an intermediary while the rest of us were all sitting in a room together. But in any case, I said I had no problem making sure that Billy got the velocities. However, I sure as heck wasn't going to fax them to Billy myself.

"I don't have time to make sure they get down to Tampa every day," I said.

"All right, all right," George said, and immediately he addressed Neil Allen. "Neil, can you get that done? Make sure that's done."

Now George wanted to know if I had any other problems with

Billy, so I figured this was the time to get everything out in the open. Well, not everything. I didn't want to rat out Neil Allen about the faxes, so I didn't mention anything about them. But I told George that I didn't want Billy going behind my back and talking to one of our pitchers without calling me and telling me what he was doing.

"I've talked to him about it, but he continues to do it," I said, "and it's not right."

Billy was clearly uncomfortable with this subject, looking down at the table rather than make eye contact with me or anybody else. And to his credit, George agreed with me.

"He's right, Billy," George said. "You call Stottlemyre first if you want to talk to one of the pitchers. I don't want any more problems."

And with that, George adjourned the meeting. It wasn't the first time I walked out of one of those meetings shaking my head, thinking what a waste of time it had been. I knew Billy would still be trying to get messages to my pitchers, and running to George about what our pitchers should be doing better. I'm not saying that Billy didn't have some good ideas at times. But he should have been working with me, and not going behind my back.

In any case, we all went back to the task of trying to hold the ball club together after the poor start. Personally, what I needed most wasn't advice from Billy Connors or anyone else as much as magical healing powers for all of our injured pitchers. We had signed free agents Carl Pavano and Jaret Wright during the off-season, and by June both of them were out with shoulder injuries. In Pavano's case, he never returned in 2005, or even in 2006, as he was sidelined by a number of injuries. I know there was considerable speculation that he never felt comfortable in New York, but I can't say that I ever saw evidence of that. If he thought he made the wrong decision, signing with the Yankees, he didn't give off that kind of vibe in the spring of 2005. He looked like he was going to be fine, though we did have concerns about Pavano right from the start. It wasn't a character issue, but rather a velocity issue, as he didn't have the fastball that we'd seen two years earlier during the 2003 World Series, or the one our scouts saw while he was winning eighteen games for the Marlins in 2004. His velocity was down, and that turned out to be a sign that he had a shoulder problem. As for everything else, the back problem, the bruised buttocks, the broken ribs from his car accident, all I can tell you is that from a distance in 2006 I was wondering what was going on with him myself. The Yankees invested $40 million to sign him for four years, and if he had delivered as expected, who knows, he might have made a difference the last two Octobers.

As it turned out, Pavano and Wright were only the beginning of our injury problems in 2005. Kevin Brown returned for the final year of his contract and his back was only getting worse, forcing him to miss much of the season, while Mike Mussina had an elbow problem. We had so many guys go down that we used fourteen different starting pitchers that season, including marginal major leaguers like Tim Redding and Darrell May that you may never hear about again. Even when we uncovered a potential gem in Chien-Ming Wang from our farm system, our luck didn't last as he too went down with a shoulder injury. As a result, we were patching things together all year in the starting rotation, and I felt good about the job I was doing, helping to get the most out of guys like Aaron Small and Shawn Chacon, fill-ins who wound up being saviors for us.

The only starter who didn't miss time was Randy Johnson. George finally had landed the Big Unit, after years of trying, and I was like everyone else, thinking he could still be the dominant number one starter that we needed. In spring training I liked what I saw, for the most part. His slider was real nasty, and he demonstrated better command of it than I had expected. My only concern was the inconsistency of his fastball velocity. He'd pop a couple, and then throw one that didn't have the same zip. The dropoff was too significant not to notice, from maybe 95 miles per hour to 90. I assumed that such inconsistency would disappear as he gained arm strength in spring training and the early part of the season, but it turned out to be a sign that age was beginning to take a toll on Randy.

Because the explosiveness was missing from his fastball at times, Randy didn't tear up the American League as I thought he would. His slider became his out pitch, and he was inconsistent with that as well, mainly because he'd get out of synch with his mechanics. When he rushed his delivery, his arm would lag behind a bit, and drop down more to the side, which would take that sharp, down-and-in tilt to right-handed hitters out of the slider, and he wound up giving up a lot of home runs because it would hang in the strike zone. From there Randy had a tough time adjusting to being human. He'd been overpowering for so long, able to throw his fastball by hitters without too much worry about location or mechanics, that it was humbling for him to get smacked around at times. But as the season went on he worked harder at his mechanics and pitched more like the Big Unit of old in August and September, helping us overtake the Red Sox and win the AL East.

Because the race with the Red Sox went down to the final weekend of the season, Randy wasn't on turn to pitch until Game 3 of the division series against the Los Angeles Angels. That turned out to be a pivotal game after we'd split the first two in Anaheim, and we thought we were in great shape with our number one guy going. This was the reason that George had given Randy the two-year, $32 million contract extension he demanded as a condition to agree to become a Yankee, for him to carry us through October. Only on this night the Angels pounded him in rather shocking fashion. They seemed to be on every pitch, and, in retrospect, I'm pretty sure they were seeing something in Randy's delivery to tip them off as to which pitches he was throwing.

I never heard that for sure, the way I found out the Arizona Diamondbacks were reading Andy Pettitte's delivery in Game 6 of the

2001 World Series, but it seemed fairly obvious. Even on his off-nights, Randy was still good enough to produce some weak swings, but I don't remember an Angel hitter looking like he was fooled all night. Over the years Randy had problems with tipping his pitches, partly because his long delivery made him susceptible to certain mannerisms. Of course, when he was at his best it almost didn't matter if the other team knew what was coming because they still couldn't hit it, but he didn't have that kind of stuff anymore. So he was hit hard, knocked out in the fourth inning as we lost 11–7, and we wound up losing the series in five games. Randy pitched effectively in relief in Game 5, after we talked about changing the position in which he held his glove during his delivery, so that left no doubt to me the Angels knew something in Game 3.

It was a shame because it probably cost us the series, and as a result we were going home earlier than expected. It was bitterly disappointing because we felt we were playing well enough to win another championship, but at the same time, it had been a very rewarding season. With all of our pitching injuries, I thought we'd showed tremendous character by hanging in there, finally overtaking the Red Sox and winning our eighth straight AL East title. I was proud of the job I did, piecing the pitching together, and I thought it was definitely Joe's best job of managing the Yankees, keeping the club from falling apart at times when it seemed that nothing was going our way.

The problem is, you're not allowed to feel good when you work for George unless you win it all. Believe me, I want to win as much as anybody, and it killed me to lose to the Angels. But that doesn't mean you condemn the season as a failure. I understand the huge expectations that come with having the highest payroll in baseball. Still, you have to consider the circumstances on a year-to-year basis, regardless of player salaries, and with those circumstances in mind, I did think of the 2005 season as at least a qualified success.

By the end, I still had the same mind-set that had taken shape back in May. I was retiring, not with bitterness but a sense of accomplishment. I didn't want to make a big deal of it, and I wasn't even planning on saying anything about it publicly for a while. I figured I'd go home, wait a couple of weeks, then make an announcement that I wasn't coming back. I preferred to slip away quietly.

Ah, but then George managed to get me riled up one last time. A day after we returned from Game 5 in Anaheim, I went to Yankee Stadium to clean out my locker, and I saw that George had made headlines by congratulating and praising Angels manager Mike Scioscia for the job he'd done in the series. It was such an obvious slap at Joe that it really ticked me off. First of all, how would he know if Scioscia had done a good job? To me it was just another dig, a way of throwing blame at Joe and the coaches.

So when reporters cornered me at the stadium that day, I told them that I was definitely retiring, partly because of comments like those from George. I also said that I'd love to sit down with George for thirty minutes or so and make him understand the need for better communication between the Tampa and New York arms of the organization. But I knew that wouldn't happen, as George didn't grant such audiences with the coaches. Mostly I wanted to make it clear I was leaving because I knew that Joe was feuding with George at the time, and I didn't want to give George the opportunity to fire me as a way of sticking it to his manager. I don't know if George would have fired me or not, but I didn't want my career with the Yankees to end that way.

Neither did I want to leave the way Zim did, full of anger and bitterness. I was upset at those comments in the newspaper that day, but overall I had good feelings about the season and the organization. I had too many friends within the Yankees to walk away mad. It was kind of odd, though, the way the organization handled me leaving. I guess they read in the newspapers that I was definitely retiring, but nobody called me to make it official or anything. The next conversation I had with Brian Cashman was a month or so later when I called to ask him about the possibility of coming to spring training in 2006. It wasn't that I couldn't walk away from the game at that point as much as I just wanted to be there to help Ron Guidry make the transition from spring training instructor to pitching coach. Guidry and I had become very friendly over the years, and I knew that he was all for me being around to answer questions and offer information.

George signed off on the idea, and he was very friendly toward me when I saw him in Tampa the next spring. He and Joe had patched up their relationship—again—over the winter, and, much like 2004, George once again seemed comfortable hanging around both the manager's office and the coaches' locker room in spring training. He made a point of coming over the first day he saw me and told me how glad he was that I was there.

"Are you sure about that?" I said with a laugh.

That was my way of seeing whether George would be inclined to discuss his role in pushing me toward retirement. For all of the criticism he'd sent my way during my last few years, publicly and privately, George had never said a word to me directly, questioning why I did this or why I didn't do that. I often wished he had because I would have loved to engage him in a discussion about pitching, listened to his concerns, and given him answers that may have helped him understand why we were having problems or whatever. He preferred to relay his criticism either internally through Brian Cashman or externally via the media. I think he would have been uncomfortable actually confronting me about a pitching issue because I just don't think he was very knowledgeable about it. We'd often ask jokingly in the coaches' room, upon hearing the latest criticism about some facet of the ball club, if this was actually coming from George or the maintenance man at Tampa headquarters who'd cornered

George in the men's room. Some things you just knew he couldn't have come up with himself, and at times we felt he'd listen to anyone who caught his ear in Tampa.

In any case, George didn't take the bait when I returned his greeting.

"No, no, I really mean it," he said. "It's great to have you here. You'll always be part of the Yankee family."

I thanked George and let it go at that. That's his way. He seems to have a very difficult time complimenting you personally when you work for him, even to the point of allowing it to destroy a relationship, as in the case with Don Zimmer. Yet he has no trouble expressing such thoughts once you've parted company. Still, I have to admit, it felt good to hear George welcome me back. Despite our differences, I loved being a Yankee, as both a player and coach, and I'll always think of myself as one. So it meant a lot to me that George wanted to maintain a relationship.

After all, when I look back, I'd have to say my ten years coaching with the Yankees were the greatest of my professional life. Knowing George's track record with pitching coaches before me, I took the job thinking I'd last a couple of years at most, and instead wound up enjoying a fabulous ride. There were so many great memories. Winning the '96 World Series, getting that ring I'd missed out on as a player, will always be at the top of my list. The '98 team forever will be recalled as one of the best in baseball history, so it was an honor to be a coach on that team. Above and beyond those memories, however, the personal relationships matter the most to me. Having guys like Andy Pettitte, David Cone, Mariano Rivera, Roger Clemens, and others say thanks for working with them meant the world to me. There was nothing more rewarding than watching young guys like Andy and Mo develop into stars over the years. But then again, being a part of Roger's three hundredth win was something I'll never forget.

Without a doubt, however, I can say the greatest thing about those ten years was getting the opportunity to work with somebody like Joe Torre. He's the best, personally and professionally. He trusted me from the day I started working with him, and in ten years we never had a problem. If we disagreed about a pitcher or a pitching decision, Joe was always willing to listen to my reasoning, but even that was rare because we seemed to think alike and agree on most everything. That was one of my only regrets about retiring when I did, because for years I thought I'd go out with Joe, the two of us riding off into the sunset.

Now I just hope that Joe gets to stay as long as he wants. I was sick when I heard the reports that Joe might get fired after the 2006 season. I don't know exactly how close it came to happening, but if, as it seemed, George did step back from his anger over losing to the Detroit Tigers in the playoffs and listen to Brian Cashman and others in the organization, that's a good sign for the future of the Yankees. I think Joe is still the perfect man for that job. I can't imagine anyone else handling everything that comes with managing in New York, including a locker room full of superstars, better than him. People think the high payroll guarantees that the Yankees will be in the playoffs, but with all of the injuries, as well as the crisis mentality that both George and the media create, I can't see how anybody could have done a better job last year keeping the club on track to reach October.

In the playoffs it boils down to dominant pitching and timely hitting, and the Yankees haven't had enough of either one the last couple of years. Is that Joe's fault? I don't think so. I'm just glad he is staying because, during the times I saw him in 2006, in spring training and then on a few trips I made to New York, he seemed to really enjoy the job. He had taken it upon himself to clear the air with George again following the 2005 season, flying to Tampa to meet with the Boss in person, so that was part of it. But then, just as important, Brian Cashman's contract as GM was up at that time, and he was in a good position because George had come to lean on him heavily to handle the day-to-day operations of the ball club. Brian knew it, and he used the leverage to do something about the constant power struggle between the New York and Tampa factions of the organization. As part of his deal to sign a new contract, Cashman demanded more control, and as far as I could tell, George did step back and allow Brian to become the primary decision maker in the organization. That gave Joe more power as well, because he and Brian are close, and the Guidry decision was an obvious example. If it had been up to the Tampa end of the organization, I'm sure Billy Connors would have convinced George that Neil Allen was the man for the job as new pitching coach.

In any case, I talked to Joe a few days after George announced he was bringing him back for 2007, and he was in good spirits. I don't think he liked the TV camera crews camping out at the bottom of his driveway while George kept everyone waiting on a decision for a couple of days, but overall Joe didn't seem very concerned that his job status became such an issue. People who think that he begged George to keep his job, a notion that seemed to become a popular media opinion, just don't know the man very well. That's just not Joe's nature. He was ready to walk away a few years earlier when it seemed that George didn't want him around any longer. He knows it can't work if George doesn't really want you there. If anything, George probably wanted to hear Joe say that he thinks he can win a championship in 2007, and I'm sure he said yes. There's no reason he can't.

For the first time in years, in fact, I saw signs that the organization is developing some good, young pitching of its own, and that's vital. Chien-Ming Wang looks like he could be a dominating number-one-type ace, while top prospect Philip Hughes was impressive when I saw him in spring training, as were a few other young power arms that caught my eye. The hardest part of winning a championship is getting to the playoffs, and if the Yankees continue to do that every year, power pitching is going to give them a better chance of winning it all again one of these years. Add a young pitcher or two and it can do wonders for the veterans as well.

The Detroit Tigers were a perfect example last year. Those hard-throwing kids seemed to breathe new life into Kenny Rogers. I coached Kenny when he was with the Yankees in 1996 and 1997, but I never saw the Kenny Rogers that was challenging hitters and pumping his fist for the Tigers in the 2006 playoffs. When he was a Yankee he always seemed to try to suppress his emotions, so maybe the young guys brought out the leadership in him. Expressing those emotions made him a more confident pitcher, where he'd failed miserably in the playoffs with us because, to me, he pitched tentatively, as if just trying not to lose.

Just as surprising, I saw Jeff Weaver become reborn last October as well, three years after we gave up on him, and just a few months after a 3-10 record caused the Los Angeles Angels to give up on him, too. Weaver always had the talent, but he'd been hardheaded at times when I had him as a Yankee, a guy who would get flustered and become more of a thrower than a pitcher when the heat was on him. Yet there he was, looking like Bob Gibson for the St. Louis Cardinals in closing out the World Series against the Tigers last fall. So you just never know how things might fall into place once you get into the playoffs.

In any case, I'll be rooting for the ball to bounce Joe's way again. I'll always be a Yankee at heart, but I enjoyed my first year of retirement. Of course, I can't say I didn't miss my old job at times. I missed the guys a lot, and I missed being in the trenches at game time. I had DIRECTV installed at home in Seattle so that I could get the YES Network, and early in the season, I have to admit, while watching the games I found myself sitting there thinking, *Okay, what do we need to do here? Who should we get up in the bullpen?* That sort of thing. But as the season went on I was able to pull back and just watch the games and root for the ball club. It was nice to see guys I worked with pitch well. I felt really good for Scott Proctor, seeing him develop into an important reliever after he'd struggled to harness his talent for a couple of years. And I loved seeing Wang enjoy a breakthrough year, especially because he reminds me of myself, throwing that sinker and inducing all those ground-ball outs. Not that I ever threw 95 miles per hour as he does, but I was able to help him a little bit in developing more command of his sinker, so I get a kick out of watching him. I think he's going to be a star for years to come.

I still love baseball, but summers in Seattle are beautiful, and I enjoyed every minute of it. I played a lot of golf, did plenty of fishing, visited with my sons and their children, and made it back to New York a few times for charity golf tournaments, including my own that I still run in New Jersey. Every so often I'd get a phone call from Joe, or our trainers, Gene Monahan or Steve Donahue, or one of the coaches, when they'd be on a road trip somewhere, having one of those group dinners that I enjoyed so much over the years. Or they might be on the bus, going to the hotel or the airport. I know how that works. Somehow, my name would come up in conversation and Joe would pull out his cell phone and say, let's see what he's doing. It's nice to feel connected in some way, but I don't miss all that travel, especially the 3 A.M. arrivals in some city.

That's the thing about the way baseball teams travel. Having a chartered jet makes flying much easier than commercial travel, but because we're usually leaving after night games to go from one city to the next, more often than not we're checking into our hotel in the predawn hours. It can wear on you at times, especially as you get older, and especially for someone like me because, as a hunter and fisherman, I've always been an early riser. In fact, it was kind of funny, last summer I'd be getting up before dawn at times to go fishing, and I'd find myself chuckling, thinking the ball club was probably just getting into Baltimore after a night game in Texas, or something like that.

By summer's end I'd pretty much decided that I couldn't go back to all of that travel. But I have to admit there was still a part of me that wanted to be around the game. Last August when I went to see my son Mel Jr., who is a minor-league pitching coach with the Arizona Diamondbacks, he laughed at me because I wound up charting pitches while sitting in the stands, watching his game. Hey, it's in my blood, what can I say?

So I decided to look for a way to stay involved in baseball in a part-time role. The Yankees were still my first choice, but GM Brian Cashman told me he didn't have such a position available. The Diamondbacks were more enthusiastic when I approached them, and I signed on to become an organizational pitching coach who will work with both major and minor leaguers. I'll be involved as an adviser to Bryan Price, the Diamondbacks' pitching coach, and I'll get to work with Mel Jr., who was promoted during the winter to be Arizona's organizational pitching coach, which means he'll instruct minor leaguers on all levels. I'm excited about it because I'll be working at a job I love again while traveling only occasionally, and mostly on the West Coast near my Seattle home. It might feel a little strange wearing something other than a Yankee uniform again, but I'm also looking forward to returning to Yankee Stadium for Old-Timers Day each summer. There will always be something special about putting on the pinstripes. Sometimes it still makes me feel like that twenty-two-year-old kid who was thrown into a pennant race all those years ago. Well, almost anyway.

Acknowledgments

Behind every book there are a lot of people who deserve credit for making things or events happen. Here is my chance to say thank you to them.

Thanks to my parents. Certainly no one has had more influence on my life than my mother, Lorene, who left us in 1995, or my father, Vernon, who, at 91, is still with us.

Thanks to BoBo Brayton, my coach at Yakima Junior College, for convincing me that I had a chance to make it in professional baseball.

Thanks to Eddie Taylor, the Yankee scout who signed me in 1961, for seeing some hidden talent that no one else saw.

Thanks to Arthur Richman, an old friend, for convincing George Steinbrenner to hire me to return to the Yankees in 1996, ending a twenty-year period of estrangement with my old ballclub.

Thanks to George Steinbrenner for the opportunity to work with Joe Torre for ten years.

Thanks to Joe Torre for always being there for me, for being in my corner at the ballpark, and for his support in my battle with cancer.

Thanks to John Harper for all his work on this book and for allowing me to beat him on the golf course.

Thanks to Mauro DiPreta, my editor on this project, and his assistant, Jennifer Schulkind, for their guidance and support.

Most of all, thanks to my wife, Jean, and two sons, Mel Jr. and Todd, who have always been there for me when I needed them.

Appendix: All-Time Rotation

O ver the years people have often asked me who would make the cut on my all-time starting rotation among the pitchers I've coached, and I've always said it would be too hard to choose. I mean, I can't imagine another pitching coach has ever had the good fortune to work with the roll call of stars and superstars that I did, especially during my twenty years with the two New York teams.

But now that I'm retired and the guys I leave off won't be able to find me—I hope anyway, especially if Randy Myers still subscribes to *Soldier of Fortune* magazine—I'm going to answer the question by choosing the pitchers I'd use if I had to win a seven-game playoff series. The caveat is that my choices are based on the way these guys pitched when I coached them, not necessarily when they were at their peak. In other words, Randy Johnson in his prime probably would be the guy I'd take over everybody else, but by the time I coached him with the Yankees, well, yes, he missed the cut.

Before I give you my personal dream team, however, let me build the suspense by reminding you of just how many top-flight pitchers I've coached over the years, with some personal memories about each of them. I'll spend less time on the guys I've covered in other chapters of the book.

Let me start with the Mets, whose staff in the mid-to-late 1980s was one of the best ever.

METS STARTERS

Dwight Gooden: As I noted earlier, Doc was like a son to me because I coached him from the time he was nineteen years old and watched him grow up. Obviously he should have been a Hall of Famer, and it bothers me that he wasted some of that talent, but that's secondary to my concern for him as a troubled soul who can't seem to overcome his problems with drug addiction. Looking back, I wish I could have done more to steer him in the right direction, but I don't honestly think anything would have helped.

Sid Fernandez: Ah, El Sid. For years I was convinced that Sid was going to be the guy to pitch the first no-hitter in the Mets' franchise history. Doc or David Cone obviously had the stuff to do it, but there were nights when Sid was untouchable. He didn't throw as hard as those guys, but the big left-hander threw that fastball from an angle where it looked like it was coming right out of his body, making it tough to pick up, so that 88 miles per hour seemed more like 95 to the hitters. Sid had a nice career but the potential was there for much more, only he had weight problems and he wasn't very mentally tough. You couldn't help but like Sid because he was really just a big kid, but you constantly had to work on his self-confidence.

Sid would be distraught after a bad outing, to the point where he seemed ready to turn in his uniform. I had to talk him down from the ledge, so to speak, more than a few times. I remember once in spring training, in 1985, after a rough start he started packing his stuff at his locker, telling everyone that he was going home to his native Hawaii. I called him outside, away from the clubhouse, and asked him what he was doing.

"I'm going home," he said. "I'm terrible. I can't take it anymore."

"Home?" I said. "You can't go home. You have too much ability, Sid. Sometimes things go wrong, but you've just gotta keep working on them, and things will get better."

"No," he said. "I'm done. I already called my mother and told her I'm coming home. I'm getting a flight and I'm going."

I was starting to think he really might go, so instead of trying to reassure him he'd be okay as I usually did, I decided to try some tough love. Sid was very sensitive, and I knew he'd never forgiven the Dodgers, his first team, for trading him to the Mets a few years earlier. So I used that against him.

"You know what, Sid," I said, "that's exactly why we were able to get you. The Dodgers told us the first time things went wrong, that's exactly what you'd do, you'd pack your bags and go home."

"No, they didn't," Sid protested halfheartedly.

"Yep, that's exactly what they told us," I said. "So if you want to prove the Dodgers were right, that you'd never amount to anything, then go ahead, go on home."

With that I turned and walked off and left Sid standing there close to tears. I guess it hit home because within a half hour he was putting his stuff back in his locker. The Dodgers hadn't told us that, of course, but we knew that's what they thought of Sid, that his immaturity would keep him from becoming a winning pitcher in the big leagues. They were wrong, but those were the kind of mind games you had to play with Sid. A couple of months later he asked me if I'd really heard that from the Dodgers, and I said, "Well, not exactly in those words. But that's what they thought of you. And you have to prove them wrong."

His mood swings aside, I loved working with Sid because at the ballpark he worked hard and he was willing to do anything I asked to get better. I think he really wanted to be great, and he was at times. In 1989 he was 14-5 with a 2.83 ERA and could have won twenty games with better run support. But he couldn't stay on that elite level, and it was more mental than anything, although his weight problems cost him stamina in the late innings. He was very sensitive about his weight, and he'd get mad whenever we would make him meet a certain weight, under the threat of a fine. I never had a problem with Sid doing his work at the ballpark. But I knew he was always stopping on the way home for a pepperoni pizza and a six-pack or two. He couldn't help himself. I wasn't worried that the weight affected his pitching so much as it was putting a strain on his knees, which gave him trouble from time to time and wore him down.

One thing people forget about Sid, though. He came into Game 7 against the Red Sox in '86 early in relief and shut them down for two and a third innings after they'd taken a 3–0 lead. He was the unsung hero that night, giving us a chance to come back and win the game.

Bob Ojeda: Bobby O was a thinking man's pitcher who won big games with heart and guile and a great changeup that made a lot of good hitters look bad. Mets GM Frank Cashen made a brilliant trade, acquiring him from the Boston Red Sox in the winter before the 1986 season; his finesse style was a perfect complement to the other power arms we had, and he brought a toughness that carried over to the other guys on the staff.

He had a huge year for us in '86, going 18-5 with a 2.57 ERA, and he had the season on his shoulders when he started Game 3 against the Red Sox in Boston after we'd lost the first two games of the World Series at home. I don't know many guys who would have handled the pressure of that situation so well, especially with all the hoopla over him returning to Boston, pitching in a ballpark that could be death to left-handers. The Boston newspapers were predicting doom for him, and Bobby was the kind of guy who thrived on that stuff. For years he'd been told as a young pitcher that he wouldn't make it to the big leagues because he didn't have a big fastball, and basically if somebody told Bobby he couldn't do something, his attitude was, yeah, well watch this. That's kind of the way he went into that game in Boston, and to me, he turned that Series around by holding them to one run over seven innings, as we won 7–1.

I just wish Bobby would have hired someone to trim his hedges in 1988. If he hadn't cut off the tip of his finger that September and missed the playoffs, I'm convinced we would have beaten the Dodgers and gone to the World Series. He would have pitched Game 5, some twelve hours after Mike Scioscia had stunned us with that famous home run against Doc to even the series at 2–2. We needed somebody with Bobby's grit to regain the momentum at that point, and Sid Fernandez wasn't up to it. He gave up six runs in four-plus innings, and the eventual 7–4 loss proved pivotal.

Ron Darling: He was a very intelligent pitcher, which I guess you'd expect from a guy who attended Yale University. But sometimes I think that actually worked against him because he wanted to make the perfect pitch all the time, and there were days when he was just missing the corners, getting in trouble with walks. In fact, he used to drive Davey Johnson nuts at times because Davey wanted him to trust his stuff and throw more strikes. In 1985 Ronnie led the National League in walks with 114, and I was constantly talking to him about the need to throw more strikes. Ronnie was a great kid and a hard worker, but he could be hardheaded at times, and sometimes I didn't think he was listening much. But we had a long talk at the end of the '85 season about being more aggressive, and he committed to that style in '86 and cut his walks down to 81. Though his overall numbers were about the same for both years—he was 16-6 in '85, 15-6 in '86—he was a much better pitcher in '86, going deeper in games and pitching with more dominance.

Ronnie was a tougher competitor than people may have realized because of his image as the good-looking kid from an Ivy League school. He always wanted the ball and seemed to welcome pitching big games. People tend to remember that he was knocked out early in Game 7 of the '86 World Series, but, like Ojeda, he made a huge start for us in Boston, throwing seven shutout innings in Game 4 to get us even at 2–2 in the Series.

David Cone: As I noted earlier, David was as fierce a competitor as anybody I ever coached. He'd battle you until his arm fell off. He never, ever wanted to come out of a game, no matter how many pitches he'd thrown, and always argued that he had something left in his tank, even when he was pitching on fumes. By the time I coached him with the Yankees he'd matured into a team leader as well, and he was a big reason for the winning chemistry that seemed to carry us through in the postseason.

Frank Viola: He came over to the Mets in a trade in 1989, the year after he won the American League Cy Young Award with the Minnesota Twins. Frankie had one big year for the Mets, winning twenty games in 1990. A left-hander, he relied on a great changeup as his out pitch. He was one of the best pitchers in baseball for a few years, but when he lost a few miles per hour off his fastball, he slipped quickly. It happens to a lot of changeup pitchers because when that separation between the fastball and changeup shortens up, hitters aren't fooled as much by the off-speed pitch.

Frankie was very professional, easy to coach, but he needed a kick in the backside occasionally because he had a tendency to mope when things weren't going well for him. I remember a game where he seemed to be getting tired, but we were trying to get him through a particular inning. He gave up a couple of hits and I think he was ready to come out of the game, but we didn't have anybody ready. I went to the mound to talk to him, and after I said a couple of things, he turned and walked off the back of the mound. I guess he thought I was through talking, but I was still there when he turned around again, and he seemed surprised. He walked back up the mound and I said, "Are you ready to get down to business?" He seemed to need a jolt like that from time to time, and I remember he wound up getting out of trouble that day. Afterward he apologized and said he didn't mean to walk away from me. I just told him not to let it happen again. I never held it against a pitcher when something like that happened in the heat of the battle. I always tried to remember how emotional you could get during a game, especially when things weren't going well.

Bret Saberhagen: I just wish I'd had the opportunity to be around him when he was 100 percent healthy. Bret had tremendous stuff, pinpoint control, and had a good feel for pitching. He won two Cy Young Awards with the Kansas City Royals before coming to the Mets for the 1992 season, and he could have been a Hall of Famer if he hadn't been sidelined by a number of different injuries. I only saw him at his best a handful of times during the two seasons I coached him, but those glimpses were memorable because he could totally dominate a game with just a fastball and a changeup.

He didn't show it on the field, but Bret was a very emotional guy when he was pitching. When he'd have a rough inning, he'd go back to the clubhouse between innings and he'd throw stuff around, occasionally punch a wall. I worried about him breaking his hand or something, but fortunately it never happened. He got a bad rap with the Mets as a troublemaker because of an incident where he sprayed bleach in the locker room toward a group of reporters, but he was a playful guy and I think he just thought of it as a gag to get some laughs. He was wrong for doing it, but his timing made it worse, because that was in 1993 when the team was awful and player-media relations were strained, the result of a number of incidents, so Saberhagen paid a price for doing something stupid.

He went on to have a couple of good seasons in Boston, but shoulder problems followed him around. Bret won 92 games by the time he was twenty-five years old, after his first six seasons, and just 72 over his final thirteen seasons before injuries finally forced him to retire.

METS RELIEVERS

John Franco: Johnny was a fearless competitor who carried himself with the cockiness that you need as a closer. He was a little guy who never would have reached the big leagues, let alone racked up 424 saves in his career, if he didn't have that tough-guy-from-Brooklyn persona and an unshakable belief in his ability.

I've never seen a relief pitcher have the kind of influence in the clubhouse that Johnny did. He was the king of the wisecracks, which kept everybody loose, but he could use his zingers to make a point if he thought somebody wasn't playing all out, that type of thing. Basically Johnny was like the union boss in the clubhouse, to the point where I tried to use him if I wanted to get some sort of message across to one of my pitchers without confronting the guy myself. Johnny worked hard and cared about winning, so I never had a problem with him, which was good because, just as he could help a coach or a manager with his influence on the other players, he could get guys stirred up and cause trouble if he didn't care for someone.

On the mound the little left-hander was as gutsy as they come, relying on that screwball/changeup of his as his out pitch. He'd throw it in any count, against any hitter, and he had a lot of success with it. He had his best years with the Cincinnati Reds, before the Mets traded for him after the 1989 season. His only problem was that he wasn't a swing-and-miss guy but relied on getting guys out with contact, which made him vulnerable at times. Sometimes he could make the pitch he wanted, but ground balls would find holes or someone would get just enough of his changeup to dunk it into the outfield for a single that would cost him. He could give up two or three of the weakest hits you've ever seen that might cost him a save. For that reason, I don't know that I could call him an all-time great. His save total is a testament to his grit and his staying power, but I can't put him in a class with Rivera or some of the other dominant closers who had overpowering stuff.

Randy Myers: In 1989 Myers was a promising, young, hard-throwing left-handed closer—in other words, one of the rarest commodities in baseball. Yet the Mets traded him for Franco, a more proven closer at the time, but a finesse pitcher. All because Randy was something of a rebel who worried the organization with his interest in military-related paraphernalia and angered the brass with his adherence to an unorthodox weight-training program. Weight training of any kind had long been taboo in baseball, the antiquated theory being that it would make players too bulky, and at the time such thinking was just beginning to change. But Randy pushed the envelope, working with heavy weights, mostly for his legs, before games, and at various times he ignored then-GM Joe McIlvaine's requests that he conform to the team's more orthodox strength and conditioning routine. Maybe Randy was ahead of the curve, because the weight work didn't seem to hurt his performance. He had great talent and could thread the needle on the outside corner to right-handed hitters with a 95 mph fastball.

Randy liked people to think he was way out there, with his military obsession and everything, wearing camouflage T-shirts and a Rambo-style cloth headband, but I think it was more of an act than anything. He worked hard, cared very much about the team, and was always ready to take the ball. I don't know if you can say that trading him for Franco was a mistake, but Randy definitely was more dominant over the next few seasons, helping the Cincinnati Reds win a world championship in 1990 as part of the Nasty Boys bullpen, along with Rob Dibble and Norm Charlton.

Jesse Orosco: When it comes to Jesse, my lasting image of him is probably the same as it is for so many Mets fans: flinging that glove into the air after striking out Marty Barrett for the last out of the 1986 World Series. It kind of captured the moment after those back-to-back, nerve-racking series against the Houston Astros and then the Boston Red Sox. Actually, the game I'll always remember Jesse for was the clinching Game 6 against the Astros, when he gave up the lead on a fourteenth-inning home run to Billy Hatcher, but then hung in there for two more innings and closed out the win in sixteen innings.

Jesse was a dominant closer at that time, but he didn't rack up huge save numbers, partly because those Mets teams won so many lopsided games, and partly because he did his best work before the dawn of the one-inning closer era that began in the late 1980s with Dennis Eckersley of the Oakland A's. Above all else, Jesse proved to be a testament to the long-life expectancy for a left-hander with a great breaking ball. He wound up playing twenty-four years in the big leagues, the last ten strictly as a situational reliever who was used to get out one or two left-handed hitters in the late innings. But in his prime, Jesse was as good as any left-handed closer you want to name.

YANKEES STARTERS

Andy Pettitte: As I noted earlier, I became closer to Andy than maybe any other pitcher I've coached. We argued a lot early in his career, but soon developed a trusting relationship that went beyond base-ball, first when Andy needed somebody to talk to about his father's health problems, and then when he returned the favor for me the year I dealt with cancer. It crushed me to see him leave the Yankees as a free agent after the 2003 season. I really wanted to see him stay and put his mark in the record books as one of the greatest pitchers in Yankee history. Andy's elbow problem notwithstanding, I still think George Steinbrenner made a mistake by not treating him as a top priority the winter he signed with the Houston Astros. On the other hand, I think it was a smart move to sign him as a free agent last winter and bring him back for 2007.

Jimmy Key: Jimmy was the consummate professional, a crafty left-hander who was in the twilight of his career by the time I coached him in 1996. I spent considerable time just talking pitching with Jimmy, because he enjoyed the give-and-take and had some interesting ideas himself. I rarely messed with either his mechanics or his approach because he was such a bright guy who knew exactly what he was doing on the mound.

Jimmy was an important influence on young guys like Pettitte and even other veterans such as David Cone, and everybody was thrilled that he earned the victory in the 1996 World Series clincher, when he outpitched Greg Maddux in Game 6.

David Wells: Unless you've skipped ahead, you've read plenty by now about my sometimes-contentious relationship with David. Not that I think he's a bad guy; I just think he could have been a Hall of Famer if he had worked harder to get the most out of his talent.

Roger Clemens: As I noted earlier, Roger turned out to be one of my most pleasant surprises in coaching, quite the opposite of the big-ego superstar I thought I saw as an opponent for years. He enjoyed talking about pitching, exchanging ideas with me about how to throw different pitches. Roger occasionally would come to me with an idea to help one of our younger pitchers, and I was more than willing to have him pass it along. He was happy to do it, but he wasn't going to waste his time on anybody who he thought wasn't as dedicated to his craft as him. Sometimes he'd come back to me after trying to pass something on to one of our younger pitchers, and he'd say, "Sorry, Mel, I can't do anything with him." He just didn't have any patience for guys who weren't willing to work hard. That's why he didn't care much for David Wells.

Once everybody got to know Roger, he became a leader in our club. I think he won over any skeptics when he matched Curt Schilling pitch for pitch in Game 7 of the 2001 World Series, the game that Mariano Rivera let get away at the end. But I'll remember Roger most for a regular-season game that showed what he was all about. We were in Detroit, short a pitcher because of an injury, and we called up Adrian Hernandez from the minors to fill the spot in the rotation. But on the day he was supposed to pitch, Hernandez came down with the flu, and suddenly, we needed a starter. Roger was supposed to start the next day, but he came to me and said, "Give me the ball. I'll pitch."

It was the farthest thing from my mind. Roger was forty years old at the time and we wanted him getting his full rest between starts, but he insisted. He said he felt good and would have no problem pitching on three days' rest. I approached Joe about it and we agreed we didn't have a better option, so we took Roger up on his offer. He didn't pitch great, giving up five runs in five innings, but we ended up winning the game, and it really made an impression on the rest of the team. A lot of guys are willing to pitch on short rest in a crucial situation, late in the season or in the postseason, but not many would have volunteered for a ho-hum game in June. By this point Roger had long since been accepted, so he wasn't trying to win friends, just the game.

Orlando Hernandez: As I noted earlier, El Duque was one of a kind, from his swagger that made him such a great postseason pitcher, to his temperamental ways, which made him difficult at times to handle. He made his mark with one game, in particular, beating the Cleveland Indians in Game 4 of the 1998 ALCS when we were trailing 2–1 in the series and feeling the pressure of validating our 114-win regular season.

Randy Johnson: The Big Unit was different—that might be the best way to put it. I got along fine with him but suffice it to say there was an adjustment period for both of us. I think he spent most of his first year with the Yankees, in 2005, learning the way Joe Torre did things. Randy seemed to be accustomed to everything revolving around him, in terms of pitching plans, but Joe doesn't take that approach, and it seemed to take a little while for Randy to accept that.

Randy was open to ideas and he wasn't afraid to try things I might suggest. He was very much in tune with his mechanics and wanted me to watch closely for signs to ensure that he wasn't getting out of synch. He knew how important it was for him to find the right arm slot, to make sure his arm wasn't dropping down and taking the tilt out of his slider. Randy was constantly worried about tipping his pitches, which he did at times by the way he held his glove for a certain pitch, that type of thing. In the past his stuff was so dominant that he didn't have to worry about such issues, but during his first year with the Yankees he began to realize that he needed every advantage to win consistently. So there was plenty to work on with Randy, and that was never an issue. He was just kind of tough to get to know. He kept to himself a lot, and I never felt there was a strong trust between us. It was hard for him that first year because so much was expected, and though he wound up winning seventeen games, I think he was disappointed overall.

The only time we clashed was when Randy tried to establish his own ground rules and I had to object. After a tough inning early in the season, I asked him if he'd pitched around a particular hitter whom he had walked, and Randy informed me of his two commandments.

"There are two things I don't do," he said. "I don't pitch around anybody and I don't tell anybody if I'm tired."

The second commandment quickly became a problem. After six or seven innings, depending on the pitch count, I'll always go to my pitcher and ask him how he feels, how much he thinks he has left in the tank, and so on. When I did that with Randy he would recite his second commandment and make it clear he didn't want me asking how he felt.

More than once I told him, "Randy, you might as well get used to it. It's part of my job. Joe always asks me to check at this stage of the game, so don't let it bother you. But you're going to have to get used to it."

He grudgingly agreed, but from time to time he would still come back to his two commandments and reiterate that basically he never admitted to being tired.

It was kind of funny because there was a game at home against Minnesota in July where Randy was dominating the Twins. He'd given up two hits and struck out eleven through seven innings, and he'd thrown ninety-seven pitches. Leading 4–0, he seemed to be cruising, to the point where I wasn't even going to check with him after the seventh, but this time he came to me and said, "Do you have somebody to pitch the eighth?"

I remember it well because his previous start had been one of those days when he told me he never gets tired—or at least he never tells anyone he's tired. And now he was asking if we had someone ready to take over.

So I said, "Yeah, Randy, I have somebody to pitch the eighth. You. You need to give me one more inning."

He didn't argue or anything. He said okay, went out, and pitched another shutout inning, and Tom Gordon finished up in the ninth.

The next day I went to him and told him that any time he was pitching with that kind of dominance, I never wanted him even thinking about coming out of the game unless it was for Mariano Rivera in a save situation. Randy agreed, but he didn't give me any insight into why he'd gone from saying he never gets tired to suddenly asking about possibly coming out of a game. That was Randy—he could be a little strange sometimes. I felt for him because it wasn't easy having such huge expectations at an age when his body wasn't allowing him to be quite the same pitcher he'd been for so many years.

Mike Mussina: If there's one pitcher in the big leagues who doesn't need a pitching coach, it has to be Moose. He's a bright guy who attended Stanford University, very much a thinking man's pitcher who understands his body and his mechanics very well, and he is so meticulous about his routine that he throws the same number of pitches when he warms up before every start. I don't think he counts them, but he'll be within one or two of the same number every time. He banks on his routine to keep himself in synch throughout the season, and he hates if something messes with it. He wants to pitch every fifth day—he frets if he goes an extra day between starts and never wants to pitch on three days' rest.

I don't think it was a coincidence that he had his worst season with us in 2004, the year we opened the season in Japan in March, then returned to Florida for the end of spring training before reopening a week later. He wasn't happy that he had to change his routine to be ready to pitch in Japan, and then adjust again when we returned. He lost his start in Japan and I really think he let the trip get in his head and bother him, to the point where I think it had an impact on his entire season, as he went 12-9 with a 4.59 ERA.

Mike was easy to coach, but he wasn't easy to get to know and understand. He works hard, goes about his business very seriously, and holds everyone a little bit at arm's length, I guess you'd say. When he came over as a free agent from the Baltimore Orioles, he told me that he never relied too much on pitching coaches, mainly because he'd had a bunch of different ones with the Orioles and had to learn to know himself very well. He enjoyed talking about pitching, but I learned that if I had something I thought would help him, I had to suggest it in a roundabout way. I couldn't just tell him to try something during a bullpen session between starts because he was very analytical and needed to think it through first, before deciding if it applied to him. So I got in the habit of sitting and talking with him, planting a seed about something a couple of days before he was scheduled to throw between starts. It was always hard to tell what he thought about such an idea. He wouldn't always agree but he'd always give it some thought, which is all I asked. And often I saw him incorporate my idea, whether it was in his next bullpen session or sometimes in his next game.

I'll always remember Moose for two games: The first was his 1–0 victory over the A's in Oakland in Game 3 of the 2001 playoffs, when he outdueled Barry Zito to keep us alive after we'd lost the first two games of a best-of-five series. That was about as clutch as it gets for a starting pitcher. Then there was his near-perfect game in 2001 against the Red Sox in Boston, when he came within one out of pitching a perfect game, only to have it broken up by a pinch-hit single by Carl Everett. He made a great pitch, a fastball on the outside corner, and Everett just reached out and poked it into left center. It was the fourth time he'd carried a no-hitter as late as the eighth inning without getting it, and Mike was really devastated afterward. He's such a perfectionist that it would have been fitting for him to get the perfect game, but it wasn't meant to be.

Kevin Brown: Unfortunately, as I noted earlier, because of age and chronic back problems, Kevin wasn't nearly the dominant pitcher as a Yankee that he'd been for much of his career. More unfortunately, I'll remember him for breaking his hand on the clubhouse wall more than anything he did on the mound for us.

YANKEES RELIEVERS

Mariano Rivera: I've already written about how much Mariano means to me, but all you really need to know is that when I retired, the guys who'd been there for all ten of my years with the Yankees chipped in to buy me a fishing boat and gave it a name that is painted across the back: Mo In The Ninth.

Not that I want to see him retire anytime soon, but I look forward to the day when I go to Cooperstown for his Hall of Fame induction.

John Wetteland: We liked to call John a top-stepper. As a closer, he almost always got the job done, but often only after getting into some type of jam, to the point where he had the manager on the top step of the dugout, ready to come get him any minute. John had a great fastball but sometimes very little command of it, and that's what often got him in trouble. I think John liked that, though. He loved the competition and the challenge of getting the last three outs, the tougher the spot the better. He was one of the few guys I've seen who truly seemed to enjoy the pressure of getting a tough save. He had a way of keeping baseball in perspective, and I think that was part of his success—he handled the pressure better than the hitters.

John believed there was more to life than baseball. I guess you'd call him a little flaky, like a lot of closers. In the afternoons, hours before the game, he loved to Rollerblade around the stadium and even the parking lot in some stadiums on the road. He was a little reckless at times, to the point where the front office finally ordered him to stop the Rollerblading at the ballpark.

I'll always remember him for—what else?—the pop-up from Mark Lemke that landed in Charlie Hayes's glove near the third-base stands at Yankee Stadium for the final out in the '96 World Series. He went to the Texas Rangers as a free agent that winter, only because we couldn't justify spending big bucks to keep him when we had a young—and inexpensive at the time—Rivera ready to take over as closer.

Jeff Nelson: Jeff was the right-handed half of our setup relief tandem that helped win three straight championships. He was intimidating to right-handers because he threw sidearm and had that big-breaking slider, as well as a good fastball that moved down and in, just the opposite of his slider, on righties.

As dominating as he could be in that role, Nellie could be exasperating to watch because he wanted to strike out every hitter he faced, and he wasn't happy unless he did. The problem with that was he'd too often try to make the perfect pitch, usually with his slider, and he'd wind up falling behind hitters, or walking more of them than he should have. I used to preach to him to throw more strikes and let the natural movement on his pitches help him get outs early in the count, but Jeff wasn't a great listener. He had his own ideas and thought his success was measured by strikeouts. So if he got ahead in the count, invariably he'd nibble at the corners and wind up going to a 3-2 count. Don Zimmer used to sit there in the dugout, muttering "three-and-two, three-and-two, three-and-two." It drove Joe crazy as well, and he had his own conversations with Nellie, but nothing seemed to get through to him. He wound up issuing far too many walks, but he also managed to get out of most of his jams and was a big part of our success.

Mike Stanton: Mike was the left-handed part of that late-inning tandem. He was a real pro who knew how to set hitters up, and he seemed to be at his best in the toughest situations. He had been a closer with the Atlanta Braves for a couple of years, and when he came to us in 1997 I think he believed he would inherit John Wetteland's job. But when he realized that Mariano was going to be our closer, he adapted well as a setup man. He hated giving up the ball when we'd go righty-lefty, but eventually he understood it was a winning formula, and he was a guy who put winning ahead of everything else.

ALL-TIME ROTATION

All right, here we go. Given my pick of every pitcher I've coached, here's how I'd set up a rotation for a playoff series.

Starters

Game 1: Dwight Gooden. A young Doc. At age twenty there was nobody better.

Game 2: Roger Clemens. Nearly as dominant when I had him, at forty, as he was at twenty-five.

Game 3: David Cone. The younger version that I had with the Mets. Not that he wasn't still very good as a Yankee, but in 1988, the year he went 20-3, he left more batters shaking their heads than I've ever seen.

Game 4: Andy Pettitte: His 1–0 victory in Game 5 of the '96 World Series, when he outdueled John Smoltz, was proof of a toughness that he demonstrated again and again in the postseason.

Relievers

Closer: Mariano Rivera. The greatest postseason closer in history. Enough said.

Setup man: Jesse Orosco. Jesse was a closer for the Mets but for this team he's my eighth-inning guy. He was overshadowed by all the stars on that '86 team, but he had a couple of Rivera-like years.

So there it is. As I said earlier, this is all based on when I coached each guy. If I had to win one game for my life, when they were all at their peak, I'd have to go with Randy Johnson. It'd be a tough call over Doc or Roger, but nobody was more intimidating in his prime than the Big Unit. He just wasn't at that level anymore when I coached him with the Yankees.

Index